Crimes of the Art World

THOMAS D. BAZLEY

PRAEGER

AN IMPRINT OF ABC-CLIO, LLC
Santa Barbara, California • Denver, Colorado • Oxford, England

Library of Congress Cataloging-in-Publication Data

Bazley, Tom.
  Crimes of the art world / Thomas D. Bazley.
      p.   cm.
  Includes bibliographical references and index.
  ISBN 978-0-313-36047-3 (hard copy : alk. paper) — ISBN 978-0-313-36048-0 (ebook)
1. Art thefts. 2. Art—Forgeries. 3. Art—Mutilation, defacement, etc.   I. Title.
  N8795.B39   2010
  364.16'287—dc22   2009044854

ISBN: 978-0-313-36047-3
EISBN: 978-0-313-36048-0

14   13   12   11   10   1   2   3   4   5

This book is also available on the World Wide Web as an eBook.
Visit www.abc-clio.com for details.

Praeger
An Imprint of ABC-CLIO, LLC

ABC-CLIO, LLC
130 Cremona Drive, P.O. Box 1911
Santa Barbara, California 93116–1911

This book is printed on acid-free paper ∞
Manufactured in the United States of America

Contents

Boxes, Figures, and Tables

Preface

This book is an introduction to art crime, researched and written from the perspective of criminology (and to a lesser extent, from insights gained through a career as a federal criminal investigator). However, long before my days as a federal agent, graduate student, and now college instructor, I studied art history as an undergraduate. This coursework laid a foundation for a lifelong interest in art and art history, which in turn, prompted this undertaking. To be very clear, however, this is not a work of art history. I leave such endeavors to those who have acquired the requisite education, training, and experience in that highly specialized field. However, as a work that attempts to explore the intersection of art and crime, it will hopefully be of interest and value not only to those who study and/or follow crime but also to those who study and/or follow art as well. If this goal is met, the interests of a broad segment of readers should be addressed.

Criminology is a social science that examines crime as social phenomenon and society's reaction to it. While it is rooted in sociology, it readily brings in knowledge from other fields such as psychology, law, economics, political science, and philosophy in its attempt to better understand the process of why and how we have laws that label some conduct as crimes, why some people break these laws, and what we as a society do when such conduct occurs. This inclusive approach has extended the reach of criminology in many directions ranging from theoretical explanations to analyses of various types of offending to policing and correctional practices. Nevertheless, the literature in criminology has been relatively silent on crimes that affect art and those who create, own, and/or have custody of art objects. This relative lack of attention is all the more surprising when confronted with the highly ranked position that art crime occupies in international crime estimates. The chapters that follow will detail the obstacles encountered when attempting to apply many of the standard criminological research practices. As will be repeated throughout this volume, the lack of any comprehensive database precludes the type of statistical analysis that is so frequently reflected in criminological literature. However, such obstacles are not unique in the study of crime. For instance, there is no comprehensive database on serial killing or mass murder. Moreover, perhaps the most costly form of crime and certainly one of the most pervasive, white-collar crime, also cannot be broadly studied through quantitative analysis due to the lack of comprehensive data. So do we give up? Of course not! We rely on what information we can glean from other sources: very frequently through case study analysis, data often emanating from media reports. Such approaches are adopted here as well.

Aside from data problems, another impediment to studying art crime is the unique environment in which a criminologist is likely to find him/herself. Some knowledge and interest in art and art history are necessary prerequisites if one wishes to study crime within the art world. This type of background and interest is not universally found among criminologists; folks who are more likely comfortable when dealing with homicide, drug use, rape, prisons, and other topics that reflect the less charming aspects of humankind. Nevertheless, crimes that affect art and those who create, own, or have custody of art should fall squarely within the concerns of criminology. The present undertaking is premised on the (hopefully correct) notion that one need not be an art historian to study and write about art crime. The goal here is straightforward but also ambitious and challenging, whether approaching it as a criminologist or art historian, that is, to bridge the gap between the two fields and to add to the relatively small body of literature on crimes in the art world.

While written from a criminological perspective, this volume hopefully does not dwell on the parochial characteristics of social science texts, that is, theory discussion and statistical analysis (there isn't much to work with here in this regard anyway!). As the introduction to the volume, chapter 1 provides an overview of the art world that we will be exploring and a glimpse of the crimes that will be covered in the chapters that follow. Chapters 2 and 3 deal with art theft in the traditional criminal sense; that is, larceny, burglary, and robbery; with chapter 2 being somewhat more theoretical and analytical and chapter 3 highlighting some of the great art thefts through conventional criminal methodologies. When one thinks about art crime, art theft often first comes to mind, quickly followed by art forgeries, fakes, and counterfeits. It is fitting then that this subject is discussed next in chapter 4. Chapters 5 and 6 bring us back to theft scenarios, but in special contexts. Chapter 5 deals with art theft incident to wars and civil/religious unrest while chapter 6 focuses on the theft and trafficking of cultural-heritage objects. Chapter 7 breaks new ground with regard to the literature on art crime as it categorizes certain misconduct that has occurred in the art world as white-collar crime. Chapter 8 concludes our examination of the various art-crime categories with a discussion on art vandalism and malicious destruction. The final two chapters, chapters 9 and 10, take us in a different but related direction when considering crimes of the art world; that is, how do we respond to it? Chapter 9 covers the legal, diplomatic, and law enforcement response to art crime while chapter 10 discusses security and prevention measures that can be taken to avoid victimization.

It is my hope that regardless of orientation and interest, all readers will find this tour of the crimes of the art world both fascinating and disturbing, but also as enlightening as I have. My sincere thanks to my family, friends, and professional colleagues for their support and encouragement throughout this undertaking; and in particular, for the much needed proofreading assistance provided by my wife, Lyn.

Thomas D. Bazley, PhD
Tampa, Florida

CHAPTER 1

Art and Crime?

"Art" and "crime?" Even without getting into exact definitions of these two terms, many readers might sense a non sequitur or lack of congruity. First, although both terms can be nouns, art is generally a tangible object (at least as we will consider it here) while crime is a form of human conduct or, more accurately, misconduct. Moreover, as a visual form of expression which many viewers find beautiful (or alternatively intriguing or thought-provoking), it could be argued that art is a *positive* contribution to our world and has been throughout the ages. Crime, however, conjures images of human behavior at its worst and would seem to stand in stark contrast to art as a positive feature in our lives. Put another way, joining the terms "art" and "crime" is as unseemly as joining the terms "sublime" and "grimy."[1]

Should it be surprising then that unlike well-established pairings such as drugs and crime or guns and crime, art and crime has received relatively little attention, beyond an occasional news story about the theft of a well-known art object (or a motion picture that glamorizes such incidents)? Perhaps not, considering how out of character these two forms of human endeavor seem to be with each other. However, our failure to recognize seemingly odd pairings is not without precedent when it comes to studying and addressing crime. Up until the mid-20th century, not only the general public but also government policy makers and the academic world ignored linkages between criminal behavior and those occupying the upper or white-collar classes of our society. It was not until Edwin Sutherland, the noted American criminologist, began to promote this concept (beginning in an article entitled "White-Collar Criminality" published in 1940 in *American Sociological Review* 5(1): pp. 1–12) that crimes committed by the business community were viewed within academic and government circles as a unified category of offenses, that is, white-collar crime. In addition to calling attention to these offenses by categorizing them under one banner, Sutherland also argued that the upper classes committed crimes in connection with their business activities, but these crimes were not looked upon as such and therefore, upper-class criminality was excluded from criminological consideration and theory. Moreover, he felt that crime statistics were skewed because they focused only on crimes committed by the lower classes and, therefore, forced theorists to work only within the framework of lower-class offenders.

For the study of white-collar crime, Sutherland's article was important conceptually in at least four respects. First, it argued for the recognition of white-collar crime as a serious crime problem. Second, it advocated for a reorientation of criminology/sociology and societal institutions concerned with criminal behavior to consider the illegal activities of both the upper and lower social classes. Third, the effect of such a reorientation would be that the study and control of this type of crime would need to consider not only the offense's characteristics but also the offender's social and class characteristics as well. As Sutherland was concerned about crimes committed by the upper classes in the course of their business activities, class and social characteristics provided upper-class individuals offending opportunities not available to lower-class individuals. Heretofore, crime was viewed as solely a lower-class phenomenon and, thus, all criminal offenders were believed to share common lower-class social characteristics.

The fourth conceptual issue raised by Sutherland was the inclusion of illegal but not necessarily criminal activities as conduct worthy of attention by both criminologists/sociologists and criminal-justice policy makers. He acknowledged that much of the conduct he considered white-collar crime was not investigated by traditional law-enforcement agencies nor adjudicated in the criminal courts. Rather, these offenses were usually handled civilly or administratively, often by regulatory type agencies. However, he felt that most of these types of actions arose because the offenders did engage in the type of conduct that would also constitute a criminal violation, usually in the form of criminal fraud. He also noted in this article that juvenile delinquency is not adjudicated in the criminal courts, but there is little public debate over whether this type of conduct is, in actuality, a criminal concern.

Sutherland's conceptual arguments to recognize white-collar crime as being within the purview of those who study and regulate crime have some interesting parallels to the seemingly odd-fellow relationship of art and crime. First, is art crime a serious problem? Later we'll examine this issue in greater detail when we discuss art-crime typologies and losses. For now, consider this: in an international survey of world governments conducted by the United Nations regarding transnational crime problems, the theft of art and cultural objects was ranked number three in terms of prevalence and seriousness (out of a total of 18 crime categories), just behind money laundering and terrorist activities. While the rationale for this ranking was largely based on the argument that the theft of cultural objects can rob entire nations and cultures of their cultural heritage, annual loss estimates attributable to the theft of *fine art* alone (e.g., paintings and sculptures) as high as $4.5 billion provide further evidence of the seriousness of art crime.[2] Second, just as Sutherland urged academics and government policy makers to reorient themselves to consider the illegal activities of both the lower and upper classes because the business crimes of the upper classes had traditionally been ignored, so too could an argument be made for a reorientation to, and fuller recognition of, the worldwide, serious impact of art crime.

Drawing a parallel between art crime and white-collar crime regarding Sutherland's offense and offender concerns is perhaps more tenuous, but an analogous situation can still be argued. Sutherland recognized that for the academic world to bring white-collar offenses within its research purview, it would need to broaden its social-class focus. No longer would only those occupying the lower socioeconomic classes be the subjects of criminal offender studies. Perhaps not surprisingly, expanding research on criminal activities to include art crime will likewise bring into focus upper-class offending. However, as we progress through this volume, it will become clear that art crime spans all socioeconomic classes ranging from the very poor to very rich. A further analogy with regard to Sutherland's offense and offender concern is an implication in his description of upper-class offending as being connected to business activities; that is, this offending and the environment in which it occurs are highly specialized. A lack of familiarity with this new territory could pose obstacles to those whose research and study had previously concentrated on violent crimes and property crimes of a more conventional nature. Needless to say, the art world is also a unique environment (i.e., the collective of those whose business is art—artists, gallery owners, museums and their related professional staff, auction houses, art academics, etc.—and those for whom art is an avocation—collectors, students, museum and gallery aficionados, and even those who simply enjoy art on a more casual basis). Moreover, some (although not all) of the crimes that occur within this world are quite unique, if not sophisticated. These factors would likely require many traditional crime researchers to augment their knowledge of art and art history in order to pursue inquiries in this area.

Finally, in his discussion of white-collar crime, Sutherland raised the still contentious issue of bringing noncriminal conduct within the white-collar crime umbrella and thus making it an appropriate concern for those who study or control crime. Specifically, Sutherland recognized that many white-collar offenses were not adjudicated in criminal courts but rather were litigated in civil or agency administrative forums. Nevertheless, he contended that the conduct being examined in these noncriminal forums was essentially the same conduct that could also form a basis for a criminal prosecution. As we shall see in later chapters, the resolution of crimes that occur in the art world is not always accomplished in criminal courts. Rather, civil proceedings and even international treaties and diplomatic negotiations have been used to correct wrongs that are akin to crimes such as theft, smuggling, conspiracy, and so forth.

The point to this discussion is this: just as crime and upper-class status was at one time overlooked by those who studied and controlled criminal offending, the association between art and crime has likewise suffered from a lack of attention; and Sutherland's framework for reorienting attention to upper-class offending can be similarly applied when arguing for a greater recognition of misconduct in the art world.

TWO INTERSECTING PERSPECTIVES: ART AND CRIMINOLOGY

This volume is not an art or art-history book per se, nor is it simply a collection of true-crime stories. Rather, from a criminological perspective it explores the intersection of art and crime (i.e., the occasions/situations where these two starkly different human endeavors meet or even collide). It follows then that a common understanding of these intersecting perspectives needs to be established. We'll start first with defining criminology and then move on to defining art.

What Is Criminology?

While variations in defining the term "criminology" may be found, these differences tend to reflect semantics more than substance. For instance, in their text entitled *Criminology* (6th ed.), Adler, Mueller, and Laufer defined criminology as "the scientific study of the making of laws, the breaking of laws, and society's reaction to the breaking of laws" (p. 1). An earlier text by Barlow described criminology as the scientific study of crime and criminals.[3] If one simply consults *Merriam-Webster's Collegiate Dictionary*, the definition provided is the scientific study of crime as a social phenomenon, of criminals, and of penal treatment.[4] Sutherland's definition as put forth in 1934 is still widely accepted: "Criminology is the body of knowledge regarding crime as a social phenomenon. It includes within its scope the process of making laws, of breaking laws, and of reacting toward the breaking of laws."[5]

Drawing from a composite of these definitions, the criminological perspective undertaken here will include a systematic examination of (1) the law making process, (2) law breaking, and (3) society's reaction to it, to the extent these dimensions impact the art world. Among the specific topics to be considered that fall under this general outline are:

1. Prevailing laws or lack thereof
2. Types and frequencies of crimes
3. Victimization
4. Offenders
5. Enforcement and prevention responses

What Is Art?

While for many the term "art" may be more familiar than criminology, it nevertheless requires definition in order to provide a framework for the discussions that follow. If there is any doubt about this, review a dictionary definition of this term. For instance, *Merriam-Webster's Dictionary* [6] offers several alternative definitions for art (as a noun):

1. Skill acquired by experience, study, or observation
2. A branch of learning
3. An occupation requiring knowledge or skill
4. The conscious use of skill and creative imagination, especially in the production of aesthetic objects
5. A skillful plan
6. Decorative or illustrative elements in printed matter

While each of these alternatives might apply to our concerns at one point or another, items number four and number six most closely describe the "art" perspective of the art/criminology intersection we are exploring. However, as will soon become apparent, defining art as "decorative or illustrative elements in printed matter" is too limiting. On the other hand, "the conscious use of skill and creative imagination, especially in the production of aesthetic objects," comes closer to the "art" perspective of the art/criminology intersection. However, our exploration here would seem to require a more structured framework to guide our journey, a concern expressed by those (few) others who have ventured into the intersection of art and criminology. For instance, in research conducted on art theft, John Barelli referred to the definition of art as "complex" and as having a "wide extension of meanings." His resolution to this definitional dilemma was to rely on a typological list of objects generally considered to be art. In this case, he adopted an art typology that is reflected by the 16 curatorial departments at the Metropolitan Museum of Art in New York City.[7] This typology in a more recent form is contained in table 1.1.

Criminologist John Conklin followed this same path in his book *Art Crime* (1994). In this volume, the typology used by the International Foundation for Art Research (IFAR; a private organization that tracks stolen art works) formed the definitional basis for "art."[8] Again, this typology is contained in table 1.1. Another art typology is put forth by the Federal Bureau of Investigation's *National Stolen Art File* (NASF; to be discussed further below). Like the IFAR list, this typology serves to describe the type of stolen objects that will be considered for investigative attention as art.[9] This typology is also contained in table 1.1.

The typologies of art objects as detailed in table 1.1 are by no means the only authoritative or recognized classifications of art objects. Other typologies

Table 1.1
Art Typologies

Metropolitan Museum of Art	IFAR	FBI
American decorative arts	Fine arts (including paintings photographs, prints, drawings and sculpture)	Fine arts
American painting and sculpture		Decorative arts
Ancient Near Eastern art	Decorative arts	Antiquities
Arms and armor	Antiquities	Asian art
Arts of Africa, Oceania and the Americas	Ethnographic objects	Islamic art
Asian art	Oriental and Islamic art	Native American art
Costumes	Miscellaneous items (including armor, books, coins, and medals)	Ethnographic objects
Drawings and prints		Archeological material
Egyptian art		Textiles
European paintings		Books and manuscripts
European sculpture and decorative arts		Clocks and watches
Greek and Roman art		Coins
Islamic art		Stamps
Medieval art		Musical instruments
Modern art		Scientific instruments
Musical instruments		
Photographs		
Textiles		

(See appendix A for a description of many of these categories.)

have been compiled by any number of organizations that have a need to categorize art objects (e.g., museums, educational institutions, art galleries and auction houses, government agencies, etc.). However, those detailed in table 1.1 represent a cross section of such classification efforts that have been put forth by renowned organizations, although each has a different role within the art world. The Metropolitan Museum of Art typology reflects the different components of its collection as well as its organizational structure in terms of curatorial departments. The IFAR typology was developed as a framework for its mission as a private, worldwide clearinghouse for stolen art. The FBI typology was devised to define its role as a public agency tasked with the investigation of art crimes. Essentially, however, the three typologies are quite similar, if not overlapping. The Metropolitan Museum of Art list is quite detailed while IFAR's list is more concise, relying on broad, catchall categories of Fine Arts, Decorative Arts, and Antiquities. The FBI list tracks more closely with IFAR although it specifically includes collectibles such as stamps and coins which could fall under IFAR's miscellaneous category. Also, the IFAR and FBI lists, unlike that of the Metropolitan Museum of Art, specifically include an ethnographic category (while the FBI also includes a separate archeology category).

In any event, for our purposes if we are to follow the practice of defining "art" through a typological list of objects generally considered to be art, basing our "art" definition on a composite of the three typologies in table 1.1 would seem to be an arguably sound rationale. Further, in doing so the *specific* types of objects that occupy the realm of our focus, that is, the art/criminology intersection, are now more clearly identified. Having said that, our emphasis will be more on items that fall into the broad categories of Fine Arts (paintings, sculpture, photographs, prints, and drawings), Decorative Arts (jewelry, furniture, ceramics), and Antiquities/Ethnographic/Archeological objects; and less so on such items as coins, stamps, and musical and scientific instruments.

ART: WHY IS IT IMPORTANT? WHY IS IT VALUABLE?

While defining art on a typological basis provides a necessary practical framework for our explorations here, more general definitions hint at why art can be important and valuable. For instance, referring back to the *Merriam-Webster's* definitions above, alternative number four defines "art" as the conscious use of skill and creative imagination, especially in the production of aesthetic objects. Whether it is a worker, a student, an athlete or an artist, we tend to elevate and, in turn, attach value to those whose efforts or work products exhibit or demonstrate skill in appreciation for their uncommon or rare qualities. Likewise, creative imaginations can produce sources of entertainment and pleasure, but not all individuals possess this talent. Again, we tend to elevate and attach value to those with creative imaginations in recognition of their uncommon abilities to provide us enjoyment. Finally, human history provides a long record of engagement with visual media. While the communication role that visual media has played is undeniable (especially before the advent of the written word), ascribing aesthetic qualities to some visual images and objects (i.e., beauty, pleasing to the eye, etc.) has a lengthy tradition that has continued unabated. Visual objects and images with aesthetic qualities have value because of the viewing pleasure they provide in addition to being manifestations of the valued attributes of skill and creative imagination. Thus, art can be valuable as a personal experience simply because we like to look at it. We may see beauty in a piece of art or otherwise derive viewing pleasure from it (e.g., it is thought provoking; it tells an interesting story, etc.). We may also admire the skill and creative imagination of the artist that produced the piece. Does that make art valuable or important? Arguably yes, on both counts! Art is the product of uncommon skill and creative imagination and possesses aesthetic qualities, all of which are attributes of value. We will address the importance of art further before we conclude this discussion, but suffice it to say for now that art has been an essential facilitator of communication as well as a popular form of entertainment throughout human history. But when considering the value and importance of art, other dimensions must be examined as well, especially within our context of the art/criminology intersection.

Monetary Value

William Grampp, in his economic analysis of art (he focused primarily on paintings), applied perhaps the most well-known law of economics to explain the pricing of these objects: the law of supply and demand. As he explained, when something is desired and also scarce, it will have a price.[10] J. E. Conklin, from his perspective as a criminologist, observed that the value of art is not intrinsic but is rather socially constructed.[11] Thus, if we adopt the view put forth above about the value and importance of art, by implication we can argue that at least to some individuals, art is a desirable commodity, which in turn creates a demand for it. However, because objects considered as art have aesthetic qualities that are the product of uncommon or rare skills and creative imagination, works of art are not in abundance but rather are scarce, thereby giving rise to prices being attached to art objects.

While we will forgo a detailed economic history of art, studies of art pricing and art as investment have examined periods as far back as 1650.[12] Grampp assessed five such studies of art and found three that reported long-term upward trends with annual increases at 3.3 percent, 10.5 percent and 11 percent (Old Masters only); one that found the increase to be at 0.55 percent when an adjustment is made for the value of money; and one with a reported increase of 1.5 percent after adjustment. He concluded that for investment purposes, art is great for those who love risk and love art. It is not for the risk-averse or risk-neutral investor. Moreover, these studies tended to show that art as an investment returned less than the stock market. Accordingly, his recommendation was that the art lover should buy art for the pleasure of owning it.[13]

However, these studies deal with comparisons of art values on a year-to-year basis, or even longer intervals, and do not focus on specific prices and/or landmark sales. For our purposes, this latter perspective is important because high prices for art encourage a variety of art crimes.[14] Simon Houpt in his book *Museum of the Missing: A History of Art Theft* (2006) supported this assessment when he described art theft as an epidemic and attributed it to skyrocketing art prices over the past few decades. He traced these dramatic increases to the sale of Cézanne's *Le garçon au gilet rouge* (1890) at auction in London in 1958 for $610,000, a price that was more than five times higher than the amount any painting previously sold for.[15] While differing in the specific watershed sale, researcher Truc-Nhu Ho concluded similarly: art theft did not start to become widespread until 1961 when Rembrandt's *Aristotle Contemplating the Bust of Homer* was sold for $2.3 million, after which art prices increased 10 to 11-fold.[16] Throughout the remainder of the 20th century and into the new millennium, the values of prized pieces of art continued to climb, as evidenced by the sale of Picasso's *Garçon à la pipe* that sold at auction for $104.1 million in May 2004.[17]

Prior to the middle of the 20th century art theft was not common because art collecting was limited by the constraints of the art market. For example, until the advent of Impressionism in the mid-1870s, private art galleries did not promote artists; this practice changed when Impressionist painters, scorned by the prevailing art establishment, organized their own showings. Other factors reported by Truc-Nhu Ho that removed constraints from the U.S. art market included growing prosperity coupled with wider art literacy and increases in the number of museums, art professionals, and art patronage by corporations.[18]

With a few exceptions, the value of art depends on the name of the artist, the quality of the piece, and the period in which the work was produced. Again with a few exceptions, the older the work is, the higher its monetary value.[19] In Grampp's economic analysis of art values, he argued that the value the market places on works of art is consistent with the judgment which is made about their aesthetic quality, a term synonymous with beauty, historical importance, or any attribute other than price.[20] Art-theft investigator Robert Spiel claimed that objects classified as fine art (i.e., paintings and sculptures) constitute the most valuable category of art; and that within this category oil paintings are considered the most valuable pieces.[21]

But just where is "the art market" and how are prices established? As used elsewhere to describe a universe of buyers and sellers of a particular commodity (e.g., the "real estate market"), there are no specially designated places/physical locations known as the "art markets," per se. Rather, we are referring to the abstract concept of a collective group of individuals engaged in the sale and/or purchase of art; whether on a one-time basis or more frequently, to include those who are professionally involved in such transactions. To be clear, however, there are an infinite number of physical locations worldwide where the art market plays out, that is, where art is bought and sold, including art galleries, auction houses, museums, retail outlets, as well as in private, nonpublic settings.

An initial price for a piece of art is usually established through an appraisal process that takes into consideration the sales history of similar objects, value of the medium, investment potential, rarity, craftsmanship, identity of maker, identity of subject, identity of prior possessor, historical significance, condition, size, and subject matter.[22] Whether any given piece is sold for the appraised value, however, will vary with the vagaries of the market; for example, factors such as the motivation of a seller, the eagerness of a buyer, and any competition for the same piece can all influence whether the piece sells at, above, or below the appraised value. Given the nature of art pricing, it should not be surprising that one of the primary trading venues is the auction. Charles W. Smith, author of *Auctions: The Social Construction of Value* (1989), indicated that auctions flourish in situations where conventional ways of establishing price are inadequate for a number of reasons, including when there is something special or unusual about the item.[23] As art objects generally meet these criteria, they are routinely bought and sold at auction, a phenomenon that has given rise to an art-auction industry that includes such giants as Sotheby's and Christie's. Even in this environment, however, bidding starts at a "reserve," or minimum price.[24] For example, Sotheby's describes its reserve as a confidential minimum price below which the item will not be sold. The reserve is established through a presale estimate process that produces a price range (as opposed to a specific appraisal value) that the piece would be expected to sell in, and the reserve price is then fixed at or below the low end of this range.[25]

Cultural/Historical Importance

In addition to art objects being of importance because of their aesthetic qualities, which in turn influences their monetary values, some art is important because it represents the culture of an entire society or civilization and/or has particular historic relevance within a society. In this context, we are usually talking about art that is contained within the following categories identified in table 1.1: Ancient Near Eastern, Egyptian, Greek and Roman, Medieval, Islamic, Antiquities, and Ethnographic and Archeological Material. These types of objects represent the remaining vestiges of civilizations that are foundations for modern societies. In addition to providing a primary means to learn about and study these civilizations, many of these objects exhibit the skill and aesthetic qualities that would place them within the realm of art regardless of their cultural or historic significance. For example, in chronicling the looting of antiquities in Italy, Peter Watson and Cecilia Todeschini called Greek vase paintings the highest achievement of human art until at least the great cathedrals of the High Middle Ages more than a millennium later. They further asserted vase paintings are one of the reasons the ancient Greeks are held in such high esteem. However, they identified other Mediterranean civilizations as well as those in Central and South America, West Africa, and Asia—as sources of objects with cultural and historic importance.[26] And to be clear, while historically and culturally important, the rarity and beauty of many of these objects have resulted in their substantial, if not incalculable, monetary value as well. For example, a wood and ivory carving of Phoenician origin known as *Lioness Attacking a Nubian* (720 B.C.E) was stolen from the Iraq National Museum in Baghdad in April 2003 following the U.S. invasion. It is considered priceless.[27] A life-size ivory carving of the head of the Greek sun god Apollo from the fifth century B.C.E has been valued at $50 million.[28]

The Value and Importance of Art: In Summary

Art is valuable because it is the product of rare skill and creative imagination, which in turn results in aesthetic or otherwise desirable qualities. Art has monetary value, sometimes substantial in nature, because by its nature (i.e., rare skill and creative imagination that produces objects with aesthetic qualities), it is in short supply relative to the demand for it. Finally, art is valuable and important because it portrays the culture and sometimes history of societies; and in many instances, it provides the extant evidence of great early human civilizations. As has been suggested throughout this discussion, as the value and importance attached to art has increased, criminal activity associated with art has done likewise. It is the nature of this activity that we will now turn our attention to.

ART CRIMES

In exploring the intersection of art and criminology, we will focus on the following types of misconduct:

- Larceny
- Burglary
- Robbery
- Forgery, fakery and counterfeiting
- Theft of and/or damage to art incident to wars and civil/religious unrest
- Illicit trafficking in objects of cultural-heritage and/or historic importance

- White-collar crime within the art world
- Vandalism and malicious destruction of art

These categories of misconduct in their more general or common manifestations are probably not unfamiliar to those who have studied or who have responsibilities for controlling crime; however, here each of these offenses will be explored within the unique context of the art world. This unique context also requires that we expand the reach to include consideration of illegal but not necessarily criminal conduct, that is, conduct that is defined statutorily as a crime and punishable by fines and/or imprisonment. While conduct that constitutes larceny, burglary, robbery, or vandalism/malicious destruction of property is generally considered to be criminal in nature and is usually investigated and prosecuted as such, the remainder of our misconduct categories may or may not be pursued in this manner, depending upon the circumstances in each case. What will become apparent is that when criminal proceedings are not undertaken, civil remedies have been applied; and in some instances, diplomatic efforts have resulted in international treaties to address the misconduct.

As may be recalled from the outset of this chapter, taking this approach when examining illegal conduct is not without precedent. Criminologist Edwin Sutherland argued for the study of white-collar crime in this manner because much of this type of misconduct was not sanctioned through the criminal court system.[29] Moreover, Adler et al.'s definition of criminology (i.e., the scientific study of the making of laws, the breaking of laws, and society's reaction to the breaking of laws[30]) supports this broad approach.

In the chapters that follow, each of the types of art crime identified above will be examined in detail, including victimization within each category. However, within this introductory chapter some general observations about criminal victimization in the art world will be put forth.

Victimization: A Worldwide Impact

The first observation that needs to be offered in this regard is that while the term "art world" has been and will continue to be used throughout this volume to refer to the collective of those vocationally and avocationally involved or affiliated with art, the art world we will be examining is also global (i.e., geographically global) in scope. One indicator of the global scope of the art world is art-auction sales data. In 1995, most of the world's art-auction sales (in terms of monetary value) took place in Austria, France, Germany, Italy, Netherlands, Sweden, Switzerland, the United Kingdom, and the United States.[31] While this listing of nations is tilted toward Western Europe and North America, when source regions of cultural-heritage objects are also considered, that is, throughout the Mediterranean, Central and South America, Africa, and Asia, the art world's global reach comes into focus. Given our modern-day environment of escalating art prices (as discussed above) and the assessment that high prices for art encourage a variety of art crimes, the United Nations' ranking of art crime as the third most serious transnational crime should not be surprising, especially since this type of activity not only manifests itself as a costly form of property crime but can also be responsible for depriving entire nations and cultures of their cultural heritage.

A second general observation is that the worldwide scope of art crime introduces a complexity when attempting to define victimization. Calculating art-crime occurrences and losses is made difficult by obstacles commonly encountered when trying to quantify crime on an international basis; for example, nations have different laws and different methods for gathering crime statistics.[32] The bottom line: there is no reliable, comprehensive data regarding art-crime victimization.[33]

Victimization: Measuring Frequencies and Losses

While there may be no reliable, comprehensive data on art crime, this is not to say we are devoid of any statistics or other indicators of the prevalence of art crimes. Surveys have been taken; estimates have been put forth; and some databases are maintained; however, most of these efforts are limited to stolen, missing, and/or lost art (and not other art crimes such as forgeries, counterfeits, fraud and vandalism, or malicious damage). Keep in mind, however, all these efforts are hindered by the obstacles cited above when attempting to quantify crime on the international level (that is, differing laws and data-collection methods). With these caveats in mind, loss estimates due to theft alone (and inclusive of cultural-heritage objects) that have been reported in the art-crime literature range from $1 billion to $6 billion annually.[34] Not reflected in this dollar loss range are the number of theft incidents and the number of stolen/missing pieces of art and cultural-heritage items. Estimates that have been put forth in regard to the latter talk in terms of tens of thousands of, if not 100,000, paintings, sculptures, and other art objects as missing.[35] Although this estimated range is not annualized and represents collective losses over time, the impact is still substantial considering the huge, if not priceless, values of some missing pieces. Moreover, as Houpt emphasized, "When a painting goes missing, we lose a piece of our common heritage."[36] In another assessment along these lines, but referring specifically to cultural-heritage objects, Watson and Todeschini stated, "Virtually half of the history of Greek, Etruscan, and Roman culture in Italy has been stolen from us."[37]

However, one of the more somber opinions (and perhaps quite accurate) on attempts to quantify art crime comes from Interpol, the international police organization. Referring to the theft and trafficking in art and cultural-heritage items, Interpol claims that it is very difficult to determine the number and value of stolen art objects. They further express doubt that accurate statistics can be gathered on this type of crime because most countries track these incidents by type of theft (i.e., larceny, burglary, robbery) rather than by the nature of the object stolen.[38] The observation being made here becomes clearer when one considers such well-established U.S. crime databases as the *Uniform Crime Report* and the *National Crime Victimization Survey.* The goal of these databases is solely to identify how frequently certain monitored crimes occur and to report on related offender and victim details. Art crime, in any form, is not a separately identified category in either of these databases, nor is it a separate crime category in the still-evolving *National Incident Based Reporting System.* In fact, even periodic international crime-collection surveys undertaken by the United Nations do not separate out art-crime data. However, Interpol does make an attempt to do so, but has found on average only 60 of 186 of its members submit replies regarding art theft, some of which are incomplete while others are simply negative reports. They also note complications in placing value on cultural-heritage items. For instance, cultural-heritage objects may have one value in their country of origin but another value in the country where they are destined. Moreover, the value of objects being removed through illicit archeological looting will not be established until they eventually appear in the international market.[39]

Art-Crime Databases

As indicated above, in addition to art-crime estimates and surveys, there are also ongoing efforts in the form of databases that track at least certain types of art crime (usually thefts and lost/missing objects). While helpful in providing some perspective on art-crime victimization, their primary purpose is not purely statistical gathering to determine frequency of offending and victimization. Rather, their primary goal is to assist in the investigation and recovery of stolen art, and to discourage its trafficking/dissemination. With the advent of computerized databases, the details of a reported incident can be made rapidly available worldwide, often with accompanying photographs to facilitate identification. Not only can such information possibly assist in the investigation and recovery of lost, missing, or stolen art, but these types of indices can also provide a means for those in the private sector (gallery owners, museums, private collectors) to check on the bona fides of an object before acquiring it. It is believed that the availability and, in turn, increased use of these indices act as a deterrent to at least some art crime. Table 1.2 identifies and describes six prominent art-crime databases. They are prominent because they are (1) widely consulted, (2) contain a sizable volume of entries, and/or (3) collect data on a broad geographical basis, if not worldwide. However, these are not the only art-loss databases operated by government, police, and private organizations. Appendix B contains a more comprehensive listing of art-loss databases that can be accessed online.

Table 1.2
Art-crime Databases

Name/Operator	Type/Scope of Data	Stated Purpose/Goals	Accessibility
Art Loss Register[1]/International Foundation For Art Research (IFAR)	The world's largest private database of lost and stolen art, antiques, and collectibles; world-wide in scope; computerized and operating since 1991. Over 200,000 listed items and instrumental in $140 million in recoveries.	Deters theft and assists in recovery of stolen items.	Collectors, the art trade, insurers, and worldwide law-enforcement agencies. Search fees apply.
National Stolen Art File[2]/Federal Bureau of Investigation	Computerized index of stolen art and cultural objects as reported to the FBI by law enforcement in the United States and worldwide. Generally limited to objects with a value of at least $2,000.	Assists investigators in art and cultural-object theft cases and provides analytical data to law enforcement.	Both listing objects in the database and requesting searches must originate through law-enforcement channels.
Stolen Works of Art Database[3]/Interpol	Computerized database that contains approximately 34,000 stolen and missing art objects. Data includes both descriptions and photos and is worldwide in scope.	Centralizes and assists in the analysis of information received about stolen/missing art and cultural-heritage objects in an effort to give it added value.	Access to the database is available to law enforcement, and to others upon application.
London Stolen Art Database[4]/New Scotland Yard	Computerized database containing over 54,000 art, antique, and cultural-property items.	Assists in the collation and dissemination of intelligence pertaining to art crime. It is not to be used for "due diligence searches."	Photos and/or descriptions of some of the included items are available online.
Stolen Art Database[5]/Italian Carabinieri	Database containing over 240,000 artifacts and artworks stolen from Italy.	Assists in the investigation and recovery of stolen Italian art and cultural-heritage objects.	Public access to database at http://www.carabinieri.it/Internet/Cittadino/Servizi/BanceDati/
Trace Looted Art[6]/Trace	A global database containing reports of art objects that were stolen during the Holocaust era by the Nazis.	Assists in the identification of these objects incident to their discovery and/or dissemination for purposes of recovery and return to claimants.	Access available to both affected private-sector parties as well as law enforcement.

[1] *Data sources:* www.artloss.com/home/content (accessed September 18, 2007); and Houpt, S. 2006. *Museum of the Missing: A History of Art Theft.* New York: Sterling Publishing, 8, 113.

[2] *Data source:* http://www.fbi.gov/hq/cid/arttheft/artcrimeteam.htm (accessed September 17, 2007).

[3] *Data source:* www.interpol.int/Public/WorkOfArt/woafaq.asp (accessed September 12, 2007); and Interpol Media Release, August 17, 2009 (accessed through http://www.interpol.int/Public/ICPO/PressReleases/PR2009/PR200978.asp).

[4] *Data source:* http://www.met.police.uk/artandantiques/index.htm (accessed September 17, 2008).

[5] *Data source:* http://www.carabinieri.it/Internet/ (accessed September 17, 2007).

[6] *Data source:* http://www.tracelootedart.com (accessed September 12, 2007).

While we will revisit in more detail art-crime investigative efforts by the organizations identified in table 1.2 (as well as others) in chapter 9, these databases do offer another perspective on assessing frequency and victimization, at least in terms of stolen and missing objects. Note that the *Art Loss Register* contains over 200,000 missing objects while the Italian Carabinieri (the national paramilitary police) database contains over 240,000 items (many of which are cultural- heritage objects). Thus, these figures are in marked contrast to loss estimates cited earlier that ranged from tens of thousands to one hundred thousand. These estimates, however, might not be fully inclusive of cultural-heritage objects, a category that has particular emphasis in the Carabinieri database, all of which serves as a reminder that we lack comprehensive, reliable art-crime statistics.

CASE STUDIES

Many of the chapters that follow contain one or more case studies to illustrate the particular crime categories being examined. The case presented here in this introductory chapter (in the form of an actual U.S. Department of Justice press release, see box 1.1) serves a twofold purpose: (1) it illustrates a case in which one of the above databases played an instrumental role in the recovery and investigation of stolen art; and (2) it provides an overview of the types of offenders frequently encountered in art crimes and the environment in which they often operate (i.e., street-crime type criminals, middle men/fences, white-collar professionals, all operating in an international setting).

BOX 1.1 CASE STUDY: A CLASSIC TALE OF ART CRIME

United States Attorney Michael J. Sullivan

District of Massachusetts
Tuesday, February 13, 2007

Retired Massachusetts Attorney Arrested On Federal Charge Of Possession And Attempted Sale Of Stolen Art

BOSTON, MA—A federal complaint was unsealed today following the arrest of a retired Massachusetts attorney on a charge of possessing, concealing, storing and attempting to sell stolen goods that had crossed United States borders, in connection with seven pieces of art stolen in 1978 from a Stockbridge home—the largest burglary from a private residence in Massachusetts history.

United States Attorney Michael J. Sullivan and Warren T. Bamford, Special Agent in Charge of the Federal Bureau of Investigation in New England, announced today that **ROBERT R. MARDIROSIAN,** 72, Falmouth, Massachusetts, and St. Paul de Vence, France, was arrested today on a complaint charging him with possession, concealment, storage and attempted sale of goods that had crossed a United States boundary that he knew to have been stolen. **MARDIROSIAN** was arrested today at Boston's Logan International Airport as he disembarked a flight from France. He will appear later today in federal court before a U.S. Magistrate Judge.

"It is extremely disheartening that an attorney charged with upholding the law, as the defendant was in this case, would disregard that duty and for decades conceal the whereabouts of priceless works of art for no other reason than greed," stated U.S. Attorney Sullivan. "As a result, the paintings have needlessly been kept from their rightful owner for nearly thirty years. The defendant is alleged to have held on to the artwork because he hoped to receive payment in exchange for their return. No one involved in the theft or concealment of art should be allowed to profit. We will continue to pursue this case until all of the stolen artwork is reunited with its rightful owner." "It is unconscionable to think that an attorney, knowingly in possession of stolen property, would negotiate the return of the paintings for a finder's fee instead of returning them to the rightful owner," commented FBI Special Agent in Charge Bamford.

On Memorial Day weekend in 1978, seven pieces of valuable artwork, including the Cezanne painting, "Pitcher and Fruits," were stolen from a home in Stockbridge. According to affidavits filed with the court, and unsealed today, **MARDIROSIAN,** now retired, practiced law in Massachusetts from the 1960's until 1995. It is alleged that **MARDIROSIAN** has secretly held the stolen paintings since 1978 after the alleged thief, David Colvin, whom **MARDIROSIAN** represented in another case, left them with him. Colvin was killed in a dispute with gambling debt collectors in 1979 at his home in Pittsfield.

It is alleged that **MARDIROSIAN** maintained possession of the stolen artwork in Massachusetts until 1988, when he moved the paintings to Monaco and later to a Swiss bank for safekeeping. It is alleged that **MARDIROSIAN** intended to return the stolen paintings to their owner in exchange for a finder's fee or 10% of their value. According to the affidavit, **MARDIROSIAN** was able to keep his possession of the paintings secret by working through lawyers in London, Monaco and Switzerland, as well as a Panamanian shell company he created, Erie International Trading Co. (Erie). It is alleged that using the cover of the Panamanian shell company in 1999, **MARDIROSIAN** attempted to sell the stolen paintings in London. However, an investigation by the Art Loss Register (ALR) determined that the artwork was stolen. ALR is a London-based company that maintains a comprehensive database of stolen artwork. Auction houses, such as Sotheby's, retain ALR's services when performing due diligence on artwork to be auctioned. ALR alerted the Stockbridge owner that his stolen paintings had surfaced and ultimately, on October 15, 1999, brokered a "contract" between the owner and Erie, whereby Erie handed over the most valuable painting, the Cezanne, in exchange for the owner's relinquishing all claims to the remaining six pieces of artwork. At the time, the six paintings were given a total value of approximately $1 million. Two months later in December, the owner auctioned the Cezanne through Sotheby's in London for $29.3 million—it had been purchased by the owner's mother for $500,000 in 1963.

In November 2004, Sotheby's was contacted by Paul Palandjian of Belmont, seeking to have the auction house sell four paintings for his client. After taking possession of the four paintings, Sotheby's was informed by ALR that the paintings were among the six remaining stolen Stockbridge paintings. The owner thereafter filed suit in the English courts against Sotheby's and Erie claiming that the 1999 "contract" he entered into with Erie was void because it had been signed under duress. Ultimately, in December 2005, the British court found in favor of the Stockbridge owner ruling that the 1999 "contract" was void. The Court also revealed that the client for whom Palandjian was trying to sell the four stolen paintings was **MARDIROSIAN.**

According to a search warrant affidavit, Palandjian told investigators that in December 2003, **MARDIROSIAN** asked him to help in selling the remaining six stolen paintings. Palandjian agreed to do so for a commission. After beginning to make arrangements with Sotheby's to sell the paintings at auction, Palandjian flew to Geneva, Switzerland and received the six remaining paintings from **MARDIROSIAN**'s friend, Henri Klein, who had been holding them for **MARDIROSIAN.** Palandjian had them brought to a Swiss bank for storage, until April 2005, when he arranged for four of the six paintings to be shipped from Geneva to Sotheby's in London—after which the owner filed his suit seeking to void the 1999 "contract" with Erie. The remaining two paintings were returned to Klein.

The four paintings, "Portrait d'une Jeune Fille" and "Portrait d'un Jeune Homme" by Chaim Soutine, and "Maison Rouge" and "Flowers" by Maurice de Vlaminck remain in the custody of Sotheby's Auction house. The remaining two stolen paintings, "Woman Seated" and "Boy" by Jean Jansen are believed to be in the possession of Henri Klein in Switzerland.

MARDIROSIAN will appear this afternoon in federal court before U.S. Magistrate Judge Marianne B. Bowler. If convicted, **MARDIROSIAN** faces a maximum sentence of 10 years in prison, to be followed by 3 years of supervised release and a $250,000 fine.

The investigation is continuing. The case is being investigated by the Federal Bureau of Investigation with assistance from the Art Loss Registry. It is being prosecuted by Assistant U.S. Attorney Jonathan Mitchell in Sullivan's Economic Crimes Unit. The details contained in the complaint are allegations. The defendant is presumed to be innocent unless and until proven guilty beyond a reasonable doubt in a court of law.

On August 18, 2008, a federal jury in Boston found Mardirosian guilty of knowingly possessing the stolen paintings and he received a seven-year prison term along with a $100,000 fine.[40]

ART AND CRIME: IN SUMMARY

Crime in the art world has received relatively little attention notwithstanding at least one report that ranks it as the third most serious transnational crime problem behind money laundering and terrorist activities. Art crime is global in scope and impact, and includes theft (larceny, burglary, robbery); forgery/counterfeiting/fraud; illicit trafficking in objects of cultural-heritage and/or historic importance; theft/damage to art incident to wars and political/religious unrest; white-collar crime; and vandalism and malicious destruction.

As art values have climbed over the past 40 years, criminal activity associated with art has also increased. However, there is no reliable, comprehensive data regarding art-crime victimization, and Interpol has expressed doubt that accurate data of this nature can be collected. At best, loss estimates in terms of dollar value have been put forth that range from $1 billion to $6 billion annually. While several art-crime databases are maintained by public and private organizations, their primary purpose is to assist in the recovery and investigation of stolen or missing art.

CHAPTER 2

Art Theft

When one thinks of "art crime," the illegal activity that probably comes most readily to mind is the theft or stealing of art. This relationship is likely due to a number of high-profile incidents in which famous pieces of art have been stolen, events that have received heavy media coverage. If real life events are not enough, Hollywood has found these incidents so intriguing that a number of movies have been made that portray art thieves as the cultured sophisticates of the criminal world. In fact, the enduring popularity of the art-theft story told in *The Thomas Crown Affair* resulted in its remake (starring Pierce Brosnan and Rene Russo) more than 30 years after the original release that starred Steve McQueen and Faye Dunaway. But before our thoughts drift to other popular-culture portrayals of art theft—OK, a couple more: Dr. No, who showed off his stolen Goya in the first James Bond movie; and Sean Connery and Catherine Zeta-Jones in *Entrapment*, an art-theft movie with a storyline curiously similar to *The Thomas Crown Affair*—let's return to real life. In fact, when viewed through the eyes of those who study crime or investigate crime, art theft is not looked upon as a singular category but rather as multiple types of offending, each of which is distinguished by the methods that were utilized in carrying out the theft. For our purposes here, we will focus on three general types of offending that result in theft: larceny, burglary, and robbery.

THEFT OFFENSES GENERALLY: LARCENY, BURGLARY, AND ROBBERY

Chapter 1 introduced two recurring themes that are inherent in the study of art crime: (1) it is worldwide in scope, (2) which results in dealing with variations in how crimes are defined from one nation to another. We have chosen to examine art theft in terms of larceny, burglary, and robbery, crimes that are defined and tracked by the *Uniform Crime Report* (*UCR*) that is compiled by the Federal Bureau of Investigation. Again, recall from chapter 1 that the *UCR* is one of the major crime-monitoring programs in the United States (the other being the *National Crime Victimization Survey*). The *UCR* reflects crimes reported to the police, and larceny, burglary, and robbery are considered major or Part I crimes within this data-collection program. Specific definitions for the monitored crimes are provided to contributing police agencies to enhance reporting consistency and standardization. The *UCR* definitions for larceny, burglary, and robbery are as follows:

- Larceny—larceny-theft is the unlawful taking, carrying, leading, or riding away of property from the possession or constructive possession of another. Examples are thefts of bicycles, motor vehicle parts and accessories, shoplifting, pocket-picking, or the stealing of any property or article that is not taken by force and violence or by fraud. Attempted larcenies are included. (*Note that under this definition larceny and theft are treated synonymously as long as no force, violence, or fraud was involved.*)

- Burglary—the unlawful entry of a structure to commit a felony or theft. To classify an offense as a burglary, the use of force to gain entry need not have occurred. There are three sub-classifications for burglary: forcible entry, unlawful entry where no force is used, and attempted forcible entry. The *UCR* definition of "structure" includes, for example, apartment, barn, house trailer or houseboat when used as a permanent dwelling, office, railroad car (but not automobile), stable, and vessel (i.e., ship).

- Robbery—the taking or attempting to take anything of value from the care, custody, or control of a person or persons by force or threat of force or violence and/or by putting the victim in fear.[1]

These crimes, of course, are not unique to the United States, but again they may be defined somewhat differently from country to country. While it would be too cumbersome (and perhaps unnecessary) to examine the definitions for these types of misconduct on a country by country basis, one way to gain a consolidated international perspective is to consider the definitions used by the United Nations (U.N.) in collecting data on worldwide crime trends. These definitions are as follows:

- Theft—may be understood to mean the removal of property without the property owner's consent and excludes burglary and housebreaking as well as theft of a motor vehicle.

- Burglary—may be understood to mean unlawful entry into someone else's premises with the intention to commit a crime.

- Robbery—may be understood to mean the theft of property from a person, overcoming resistance by force or threat of force.[2]

As may be observed, aside from variations in verbiage, the only significant difference between the *UCR* and U.N. definitions is that the latter replaces the term larceny with theft, although the respective descriptions of the misconduct involved are essentially the same.

The point to this discussion is that while studying art crime places us in an international environment where laws may differ, at least in terms of incidents where art has been stolen, there tends to be some worldwide consensus in the categorical characteristics of these cases, that is, larceny/theft, burglary, and robbery. But let's put these categories/definitions to work in the context of our focus, art crime. Consider the following case studies where art has been stolen through larceny/theft, burglary, and robbery.

BOX 2.1 LARCENY/THEFT: STEPHANE BREITWEISER[3]

Beginning in March 1995 in Switzerland with the theft of a painting valued at $2,000 by German artist Christian Wilhem Dietrich, Stephane Breitweiser stole 239 pieces of art from 179 museums and galleries in Belgium, Denmark, the Netherlands, Germany, Austria, France, and Switzerland. Over nearly eight years, he stole paintings, drawings, silverware, ivory carvings, illuminated manuscripts, and sculpture. The most expensive piece he stole was valued at $9 million, *Sybil, Princess of Cleves,* by Lucas Cranach (the elder). He also stole *Cheat Profiting from his Master* by Pieter Brueghel (the Younger) in May 1997 in Antwerp, Belgium; Corneille de la Haye's *Madeleine of France, Queen of Scotland;* Boucher's *Sleeping Shepherd* from a museum in Chartres, France, in August 1996; David Tenier's *The Monkey Ball;* and Watteau's *A Study of Two Men* from a Montpellier (France) museum in June 1999. He was finally apprehended in the winter of 2003 incident to the theft of a bugle from a museum in Lucerne, Switzerland, and although initially looked upon as a petty thief, police from Switzerland and France were able to piece together other losses that they tied to him.

Breitweiser, a native of France and a waiter by occupation, began stealing art in his mid-twenties. He claimed to be obsessed with collecting and possessing art objects, and there was no evidence that his thievery was motivated by any monetary considerations. He visited poorly guarded museums and galleries during regular business hours, and he stole small objects that could be concealed in his coat. Thus, he committed larceny or theft: he was legally on the premises and removed property that did not belong to him. In the case of paintings, he would cut them from their frames and then roll them up to accomplish this. He usually was accompanied by his girlfriend, Anne-Catherine Kleinklauss, who kept watch or flirted with any guards on duty to distract them while he engaged in theft. Breitweiser's mother, Mireille Stengel, became aware of his activities and was responsible for destroying as many as 160 of the stolen art objects, including Cranach's *Sybil, Princess of Cleves,* which she reportedly chopped up and placed in pieces in the garbage. Her other method of destruction was to toss them in the Rhine-Rhone Canal, located about 60 miles from her home. She claimed that she destroyed the objects to punish her son for this thievery, although police believe she was simply attempting to destroy evidence.

Estimates of the total value of the artworks stolen by Breitweiser vary widely, from as much as $1.9 billion to the $14–$20 million range. He, along with his girlfriend and mother, were prosecuted and convicted in France. Breitweiser received a sentence of 26 months in prison; his mother received 18 months in prison; and his girlfriend was sentenced to 6 months in prison.

BOX 2.2 BURGLARY: OSLO, NORWAY— THE SCREAM (PART I)[4]

Edvard Munch (1863–1944), viewed by many as Norway's premier artist, painted his most well-known work, *The Scream*, in 1893. Munch had actually painted four versions of this same theme, one of which was on display in 1994 in the National Gallery at Oslo, Norway. It had been located on the third floor of the gallery but then was relocated to the second floor and hung on a wall near an unreinforced window. It was neither bolted to the wall nor protected by any type of alarm system. At 6:29 AM on February 12, 1994, two men placed a ladder on the exterior of the National Gallery adjacent to the second-floor window near where *The Scream* was located. One of the men scaled the ladder, broke the window, grabbed *The Scream* from the wall, and climbed back down the ladder where he handed it to his waiting accomplice. In a total of 55 seconds, a painting valued at $72 million vanished, with the burglars using two vehicles stolen the day before to make their escape. Thus, the men committed burglary: they gained unlawful entry to the premises and then committed a theft.

While surveillance cameras were operating inside the gallery at the time of the burglary, the video images were so poor that the physical features of the burglars could not be determined, other than the fact they were wearing gloves, thus explaining the lack of fingerprints. Additionally, no witnesses could be developed and the burglars left no footprints. Subsequent investigation determined that the thieves did some advance scouting to determine the night guard's routine and the coverage of the surveillance cameras.

Efforts to recover *The Scream* and apprehend the burglars by the Oslo Police were extensive but futile. One of their initial suspects was a 26-year-old Norwegian soccer star turned criminal, Pal Enger. In February 1988, he stole another work by Munch, *The Vampire*, from the Munch Museum, also in Oslo. Other than his prior track record and the fact that the gallery's surveillance cameras filmed him on the premises five days before the burglary, police had no other evidence to tie him to the crime.

In April 1994, a British inmate with ties to the Norwegian underworld made overtures about being able to secure the release of *The Scream* for a monetary reward. Scotland Yard's Art Squad detectives evaluated this information but found the inmate to be unreliable. However, incident to providing this assistance to the Norwegian authorities, they offered their services to effect a sting operation in the event anyone else came forward offering to return *The Scream* for a price. As will be discussed here time and again, the downside of stealing a famous piece of art is the difficulty in marketing it; that is, no legitimate collector will knowingly buy a well-known stolen art object. Thus, ransom or extortion-type tactics are often employed by criminals to realize any profit from their thievery. To exploit this possibility, Norwegian authorities encouraged the gallery to make public announcements that information leading to the recovery of *The Scream* should be directed to a particular gallery official. By the end of April, these overtures bore fruit when a Norwegian art dealer reported being approached by individuals who were interested in selling *The Scream*. At this point, legendary Scotland Yard art detective Charley Hill took on the undercover persona of a representative from the Getty Museum of Los Angeles, an organization with the known resources to make such a purchase (he was accompanied by another undercover Scotland Yard detective who acted as the Getty representative's bodyguard). Hill approached the dealer and was subsequently introduced to two of the thieves with whom he conducted a transaction on May 7, 1994, that resulted in the recovery of *The Scream* and the thieves' arrests.

Further investigation by the Norwegian police determined that their original suspect, Pal Enger, was in fact the ring leader and it was he and 18-year-old William Aasheim who actually committed the burglary. The two men nabbed in the sting operation were Tor Johnsen and Bjorn Grytdal. In January 1996 they all were convicted in a Norwegian court and were sentenced to prison as follows: Enger, six years, three months; Aasheim, three years, nine months; Grytdal, four years, nine months; and Johnsen, two years, eight months. After they began serving their sentences, the thieves, with the exception of Enger, had their convictions overturned by a Norwegian Appeals Court that found the testimony of the undercover Scotland Yard detectives was not admissible because they entered Norway using false identities. Nevertheless, for the Norwegian authorities the recovery of *The Scream* was always the main objective in this case and it was successfully accomplished.

BOX 2.3 ROBBERY: OSLO, NORWAY— THE SCREAM (PART II)[5]

Munch's *The Scream* was victimized again, over 10 years later, although this time the crime occurred at the Munch Museum in Oslo and involved a different version of the painting. On Sunday, August 22, 2004, two Norwegian-speaking men armed with pistols and wearing ski masks to conceal their identities committed a daring armed robbery at 11:10 AM. While one of the robbers held 70 visitors and two unarmed security guards at gunpoint, the other removed from the wall *The Scream* and another painting by Munch, *The Madonna* (1893–1894). They exited the museum to a waiting black Audi station wagon with a masked getaway driver (but not before dropping the paintings twice as they ran out the door). Thus, this theft was accomplished through robbery: the paintings were stolen through the use or threatened use of force.

The nearest police station was a half mile away and officers arrived in minutes responding to an alarm that was triggered incident to removing the paintings. Two hours later and less than one mile from the crime scene, police found shattered wooden frames and glass from the paintings, a discovery that raised concerns about damage to the paintings. The getaway car was also later found abandoned in Oslo.

By this time *The Scream's* value had climbed to $100 million, an increase attributed to the phenomenon that once a painting is stolen and then recovered, it tends to command a higher price upon its return. Once again, however, the robbers stole a well-known, highly valuable work that would be impossible to sell in any legitimate fashion. It was feared that these circumstances could lead to the worst-case scenario of *The Scream* disappearing forever, with an alternative being a ransom/extortion attempt, absent police successful intervention.

Fortunately, the police investigation was successful in both apprehending the robbers and eventually recovering the two paintings. The paintings were recovered by police on August 31, 2006, more than two years after the robbery, and they were found in damaged condition from exposure to moisture, along with scrapes, loose paint, holes, and embedded tiny glass fragments. Police would not disclose the details surrounding the recovery. Those arrested and convicted for the robbery were Petter Tharaldsen, age 35 (sentenced to nine-and-a-half years in prison); Bjoern Hoen, age 39 (sentenced to nine years in prison); and Stian Skjold, 31 (sentenced to five-and-a-half years in prison). A fourth suspect had died before charges could be filed.

LARCENY, BURGLARY, AND ROBBERY OF ART: WHAT DO WE KNOW ABOUT THESE CRIMES?

Monetary Losses and Frequencies of Occurrence

Recall the ominous warning in chapter 1 that there is no reliable, comprehensive data regarding art-crime victimization. At best, we talk in terms of loss estimates attributable to theft, which commonly range between $1 billion and $6 billion annually. Moreover, we lack accurate information on the frequency of theft incidents; that is, what is the total number of known art thefts and/or how many occur within in any given time frame (e.g., over the course of a year)? Our only hints in this regard are reflected in limited-scope databases (i.e., those that are comprised of voluntary submissions and/or cover specific geographic areas). For instance, the *Art Loss Register* has in excess of 200,000 loss reports on file.[6]

Moreover, we lack comprehensive data on the specifics of how these losses occurred, that is, through larceny/theft, burglary, or robbery. The literature on art crime and the available data/estimates generally describe incidents of stealing art as thefts and, as suggested earlier, tend to be silent on whether we're really talking about larceny/theft or burglary or robbery. And to complicate matters further, it is often unclear whether the art-theft estimates we do have are inclusive of losses that could be attributable to lootings incident to wars or political/religious unrest and the plundering of cultural-heritage sites, or whether these estimates only reflect thefts that have occurred in the more traditional criminal-activity scenarios (e.g., stealing from museums, galleries, homes, etc.). Notwithstanding these uncertainties, this chapter will move forward in its examination of art theft in terms of larceny, burglary, and robbery committed in traditional criminal scenarios as described above (and as exemplified in the above case studies) and leave lootings incident to wars or political/religious unrest and the plundering of cultural-heritage sites to later chapters.

Along these lines, let's start out with what we think we know. Conklin's observation was that the use of force or the threat to use force to steal art is probably the least common form of art theft,[7] thus suggesting that robbery of art objects is committed with less frequency than art-related larceny or burglary. This observation is supported by the limited empirical research that has been done on art theft (i.e., research that is conducted in a systematic manner and relies on quantitative or qualitative data drawn from observation or experience[8]). Ho's study of art theft (hereinafter the New York study) examined 229 New York City Police Department reports filed between 1985 and 1988 that alleged theft of art objects. Through this examination, the study concluded that art-related robbery was a "rare" occurrence.[9] Barelli's research on art theft in England (hereinafter the England study) examined over 3,300 Scotland Yard records of art theft for the period 1980–1982 and found none that described the reported theft as a robbery.[10]

When attempting to distinguish between the frequency of art-related larceny versus art-related burglary, Conklin along with law-enforcement agencies such as the FBI and Interpol identified burglary as the most common form of art theft.[11] While the England study provided evidence that robbery of art was uncommon, it was silent on the issue of distinguishing larceny from burglary.[12] Such was not the case, however, in the New York study. Here the review of the 229 New York City police reports that alleged art theft found that larceny was the most frequent cause, followed by burglary. Additionally, this research also sought art-theft data directly from gallery owners through a self-report survey. The results of this survey (number of respondents = 45) also found that larceny was the more frequent form of art-theft victimization and, further, these results revealed that 14 of 34 theft incidents were not reported to the police. Interestingly, among the reasons provided for nonreporting included not wanting to confront a suspect employee, thus again attributing the theft to larceny as opposed to burglary.[13]

Worldwide Crime Trends

While not conclusive in resolving whether there are more art larcenies than art burglaries (or vice versa), examining offending data for these crimes generally may add some further perspective on this issue. The United Nations has attempted to track offending data on a worldwide basis. This program has standardized definitions for a variety of commonly tracked crimes (including larceny/theft, burglary, and robbery) and solicits data on offending frequencies on a periodic basis. Submission of this data is voluntary and the caveats raised in chapter 1 concerning international crime data, that is, differing laws and differing data-collection methods, must be reiterated. With these limitations and caveats in mind, what we find is that for the most recent period where complete data was available, by a wide margin larceny/theft was more frequently reported than burglary, both in terms of actual numbers as well as in terms of rate of offending per 100,000 population. In fact, larceny/theft was more frequently reported than several other commonly tracked crimes, including robbery, with substantial differences being evident in each case. Table 2.1 presents this data.

Figures 2.1 and 2.2 present this data in graphic form and provide comparisons between the world and the United States (using 2002 *UCR* data) on offending frequencies and offending rates per 100,000 population for these selected crimes. It may be observed that both worldwide and in the United States, larceny/theft was the most frequently reported crime, both in terms of actual incidents and rate per 100,000, followed by burglary and robbery.

Table 2.1
Worldwide Crime Trends for Selected Offenses: Frequencies and Rates/100,000 Population (2002)*

Offenses	Larceny/ Theft[+]	Burglary[++]	Robbery[+++]	Assault[^]	Rape[^^]	Murder[^^^]
Number of incidents	22,560,266	6,346,383	2,172,037	1,637,434	245,604	75,164
Rate/100 K	1470.66	606.22	112.62	67.68	13.59	4.98

* Data compiled from the Eighth United Nations Survey on Crime Trends and the Operations of Criminal Justice Systems (2001–2002) retrieved on October 2, 2007, from http://www.unodc.org/undoc/en/crime_cicp_survey_eighth.html.
Number of Reporting Countries: [+] N = 50; [++]N = 38; [+++]N = 48; [^]N = 40; [^^]N = 50; [^^^]N = 49

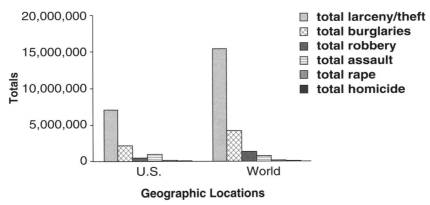

Figure 2.1 Crime frequencies: United States vs. world

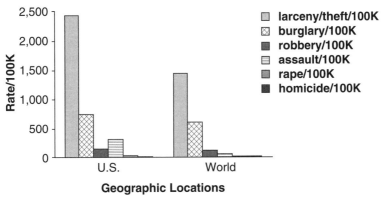

Figure 2.2 Rate per 100,000 population: United States vs. world

The point to this discussion is to demonstrate the consistency between the New York study results, which found larceny to be the most common form of art theft, and worldwide crime trends (including the United States), where larceny was the most commonly reported theft offense, both in terms of actual incidents and rates per 100,000 population. Absent empirical data to the contrary, this consistency *might* fuel speculation about whether the view that burglary is the most prevalent form of art theft is, in fact, accurate or whether most art thefts are really committed through larceny. Interestingly, interview data collected incident to the New York study provided supportive explanations for these findings. For example, respondents provided information that acts of larceny were sometimes committed on a "spur of the moment" basis, while others involved elements of planning to include prior visits to the premises and having an accomplice on hand. Burglary, on the other hand, was termed as "too much trouble" compared to larceny. Moreover, because burglars have an opportunity to be selective in what they steal, some knowledge of art was a valuable asset to have on hand in order to maximize the theft opportunity (the implication being that such knowledge among burglars was a relatively rare commodity).[14]

In any event, to return to safer havens, the consensus position regarding art-theft modalities would be to view robbery as the least frequently employed and burglary as the method of choice, with larceny occupying the number two spot (notwithstanding the mixed evidence on this issue). Although the use of each of these methods can be richly documented through anecdotal evidence (i.e., based on or consisting of reports or observations of usually unscientific observers,[15] for instance, media reports), arriving at any definitive frequency assessments is hampered by the overall lack of comprehensive art-theft data. However, this lack of data should not cast doubt on the serious harm that art theft imposes upon us, whether measured in tangible terms such as money (which in some cases can be so substantial that it is difficult to establish a value) or in nontangible terms, that is, societies being deprived of important artistic manifestations of their civilizations.

Place of Offense

While we may rely on estimates for total art-theft frequencies and losses and then grasp at straws when attempting to attribute these frequencies and losses to larceny, burglary, and robbery, we seem to fare a little better when it comes to data concerning the types of physical locations where art thefts occur. Nevertheless, whether we can make broad generalizations based on what we do know on this issue is again in question. In the big picture of stealing art, some estimates place thefts from museums, churches, galleries, and residences as accounting for only about 10 percent of stolen art, while most such incidents take place at ancient sites.[16] While we will revisit this assessment regarding art thefts from ancient sites in chapter 6, our focus in this chapter will be that portion of art theft that occurs in museums, churches, galleries, and residences.

Although the case studies presented above provide good (and high-profile) examples of art-related larceny, burglary, and robbery, they probably do perpetuate the popular misconception that most art theft occurs in museums and art galleries. To the contrary, however, law enforcement officials both in the United States and abroad claim that most art thefts occur at private residences, often incident to burglaries where art objects are stolen along with other items of value.[17] This assessment is reflected in the art-theft data compiled by the *Art Loss Register* (as discussed earlier in chapter 1). Reports of art theft maintained in this database show that 52 percent identified the place of occurrence as a residential dwelling. Museums were reported to be the next most frequently victimized location at 12 percent. Galleries were the theft sites in 9 percent of their loss reports.[18]

Other data collected incident to empirical studies of art theft has not been fully consistent with the *Art Loss Register* data (although it should be noted that these studies were limited in scope and some of the data was not recent). For instance, Barelli's England study presented statistics from government sources in Italy, France, and England. The Italian data covered the years 1972–1976 and showed that thefts from residences accounted for about 51 percent of their art thefts, with the second leading theft site being churches at about 42 percent. The more recent *Art Loss Register* data showed churches to be theft sites in only 5 percent of their cases. State and private museums accounted for approximately 8 percent. The French data covered the years 1970–1976 but had missing values for gallery locations for the years 1970–1971. This data showed that thefts from residences accounted for about 24 percent of their art thefts while churches were the leading theft sites accounting for approximately 48 percent. Museums and galleries accounted for 12 percent and 17 percent respectively. Finally, data from England spanning 1982–1984 showed that the overwhelming number of art thefts (89%) reportedly took place at private residences with museums, art galleries, and churches accounting for about 1 percent each.[19] Thus, the Italian and British data showed some consistency with more current law-enforcement assessments and the *Art Loss Register* data in that private residences are a primary art-theft site, while this type of location was the second most frequent theft site in France.

The New York study found art galleries were most frequently victimized by art theft, with theft from private dwellings occupying the second most frequent location.[20] An Australian study of art theft also found galleries to be the most frequent location for the these incidents.[21]

Thus, while the above data presents a somewhat mixed picture with regard to the locations most frequently victimized by art theft, the consensus appears to lean toward private residences as the most vulnerable locations, an outcome that can probably be attributed to the frequent absence of sophisticated security measures in private residences. Although galleries and museums might come more readily to mind as primary art-theft locations, they probably are less frequently victimized, perhaps because many of these locations are better protected against theft. Nevertheless, since these locations often have multiple holdings of high-value objects, when they are victimized by theft the loss impact can be substantial and these incidents become high-profile crimes.

What is less certain is where churches fall in the distribution of art-theft locations. While the *Art Loss Register* placed churches behind museums and galleries, early data collected during the England study bearing on France and Italy, as well as assessments that are more recent by French law enforcement officials, indicated that churches are frequently victimized by art theft. As discussed above, art-theft data/estimates are often inclusive of losses due to trafficking in cultural-heritage objects and looting/plundering incident to wars and civil/religious unrest. Whether the French and Italian data reflects this broad spectrum of art/cultural object losses is unknown. While we will be exploring the theft of cultural-heritage objects and art losses incident to wars and political/religious unrest in later chapters, at present we need to recognize that churches have been frequently victimized for their art/cultural-heritage content. To what extent these losses can be looked upon as simply larcenies, burglaries, and robberies (as opposed to being part of a cultural- heritage object trafficking network or incident war or political unrest) is unclear. For now, we know that the *Art Loss Register* placed art thefts from churches at about 5 percent of all incidents while French and Italian data indicated that churches in their locales are more frequently victimized.

A further complication that clouds any assessment of the frequency at which various physical locations are victimized by theft is the issue of reporting versus nonreporting of these events. The likelihood a residential burglary will be reported to the police would appear to be fairly strong, especially when valuable art items are stolen. Thus, the ranking of residential dwellings as the most frequent art-theft site might be skewed by the strong likelihood that such incidents will be reported to the police (and to revisit our discussion above, this same reporting bias might also be the basis for burglary being viewed by many as the most frequent form of art theft as opposed to larceny).

However, there is some evidence that thefts at nonresidential locations might be underreported. Recall that a survey of gallery owners conducted incident to the New York study disclosed that out of 34 reported incidents of theft at galleries, 14 were not reported to police. The reasons cited for nonreporting included (1) the police can't do anything about it; (2) the loss was below an insurance deductible; (3) they were not really sure if the piece was stolen or misplaced; and (4) they wanted to avoid a confrontation with a guilty employee. Another rationale presented was that when thefts are reported to the police, there is a potential loss of future consignments and thus it is better just to absorb the loss. Also expressed was the desire to avoid higher insurance premiums that might be incurred or even policy cancellation, by reporting stolen items. Museums are also reluctant to report thefts because they bring their security procedures into question, which, in turn, could discourage future loans.[22] Art-theft investigator Robert Spiel's experiences working within the art world tend to support the notion that some art theft will go unreported. His advice was to expect to encounter secrecy and confidentiality obstacles, even among those who operate legally. He found embarrassment and/or identification as a wealthy collector as reasons even legitimate people did not want to cooperate in art-theft investigations.[23]

Art theft can also go unreported simply because it is not detected. A good case in point was the theft of 221 objects from the Hermitage

Museum in St. Petersburg, Russia. A woman who had been a curator at the museum for 30 years began stealing in 1999 and her thefts, which totaled in value over $5 million, were not discovered until October 2005.[24] Another scenario which contributes to undetected and thus unreported art theft is where pieces no longer on display are in storage and warehouse facilities. Without regular inventories, thefts can occur in these circumstances and remain undetected for long periods of time.[25] Consider also the situation in print galleries where limited, yet multiple editions of the same print are offered for sale. Absent regular and careful inventories, editions could be stolen and might never be missed, or assumed to be misplaced.[26]

Thus, while our statistical data tends to support a consensus position that most art theft occurs at residential locations, we must recognize that we cannot fully assess the extent of larceny, burglary, and robbery at churches and other religious locations; and what may be a troublesome level of nonreporting might be deflating the number of thefts that are occurring at museums and galleries.

What Types of Art Are Stolen?

Once again, we must start off with the now familiar limitations and qualifications. Consistent with our focus in this chapter, we will be considering the types of art stolen incident to larcenies, burglaries, and robberies at the types of locations we discussed above, that is, private residences, galleries, museums, churches, and so forth. Within this context, our data suggests the full spectrum of objects considered to be art has been subject to theft. The *Art Loss Register*'s database contains the 11 categories of art objects reported to have been stolen/missing. These categories along with their respective percentage of the total number of stolen/missing reports are contained in table 2.2.

Evident in table 2.2 is that "pictures," that is, paintings, drawings, prints, and photographs, by a substantial margin constitute the majority of the reported stolen/missing art objects in this database, with timepieces and sculptures being the next most frequently reported categories of reported thefts. To what extent we can assume this distribution is reflective of the entire universe of stolen art objects is uncertain. However, the *Art Loss Register* database has been operating on a worldwide basis since 1991 and contains in excess of 200,000 objects. As submissions to this database are voluntary and thus less than comprehensive in nature, it nevertheless provides us one of the better worldwide assessments of types of art objects that have been stolen incident to conventional larcenies, burglaries, and robberies.

With regard to the largest theft category, "pictures," the *Art Loss Register* also tracks loss reports by artist. Table 2.3 displays the top-10 most stolen artists with stolen Pablo Picassos far exceeding thefts of works by other artists. It should be noted that with the exception of Renoir and Rubens, the

Table 2.2
Art Loss Register **Database: Top-10 Stolen/Missing Categories and Percent of Total Reports***

Object Category	Percent of Total Reports
Pictures	43
Time pieces	12.2
Sculpture	10.7
Silver	6
Ceramics	5.2
Jewelry	5.2
Furniture	4
Objects of art	3.9
Books	2.3
Textiles	1.5

* *Data source:* Maneker, M. 2009. "Art Loss Register Data Dump," *Art Monitor,* April 23 (accessed through http://www.artmarketmonitor.com/2009/04/23/art-loss-register-data-dump/ July 1, 2009).

Table 2.3
Art Loss Register **Database: Top-10 Most Frequently Stolen Artworks by Artist***

Artist	Total Loss/Stolen Reports
Pablo Picasso	699
Salvador Dali	396
Joan Miró	390
Marc Chagall	361
Albrecht Dürer	212
Pierre-Auguste Renoir	192
Andy Warhol	183
Rembrandt van Rijn	181
Peter Paul Rubens	147
Henri Matisse	138

* *Data source:* Maneker, M. 2009. "Art Loss Register Data Dump," *Art Monitor,* April 23 (accessed through http://www.artmarketmonitor.com/2009/04/23/art-loss-register-data-dump/ July 1, 2009).

other artists in the top 10 produced limited-edition prints, a medium we have already discussed as vulnerable to theft.

The highly publicized incidents of art theft usually involve valuable, well-known pieces, but actually, works of less renown and value are more at risk. Dolnick's observation was that the bulk of art that is stolen could be characterized as "good" but not "great" pieces because the former are easier to resell. However, he fully acknowledged that masterpieces do disappear through thievery and noted that three of the known 36 paintings by 17th-century Dutch master Vermeer have been stolen in recent years.[27] Matthew Hart authored *The Irish Game*, a book that chronicled the 1986 theft and subsequent recovery of one of these Vermeer's, *Lady Writing a Letter with Her Maid*. Here, he offered a similar evaluation of the nature of artwork that is subject to theft when he stated that the true art thief will bypass famous artists and steal less well-known works where there is a greater market and not a large body of documentation concerning ownership.[28] Perhaps, not surprisingly, both of these assessments imply that thieves are motivated to steal art in order to sell it rather than to satisfy their own collecting interests (Stephane Breitweiser from our case study above, being a notable exception), and this motivation enters into their targeting of certain objects and excluding others. Nevertheless, high-value, well-known art continues to be stolen, events that reflect the mind-set of some art thieves that even highly recognizable pieces can be sold to someone.[29]

Another consideration regarding the types of art stolen is the size of the object. This consideration emanates from practical and logistical concerns about carrying stolen object(s) from the premises, and frequently in the case of larceny, the necessity to conceal the object(s) to avoid detection. To be clear, there is ample anecdotal evidence of art objects of all shapes and sizes being stolen, ranging from small objects such as porcelain figures and jewelry that can easily be concealed in one's pocket to large sculptures (as evidenced by a two-and-one-half ton bronze sculpture entitled *Reclining Figure* (1970) by Henry Moore, which was stolen in England at night on December 15, 2005, by three thieves using a crane and flatbed truck[30]). But even paintings pose a "handling," if not concealment consideration to thieves, especially when they are carried off in their frames. We have read about two thefts of Munch's *The Scream*; consider that this painting measures 36" x 29."[31] Although perhaps not huge compared to other paintings, you might want to envision yourself climbing down a ladder with a rectangular object of this size in hand or running out of a public building carrying it to appreciate that stealing paintings of more than minimal size might not lend themselves to a graceful and/or stealth-like exit from the theft premises. In fact, the one painting that has been stolen most often is a Rembrandt portrait entitled *Jacob III de Gheyn* (1632), and it measures about 8 inches by 10 inches, small enough to be concealed inside a jacket. It has been stolen and recovered four times, thus far.[32]

Conversely, during the biggest art theft that has occurred in the United States there is some evidence that the size of the paintings was an unexpected obstacle. On March 18, 1990, at approximately 1:00 AM two robbers masquerading as police officers forced their way into Boston's Isabella Stewart Gardner Museum by overpowering the on-duty security guards and then stole 13 paintings that have a combined value of $200–$300 million. Many consider the paintings that were stolen to be an odd assortment that might reflect an unanticipated obstacle, that is, handling large, awkward pieces. Two Rembrandts, *The Storm on the Sea of Galilee* (1633; 63.5" x 51") and *A Lady and Gentleman in Black* (1633; 51.8" x 43"), were ripped from their frames while large, even more valuable paintings by both Rembrandt and the Italian Renaissance master, Titian, were left behind. Conversely, a Vermeer titled *The Concert* (1664–1667; 28.5" x 25.4"), a Manet titled *Chez Tortoni* (1878–1880; 10.2" x 13.3"), along with what is described as a "stamp-sized" Rembrandt self-portrait (1634; 1.75" x 2") were carried away in their frames, all of which fuel speculation that the thieves foresaw difficulties in making a clean getaway while being burdened down with cumbersome objects. Unfortunately, to date none of these paintings have ever been recovered.[33]

There is some supporting evidence that the size of objects is a consideration when thieves target art. In Dolnick's journalistic study of art theft, he observed that most incidents involve small works because they are easier to remove and get away with.[34] From survey/interview data, the New York study concluded that small marketable objects, especially realistic paintings and sculpture, were the preferred targets of art thieves.[35] The England study presented data on art thefts investigated by Scotland Yard during the period 1976–1984 that showed that 73 percent of the paintings, drawings, prints, and etchings reported stolen had dimensions less than 24 inches. Conversely, only 18 percent of the thefts during that period had dimensions that exceeded 36 inches. Two convicted art thieves (burglars) interviewed incident to this study both indicated they preferred stealing small objects because of easy concealment.[36]

ART THEFT: THE OFFENDERS

We began this chapter reminiscing about how art theft has been portrayed in the movies, that is, offenses committed by sophisticated gentlemen/criminals with a taste for art played by the likes of Pierce Brosnan, Steve McQueen, and Sean Connery. Are these portrayals accurate or do we need a reality check? Let's examine what we know about art thieves. Art expert Milton Esterow in 1973 described art thieves as an "assorted breed, from the debonair and urbane, to illiterates."[37] At least the "debonair" and "urbane" descriptors could arguably be applied to the movie characters played by Brosnan, McQueen, and Connery. And in fact, some recent cases of art theft still perpetuate this *classic* art-thief stereotype. For instance, Stephane Breitweiser from the previous case study (box 2.1), as an art lover-thief, if not "debonair" might fall into the "urbane" category.

Other "urbane" examples include a Japanese self-proclaimed art lover (and described in press reports as "gentlemanly") who was arrested in 2006 in Japan for burglaries at 11 museums between 1992 and 1996 during which he stole antiquities valued at $8.4 million,[38] and as discussed earlier, the female curator turned thief at the Hermitage in St. Petersburg, Russia.

Increasingly, however, those who steal art are being described more harshly and perhaps deservedly so. By all accounts, the Norwegian groups who were involved in the two *The Scream* thefts (see boxes 2.2 and 2.3) were aligned more with the criminal element than the debonair/urbane art lovers turned thieves. In Dolnick's account of the 1994 *The Scream* burglary, he characterized art thieves as being members of criminal gangs or thugs whose expertise lies in drug peddling and money laundering, although he also noted the involvement of "bumblers" as well. With regard to the former group, he claimed their involvement has become more prominent as art prices began to "skyrocket" in the 1980s. Thus, not surprisingly, he concluded that the lure of money is the prime motivation to commit art theft (although he acknowledged that intangibles such as the challenges sometimes presented by stealing art, the notoriety/publicity often associated with these thefts, and even contempt for wealthy owners who are victimized might provide additional motivation.[39]

Scotland Yard's assessment of art thieves was altered by the 1986 Vermeer theft in Ireland by an Irish criminal gang. At one point, they placed art thieves into three categories: (1) the thief who stole art exclusively, but at lower values that enabled easy fencing into the legitimate art trade; (2) those who stole to order because of opportunity and an ability to sell it; (3) and those who stole simply to enjoy the art. However, the Vermeer theft provided evidence to them as well of criminal gang involvement whose other activities include money laundering and drug trafficking.[40] Other more recent cases also link art theft to those involved in drug trafficking. For instance, a 38-year-old man pled guilty in September 2004 for his involvement in the theft of an 1880 Monet painting (*Paysage à Vétheuil*; valued at $4 million) and a Renoir painting (*La Place de Trinite*; valued at $2.7 million) from a home in Naples, Florida, in February 2003. He received a 2-year prison sentence that was to run concurrently with a 10-year sentence for unrelated drug charges. In another case with a similar cast of characters, French police in April 2005 recovered a 1924 Picasso painting entitled *Nature Morte à la Charlotte* that had been stolen from the Pompidou Center in Paris a year earlier. The painting was found at a known drug trafficker's home south of Paris. Investigation determined that the painting, worth $3.2 million, was stolen by another drug trafficker, who before being imprisoned, stored it at this residence for safekeeping.[41] It is worth noting, however, that an empirical study of transnational trafficking in illicit art and antiquities by Tijhuis disputed the notion that drug traffickers and art thieves have become one in the same. His findings suggest that those instances where that connection was found are limited and, thus, it should not be viewed as the norm.[42]

Empirical Research: Theft Offenders Generally

While the above anecdotal observations depict art thieves as emanating from a broad socioeconomic spectrum, those who study crime as a social problem would look to empirical studies to acquire this perspective. There is some empirical data/knowledge available on larceny, burglary, and robbery offenders generally and, of course, much less on art thieves in particular. Unlike the United Nations data that earlier provided us a global perspective on offending frequencies, information on offender characteristics is much less available and is usually limited to being national in scope. For instance, table 2.4 provides key demographic data on U.S. larceny, burglary, and robbery offenders.

Undoubtedly, buried within the numbers presented in table 2.4 are some art thieves, but, as we have already learned, we are hampered in our study of such offenders because of the lack of crime databases that specifically identify them and the limited extant empirical research in this area. So, to what extent is the data in table 2.4 useful to us in studying art thieves? Keeping in mind that this data is limited to U.S. offenders only, it does permit demographic comparisons on a *case-by-case basis* of those who steal art through larceny, burglary, or robbery with the general populations of these types of offenders. For instance, as females comprise 37 percent of the larceny offenders, we should not be as surprised to find a female engaged in art larceny as we would to find a female engaged in art burglary or art robbery. Likewise, in the United States, most robbery offenders are

Table 2.4
2006 U.S. Offender Characteristics: Larceny, Burglary, and Robbery*

Offense	Gender Distribution (%)		Racial Distribution (%)			Largest Age Cohorts of Adult Offenders (%)[b]
	Male	Female	White	Black	Other[a]	
Larceny (N = 595,446)	62.3	37.7	68.6	28.9	2.5	20–29 (36%) 30–39 (23%)
Burglary (N = 161,037)	85.5	14.5	69.0	29.2	1.9	20–29 (42%) 30–39 (21%)
Robbery (N = 67,435)	88.7	11.3	42.2	56.3	1.6	20–29 (45%) 18–19 (22%)

* Data collected incident to the arrests of alleged offenders as reported in the *Uniform Crime Report*, http://www.fbi.gov/ucr/cius2006/index.html (accessed January 2, 2008).
[a] Categories are inclusive of Hispanics; "other" includes native Americans and Alaskans, Asians, and Pacific Islanders.
[b] While those in the 18–19 year age range did not form a 10-year cohort, their involvements in these crimes were considerable; this 2-year cohort was the second largest offending group (the 30–39 age cohort contributed to 19% of the total robbery frequency). This cohort's contributions to larceny were 14 percent and for burglary 18 percent.

black and under age 30. Thus, art robbers who are white and older than age 30 would be somewhat of an anomaly compared to those who commit these types of crimes generally in the United States. Recall that the three Norwegian men convicted in *The Scream* robbery were 31, 35, and 39 years of age, an age range clearly outside the average age parameters of U.S. robbery offenders. Conversely, Stephane Breitweiser from our case study was engaged in art larceny from his mid-twenties to his early thirties, thus placing him squarely within the age cohorts where most U.S. larceny offenders (generally) are found.

Likewise, on a *case-by-case basis* we can also compare those who steal art to the general populations of thieves, burglars, and robbers in terms of average monetary gain per incident (or conversely average dollar loss to victims) derived from these types of offenses. Table 2.5 provides data that enables such comparisons. However, due to our lack of art-specific theft data, we are unable to differentiate average monetary values of art thefts

Table 2.5
2006 U.S. Offense Characteristics: Average Monetary Losses*

Offense	Average Monetary Loss
Larceny	
All sources (except motor vehicle theft; N = 5,265,007 reported incidents)	$855
Shoplifting (N = 695,387 reported incidents)	$194
Buildings (N = 661,277 reported incidents)	$1,170
Burglary	
All sources (N = 1,734,074 reported incidents)	$1,834
Commercial establishments	$1,855
Residences	$1,823
Robbery	
All sources (N = 342,268 reported incidents)	$1,268
Commercial establishments	$1,589
Residences	$1,469

* Data reflect number of incidents reported to police per the *Uniform Crime Report,* http://www.fbi.gov/ucr/cius2006/index.html (accessed January 11, 2008).

attributable to larceny, burglary, and robbery from the average losses from these crimes overall, that is, we cannot determine whether art-theft losses are, *on average*, more or less than the average losses suffered from larceny, burglary, or robbery generally. Thus, while anecdotal evidence clearly suggests that art thieves are motivated by potentially large financial gains that could be derived from stealing highly valuable works of art, the loss data from larceny, burglary, and robbery generally document relatively modest average amounts that are realized through these crimes.

Aside from demographics, criminologists who have studied thieves tend to differentiate between those who are amateurs and those who are professionals. Amateurs are characterized as occasional, opportunistic offenders who carry out their thefts with little planning and skill and often in response to a pressing financial need. Professional thieves, however, do approach stealing as an occupation.[43]

Criminologists have described both amateur and professional thieves as engaging in a variety of types of stealing, including burglary, sneak theft, forgery, and auto theft, while professional thieves add to this repertoire confidence swindles, counterfeiting, and extortion.[44] An enduring study on professional thieves continues to be Sutherland's work in 1937 in which he identified five prominent characteristics associated with this category of offender:

- They have well-developed technical skills for their particular mode of operation.
- They enjoy status, accorded to them by their own subculture and by law enforcement.
- They are bound by a consensus, a sharing of values with their own peers.
- Not only do they learn from each other, but they also protect each other.
- They are organized, however loosely.[45]

Within the ranks of criminology, robbery is often examined apart from crimes such as larceny and burglary because it is considered a crime of violence while the latter are considered property crimes. Nevertheless, Conklin categorized robbers in a manner that bears similarities to property-crime offenders. He found professional robbers to be relatively few in number and, like the professional property-crime thieves, these individuals had a long-term commitment to this type of crime, sought out high-value targets, carefully planned and executed the theft, and often acted in concert with accomplices. However, even within these professional ranks, there are those who exclusively commit robberies and those who commit other forms of theft as well, such as burglary. Paralleling the amateur thief is the opportunistic robber who has no long-term commitment to robbery as a way of life, is generally young and inexperienced, and targets vulnerable and small-value targets, such as the elderly and cab drivers. Conklin also found two other categories of robbers, the addict and the alcoholic varieties, both of which share more in common with the opportunistic robbers than professional robbers; but their substance abuse/dependency warrant separate labels for these robbery offenders.[46]

Studies that have focused on larceny are largely limited to shoplifters in retail establishments and have found that these thieves are most often amateurs, although at least one researcher on this subject estimated that 10 percent of all shoplifters can be classified as professionals based on Sutherland's criteria discussed above.[47] It appears that we can also apply the amateur versus professional differentiation to burglars as well. Studies of burglars have confirmed that those who engage in this form of offending tend to be "specialists" at least for a portion of their criminal careers, although many have been found to have committed a variety of offenses.[48] Commercial burglaries (which could include art galleries and museums) most often occur at night or on weekends.[49] "Good burglars" have been described as those who carefully select their targets, sometimes work in well-coordinated teams, and possess requisite skills and expertise, including being able to disarm security systems and crack safes.[50]

As suggested above, while robbery can result in theft of property, unlike larceny or burglary, it is purposely carried out using the threat of force/violence/and less frequently the actual use of force/violence.[51] Some statistics show the display of weapons (most frequently firearms and knives) in about 50 percent of all robbery incidents. These statistics also show that most robberies take place on the street or in or near residences (accounting for roughly one half of all robbery incidents) while commercial buildings are robbery sites in just over 4 percent of the occurrences.[52]

Empirical Research: Art-Theft Studies

When we attempt to compare what we know about the general populations of larceny, burglary, and robbery offenders with those who steal art using these modalities, we find little data to draw upon; and much of what is available comes from sources that have been cited elsewhere in this chapter, for example, the New York and England studies. Moreover, the little empirical research we do have on art-specific offenders is largely limited to those who steal art through larceny and burglary. The one observation that has been made about art robbery is that this form of art theft has become more frequent with the increase in effective security measures in museums and homes, thus shifting those who seek to steal art from larceny and burglary to this form of theft.[53]

The data presented in table 2.4 above demonstrated that, on average, thefts by larceny, burglary, or robbery resulted in losses under $2,000 per incident. However, both the New York and England studies concluded that the most common motivation for stealing art was, in fact, money/financial gain.[54] While stories abound that some art is stolen by art aficionados for their own collections and enjoyment, the data from these studies does not support this form of motivation as being a common reason for art theft.

Both the New York and England studies documented that art thieves can be differentiated in a manner similar to professional versus amateur typologies that have been used to describe thieves in general. In the England study, amateurs were described as those who do not engage in art theft on a full-time basis, do not research what objects to steal or where to obtain them, and are less familiar with the markets where they can be disposed. Falling into this category are juveniles, shoplifters, and opportunists. Professionals, on the other hand, work at stealing art, sometimes in the full-time occupational sense. They seek out opportunities to steal specific objects to be disposed of in specific markets. In doing so, they will take precautions to avoid being apprehended, which involves weighing the risk associated with the object to be stolen and the location where the theft is to take place. In addition, professionals prefer stealing art objects that are not well documented.[55]

The New York study described those who do not engage in stealing on a full-time basis as common thieves, and this category was found to be the most common type of art thief. Although common thieves were not viewed as being sophisticated in terms of art (although gallery employees can fall into this category), they were responsible for the majority of art losses identified through this study and, for the most part, thefts that could best be described as shoplifting. This study also found that common thieves usually do know of outlets for what they are stealing; otherwise, they would not do it. Alternatively, professional thieves were described as skilled burglars or shoplifters who create opportunities to steal artwork to order or otherwise believe an art theft will result in profit, as long as the piece is not so recognizable or valuable that there is no market for it (and for some professional thieves this is the extent of their art knowledge). They usually plan what to steal, from where to steal it and how to dispose of it without being caught. Moreover, many did not limit their activities to just art but applied this approach to the theft of other types of merchandise as well.[56]

Data collected incident to this study found that thieves tended to fit into the neighborhood where their targeted gallery was located (e.g., racially) and preferred those with multiple, nonvigilant employees where there is no buzzer admittance system and where the objects have price stickers affixed (presumably to document value). While some of these incidents were viewed as crimes of opportunity, in other cases suspects were recalled as being on the premises before the theft, thus suggesting some level of planning. In the New York study, paintings were preferred, and in a burglary, their size was not the same impediment as when committing larceny. (However, limiting the quantity of items stolen in any one burglary had the effect of minimizing attention drawn to the incident.) The ideal art-gallery burglary target outlined in this study would be located on the ground floor of a quiet street at night and of course without the presence of security guards. Window access is desirable as is the absence of any apartments located above the gallery.[57] With regard to these latter considerations, Conklin noted that burglars often work on holidays or weekends because they believe these days will afford more time at the targeted location and that the crime will then not be discovered for a day or two.[58]

Two professional British burglars were interviewed incident to the England study, one of whom specialized in art while the other did so when that type of opportunity was available. The art specialist was a university-educated male in his mid-forties and was knowledgeable in art through his academic course work. Stealing art had been his full-time occupation for 20 years. The nonart specialist/professional burglar was also a male in his mid-forties who acknowledged supporting himself through theft since he was 20 years of age but did not possess the level of education or formal art knowledge as the art specialist. Commonalities shared by these individuals included that they were both motivated by financial gain and both operated on the basis of being responsive to opportunities that became available. In weighing opportunities, the location of objects and the nature of the objects are factors. For instance, both found country estates to be easy targets because they frequently contained valuable art objects and were relatively unprotected by security systems. Even when alarm systems were in place they both felt that they could steal targeted objects and depart before any response would arrive. Also, both of these professionals had established outlets/markets for the art objects they stole,[59] a topic that we will now turn our attention to in concluding this chapter.

AFTER THE THEFT: WHAT BECOMES OF STOLEN ART?

One of the recurring themes regarding art theft is that stolen objects are seldom recovered. A recovery rate of about 10 percent is perhaps the most frequently cited figure in this regard, with some estimates only in the 3–5 percent range. The only good news relative to recovering stolen art is Conklin's assessment that these rates can be as high as 50 percent for well-known pieces,[60] a conclusion that should not be surprising when one considers that thefts of well-known objects result in widespread media and law-enforcement attention and would-be dealers or buyers could not feign ignorance of the origins of such pieces and/or openly display them. As Hart stated in his chronicle of the theft of a Vermeer, art is easy to steal but hard to sell, especially when by famous artists.[61] This is not to suggest that an unscrupulous collector would not knowingly buy a famous, but stolen item for personal and private viewing, but often in these cases, thieves find they have to pursue alternate routes to realize any profit. For instance, they can attempt to ransom it back to the original owners or if a reward is offered, seek this form of payment by arranging for the object's return.[62] Along these lines, acquiring insurance coverage on high-value works of art raises another interesting scenario. According to the New York study, insurance companies are willing to pay rewards of 10 percent of the value of a stolen art object for information leading to its recovery. In this sense, insurance companies are not paying a ransom but rather they are purchasing information. Whether art thieves and/or their intermediaries make a similar distinction regarding insurance-company rewards would surely be debatable.[63] From an insurance company's perspective, making such a payment and then recovering the piece would certainly seem preferable to paying a claim for its entire value; however, such payments might actually be an enticement to steal famous, high-value art. Insurance companies recognize this potential and claim they do not want to encourage art thefts based on any expectations of reward payments.[64] Alternatively, Conklin posited that not insuring art might provide a disincentive to steal it.[65]

In any event, famous or not, at least some stolen art is recovered. Data collected by the *Art Loss Register* shows that about one half of the recoveries of stolen art involve paintings. Other types of art objects fare less well in this regard with furniture (10%), silver (10%), and sculpture (8%) representing the other most frequently recovered categories.[66] However, one must recognize that our discussion here applies only to that 10 percent (or fewer) of stolen art works that are recovered. So what happens to the remaining 90 percent (or so) of stolen art? Dolnick's bleak response to this question is "most stolen art is gone forever,"[67] although perhaps more accurately, once stolen, most art doesn't return to its rightful owners. Most stolen art is sold by those responsible for the theft(s) and usually for much less than its established value, with 10 percent being a commonly cited figure although 5–7 percent might be the going rate for well-known objects and/or those from heavily publicized thefts, due to difficulties in concealing the origins of such items.[68]

The keys to success in realizing a profit from art theft appear to be twofold: (1) having arrangements or connections through which stolen art can be resold in the legitimate market and (2) stealing objects that can be more easily introduced into the legitimate market whether because they are not widely known and/or because fictitious provenance (i.e., a history of the artwork and its ownership) can be created to overcome suspicious origins. Those who offer the necessary arrangements or connections are commonly referred to as "fences," that is, individuals who engage in the business of facilitating the sale of stolen merchandise; and it is from these individuals that art thieves will often seek to acquire their profit as opposed to the ultimate purchaser. "Fencing" has been described as bridging the gap between the criminal world of the thief and the legitimate world. This type of activity provides the thief access to a market for stolen goods while minimizing the risks associated with disposing of such property, and, conversely, it provides opportunities for legitimate society to purchase goods at less than market price.[69] Thus, fences typically take on the persona/occupations of legitimate business persons while at the same time maintaining contacts with the criminal world to acquire stolen goods for resale. Two classic criminological studies followed the lives of two fences as they attempted to do this: *Professional Fence* by Carl Klockars (1974) and *Fence* by Darrell Steffensmeier (1986), both of whom operated out of retail storefronts, one of which was described as an antique and "second-hand" shop.[70] Interestingly, one of the professional thieves interviewed in the England study identified antique dealers as among his outlets for stolen art objects.[71]

Some fences specialize only in certain types of merchandise while others can be viewed as "master fences" because they have contacts and financial resources to handle the "fruits" of major thefts.[72] Both of these categories would seem to meet the needs of art thieves, depending upon the nature of the stolen objects to be fenced. The research findings on fencing stolen art contain the recurring theme of needing the "right" contacts. For instance, art thieves interviewed in Great Britain indicated they had developed ongoing business relationships with certain art and antique dealers.[73]

A study of art theft in Australia found evidence of the legitimate business world being involved in the distribution of stolen art. Persons from the art world interviewed in connection with this study pointed to incidents where commercial galleries and auction houses knowingly commingled stolen art objects with legitimate pieces for resale, and if need be, false provenances were created to facilitate sales of stolen objects. A common theme echoed in these interviews was that trust and secrecy, so characteristic in the art world, was conducive to the passing of stolen property; and in the case of public auctions that operate in the open, buyers tended to overlook the possibility of acquiring a stolen piece. This study also documented the role of secondhand and antique shops as well. Some gallery owners paid "runners" to scour these types of retail outlets for valuable art objects, a practice that was viewed as establishing a pathway for stolen art to enter into the legitimate marketplace.[74]

The second part of the equation for realizing a profit involves the nature of the objects that are targeted for theft. In this respect, the operative principle appears to be to steal "marketable" items as opposed to high-value, well-known art works. As cited above, Hart characterized a "true art thief" as one who would bypass famous artists and steal less well-known works where there is a greater market and not a large body of documentation concerning ownership. In the same vein, one of the professional thieves interviewed in the England study specifically mentioned that he avoided stealing from museums because the objects in these institutions were well documented and too difficult to sell.[75]

However, as is evident from several of the cases discussed in this chapter, high-value, well-known works of art are stolen, and such incidents result in widespread publicity. These types of events frequently raise questions about whether the thieves really knew what they were getting into because of the difficulties in disposing of such art works through traditional fencing channels. It is in these cases, however, that thieves tend to look toward rewards or ransom/extortion payments for their profit or alternatively use high-value art pieces as collateral in illegal activities such as drug trafficking or money laundering. Another possibility would be to "wait out" the statute of limitations (i.e., the time frame during which criminal charges can be brought) and then subtlety introduce the piece back into the market, perhaps with a doctored provenance. Taking this approach, however, might test the patience of many thieves since statutes of limitation, while varying from country to country, are usually measured in terms of years. Moreover, at least in the United States, the normal statute of limitations of five years can be extended if there is evidence that the theft and subsequent concealment was an ongoing conspiracy, a scenario that could keep the prospect of criminal charges alive indefinitely. More rarely would a stolen, high-value, well-known artwork be acquired by an unscrupulous collector, à la Dr. No of James Bond/Sean Connery fame, for their personal and private viewing and pleasure.[76]

ART THEFT: IN SUMMARY

Perspectives on criminal activity in general are acquired in a number of different ways. For many, the news media is their primary source of information regarding the prevalence of criminal activity and individual criminal incidents. This information source tends to focus on localized and/or short-term trends and, of course, highlight major criminal episodes. Crime is also a popular topic for television entertainment, movies, and books (both fiction and nonfiction), and thus these sources also provide perspectives on criminal activity; but again, usually the focus is on high-profile events, or at least those with uncommon or unique characteristics. Fewer of us scan police and other statistics to acquire a perspective on criminal offending. However, when we do so, we often come away with a different or enhanced understanding of crime than is portrayed in the media and popular entertainment. For instance, when taking a data-driven approach in analyzing the phenomenon of homicide, it becomes readily apparent that serial killing, a popular entertainment topic and one that receives intense media scrutiny, is in fact a very rare form of murder as opposed to the more common scenario where homicide arises incident to an interpersonal dispute between two parties who know each other. To be clear, comprehensive homicide statistics likely contain the activities of serial murderers, but this type of analysis does not focus on serial murders per se, nor those individuals who commit them; rather, this approach examines homicide in broader terms, for example, frequencies, offender characteristics, victim characteristics, and so forth. Is this to suggest that the activities of serial killers are not worthy of our attention and study? Certainly not! Moreover, any general discussion of homicide will likely recognize this rare form of murder due to its horrific nature and the fear and publicity it generates. However, because of the lack of any comprehensive serial-killing database (sound familiar?), we are likely to rely on a case-study approach to gain an understanding of these events and those who commit them.

So why does any of this relate to art theft? Although not an entirely analogous situation, we endeavored here to examine art theft in a manner that goes beyond a mere focus on high-profile incidents as reported in case studies in order to develop a broader understanding of this phenomenon, notwithstanding substantial data-source limitations. By taking this approach, the major observations we have made about art theft are as follows:

- Due to the absence of comprehensive data, we must rely on estimates and/ or limited-scope databases for monetary losses attributable to art theft and the number of objects that have been stolen. The estimated monetary losses range between $1 billion and $6 billion annually. The extent to which we can rely on the accuracy of these estimates is uncertain. Nor is it clear whether they reflect only thefts from residences, galleries, museums, churches, and so forth (i.e., the focus of this chapter) or whether they are inclusive of art objects that have been stolen in other contexts as well (e.g., theft of cultural-heritage items through illegal seizures or excavations, plunders of war or political/religious unrest).

- The absence of any comprehensive art-theft data also limits our ability to assess accurately the frequency of art theft (i.e., total numbers of objects stolen overall or within a given time frame) and the theft modalities involved (i.e., larceny, burglary, and robbery). Thus, we tend to rely on informed opinion about which of these modalities is most frequently employed to steal art. In this regard, the consensus is that art is most frequently stolen through burglary while robbery is the least frequently employed modality.

- Data on art theft collected by the *Art Theft Register* and by a limited number of police agencies indicate that art theft most frequently occurs at private residences and that pictures (i.e., paintings, drawings, prints, and the like) are the art objects most frequently stolen.

- Anecdotal and limited empirical data suggest that smaller art objects are more frequently targeted for theft than larger objects.

- Art thieves, like thieves in general, can be categorized as amateurs and professionals. With regard to the latter, criminal gangs have taken on a more prominent role in art thefts in recent years.

- The primary motivation for stealing art is financial. Most objects that are stolen can be classified as good but not great art because the former is more easily sold. Art thieves often place their stolen goods with fences to facilitate sales. Disposing of high-value, well-known works of art that have been stolen in highly publicized incidents can be difficult, and thieves often seek their profit through ransom or extortion-style tactics.

Having gleaned the above from the available data and research that have been conducted in this area, can we conclude that we know more about art theft than if we had simply relied on case studies? Perhaps in some ways, and if we had a comprehensive database, our understanding of art theft would likely be advanced immeasurably. For instance, simply having more precise frequency and loss statistics, data that is often taken for granted when monitoring other types of criminal activity, would be of great assistance. Likewise, demographic characteristics of those who commit these crimes (e.g., age, race/ethnicity/nationality, gender), though basic to many criminal data-collection programs, are sorely missing features in our efforts to study art thieves.

However, the value of case studies in enhancing our understanding of art theft should not be underestimated, even if we had a comprehensive data set. These sources can provide the rich and often unique details that tend to be lost in a data-set format. In addition, case studies typically focus on high-profile art thefts, that is, thefts of well-known and valuable art objects; and only through such a format can the significance and magnitude of these events be fully documented and conveyed. Moreover, the characteristics of high-profile incidents are sometimes at odds with the more generalized picture that data sets capture, and it is important that any unique characteristics associated with these types of events are not lost. Even the limited empirical data presented here is at variance with some of the high-profile cases discussed in the chapter starting with the finding that many who steal art avoid well-known, highly valuable objects because of difficulties in marketing such items. Thus, even with a comprehensive database to work with, our knowledge of art theft would not be complete without detailed narrative descriptions of individual events; and, fortunately, at least the major incidents of art theft are captured for us in this manner.

Before we venture into other forms of art crime, chapter 3 will review a further selection of the major art thefts (in brief case-study format) that have occurred since the beginning of the 20th century.

CHAPTER 3

Art Theft Continued: Selected Cases

Following are vignettes, presented in chronological order from the beginning of the 20th century that provide brief summaries of some of the world's most notable art thefts that were not discussed in chapter 2. Criteria for selecting these cases included the value and/or prominence of the object(s) stolen, prominence of the artist, and/or unique methodologies employed or circumstances involved.

1911: THEFT OF THE WORLD'S MOST FAMOUS PAINTING

Italian carpenter Vincenzo Perugia while working at the Louvre walked out with the *Mona Lisa* secreted under his clothing. He returned to Italy with it and in 1913 attempted to sell it to the Uffizi in Florence for $100,000, which he viewed as a reward for repatriating a looted Italian masterpiece. He was arrested and convicted, but was sentenced to only seven months in jail. Some accounts of this incident allege that the theft was the first step in a plan by coconspirators to forge and sell copies of the *Mona Lisa,* and Perugia was simply recruited as the thief. This part of the story also contends that Perugia did not know the true identities of the coconspirators nor of the forgery plans. Although he received an initial payment for the theft, he was expecting continued payments that never materialized, thus prompting him to seek his reward from the Uffizi.[1]

1967–1986: THE MOST STOLEN PAINTING

Rembrandt's *Portrait of Jacob III de Gheyn*, was stolen on four occasions between 1967 and 1986 from the Dulwich College Library in London. The small painting (12"x11") is valued in the $5–$6 million range. On one occasion, a 25-year-old visitor grabbed it from the wall and bicycled away before police caught up with him a mile from the library. It was also recovered in London on two other occasions, but in 1986, it made its way to Germany where police, acting on a tip, found it at a railway station.[2]

1969: CHURCH OF SAN LORENZO, PALERMO, ITALY

Two thieves, since linked to the Sicilian Mafia, stole *Nativity with St. Francis and St. Lawrence* by Caravaggio (1608; valued at $20 million). Purportedly, a third party who had commissioned the theft then refused to accept it because the thieves damaged the painting. The whereabouts of the painting is now unknown.[3]

1972: MONTREAL MUSEUM OF FINE ARTS

In the largest art theft in Canadian history, three burglars entered through a skylight while the roof was being repaired (and alarm shut down) and stole 18 paintings. Among those stolen were *Landscape with Cottages* by Rembrandt (1654; priceless); two paintings by Corot, *La reveuse à la fontaine* (ca 1855–1863; priceless) and *Jeune fille accoudée sur le bras gauche* (1865; priceless); two paintings by Millet, *Portrait of Madame Millet* (date unknown; priceless) and *La baratteuse* (1849–1850; priceless); *Portrait of Brigadier General Sir Robert Fletcher* by Gainsborough (ca 1771; priceless); and *Lionne et lion dans une caverne* by Delacroix (1856; priceless). None of these works have been recovered.[4]

1972: MUSÉE DE BAGNOLS-SUR-CÈZE, GARD, FRANCE

Nine impressionist paintings were stolen and never recovered. Included among them were: *The Old Port of Marseille* by Marquet (1918; value unknown); *View of Saint-Tropez* by Matisse (1904; value unknown) and two by Renoir, *Portrait of Madame Albert Andre* (1904; value unknown) and *Roses in a Vase* (1905; value unknown).[5]

1974–2002: RUSSBOROUGH HOUSE, IRELAND

Robberies of art at this country estate south of Dublin have occurred on four occasions spanning a period of over a quarter century. The first two incidents were most notable in terms of the participants and the objects stolen. In April 1974 IRA sympathizer Rose Dugdale accompanied by three men staged a nighttime home invasion of these premises during which they forcefully restrained the owners, Sir Alfred and Lady Beit and proceeded to steal 19 paintings, the world's most lucrative art theft up to that point in time. Among those paintings stolen were Vermeer's *Lady Writing a Letter with a Maid* (1610), Goya's *Portrait of Doña Antonia Zarate* (ca. 1810), Velasquez's *Maid in Kitchen with Christ and Disciples Outside the Window,* and Gainsborough's *Portrait of Madame Bacelli.* A week after the robbery, a ransom demand was made for $1.2 million and the transfer of four Irish political prisoners from Britain to Belfast. However, the day after these demands were made, Dugdale was apprehended 200 miles away in possession of all the stolen paintings. Dugdale received a nine-year prison sentence.

The second major theft of Russborough House, this time a burglary, occurred nearly 12 years later, in May 1986. However, the culprits proved not to be political activists but rather common criminals of the most notorious kind. Martin Cahill, Ireland's leading mobster at the time, accompanied by 15 associates stole 18 paintings including two by Rubens (one being *Portrait of a Dominican Monk*), two by Metsu (including *Man Writing a Letter*), two Guardis, a Gainsborough, a Joshua Reynolds portrait, an Antoine Vestier portrait, and once again, Goya's *Portrait of Doña Antonia Zarate,* and Vermeer's *Lady Writing a Letter with Her Maid.* They were in and out within six minutes, and with a value of $44 million, this haul topped the earlier Dugdale theft as the world's most lucrative. The next day 7 of the 18 paintings were found abandoned and undamaged about four miles from the Russborough House. These included the two Guardis and the Joshua Reynolds portrait, all of which were the least valuable of 18 stolen. It was not until 1993, however, that the Vermeer along with the Goyas, the Vestier portrait, and Metsu's *Man Writing a Letter* were recovered incident to an undercover police sting operation in Belgium. The fact that these paintings were in Belgium supports a contention that Cahill used some of the paintings as collateral for a $1 million loan from a diamond merchant in Antwerp, the proceeds of which were to finance a drug deal. All but two of the paintings stolen in 1986 have now been recovered. Cahill was never charged, but was murdered, gangland-style in Ireland, a year later.

The two other thefts at the Russborough House occurred in 2001 and 2002, respectively. In June 2001 two thieves staged a daylight home invasion by ramming their vehicle through an exterior door to gain entrance. They proceeded to steal Gainsborough's *Madame Bacelli* and Belloto's *View of Florence.* Within two minutes, they exited, abandoned, and set afire their getaway vehicle but then fled on foot when they were fought off by the driver of a vehicle they intended to commandeer. The two paintings were recovered in Dublin 15 months later. Finally (to date, anyway—and hopefully!) in September 2002 thieves using a battering ram smashed steel shutters covering a ground floor window and stole five paintings with a combined value of $76 million. The two most valuable were by Rubens (one for the second time, *Portrait of a Dominican Monk*—which had been stolen by Cahill in 1986). All have been recovered.[6]

1983: BURGLARS IN BUDAPEST

On November 5, $35 million worth of Italian Renaissance paintings were stolen at the Budapest Museum of Fine Arts. Burglars climbed scaffolding that had been erected incident to building repairs and then gained entrance through a window. The museum's burglar alarm was out of order at the time. Taken were two Raphael's valued at $20 million and $10 million respectively, two portraits by Tintoretto, and two paintings by Tiepolo. Five Italians along with three Hungarians were implicated in the burglary after one of the Hungarians, a minor female, telephoned her parents from Romania while driving with the thieves to Greece. However, the paintings were apparently destined to a wealthy Athens olive oil manufacturer whose brother was an art dealer in New York. He was charged with the theft and receiving stolen goods (the paintings) in January 1984. These charges were then dropped for unknown reasons, but the paintings were recovered in a monastery in Athens.[7]

1983–1989: THEFTS BY ARGENTINE POLICE OFFICERS

Three former Argentine police/intelligence officers, who lost their positions with the fall of the Argentine military junta in 1982, robbed the Estevez Municipal Museum in Rosario, Argentina, in November 1983. Dressed as plumbers, they forced their way into the museum after closing by overpowering the janitors who were on duty at the time. They stole five paintings included a Goya, a Murillo, and an El Greco. Then four years later the same gang stole six paintings at another museum in Rosario, the Castagnino, including a Titian, two works by Veronese, and a Goya. The Goya, entitled *Doves and Hens,* was recovered in Miami in 1989 through an FBI sting operation that also resulted in the arrest of a former Argentine federal police officer who was attempting to sell it (but who denied being involved in the theft itself).[8]

1987: NINE PAINTINGS REPORTED MISSING
FROM DUTCH GALLERY

In February 1987 a prominent art dealer in Maastricht, Robert Noortman, reported to police a burglary at his gallery that netted nine paintings from the 17th and 19th centuries, including works by Renoir (*La Clairière*), Pissarro (*Bords de la Seine à Bougival*), and Jan Brueghel the Younger (*Moneys*). The subsequent investigation failed to develop any leads or suspects and as the works were insured, Noortman eventually received an insurance payment of $4.43 million for his loss. Thereafter, allegations arose that Noortman had arranged the theft to collect fraudulently the insurance proceeds, but no charges were ever brought against him. He died of a heart attack in 2007. In late 2008, however, the private investigator hired by Noortman's insurance company was contacted by a German national who claimed that Noortman hired him to carry out the burglary and then burn the paintings. He told the private investigator that he burned only one of the nine stolen works and that he would sell the remaining eight back to the Noortman family for €5 million (over U.S. $6 million). Working with Dutch police, the private investigator met with the German contact and an accompanying woman and agreed to the deal. Police followed the pair to a van where they and a third accomplice began unloading six of the alleged stolen paintings, whereupon the officers arrested them. The two remaining paintings were recovered at a residence. The recovered works had not been well maintained over the intervening 20-plus years and two were seriously damaged. Taken into custody for money laundering (the statute of limitations for any other charges relating to the theft and/or possible insurance fraud had expired) was a 45-year-old German male business executive, his 62-year-old mother from Belgium, and 66-year-old male from the Netherlands.[9]

1988: DAYTIME THEFT IN BERLIN

On May 27 a daytime theft occurred at the Neue Nationalgalerie in Berlin, Germany, resulting in the loss of *Portrait of Francis Bacon* by Lucian Freud (1952; $1.5 million). The painting had been on loan from the Tate Gallery in London at the time.[10]

1988: VAN GOGHS STOLEN IN HOLLAND

A theft of three Van Gogh paintings occurred at the Kroeller-Mueller Museum in the Netherlands in December. The paintings had a collective value of between $72 million and $90 million. They were subsequently recovered by the police.[11]

1991: VAN GOGH MUSEUM ROBBED

In April, the Van Gogh Museum in Amsterdam was robbed by two masked men who stole 20 paintings with an estimated value of $10 million. They were all recovered within an hour in the getaway car.[12]

1993: SWEDISH MUSEUM THEFT

At the Moderna Musset in Stockholm on November 3, works by Braque and Picasso were stolen in a $53 million theft. Three Swedes were later apprehended and sentenced to prison in 1995, but *Still Life* by Georges Braque (1928; value unknown) remains unrecovered.[13]

1994: PICASSOS STOLEN IN SWITZERLAND

Seven Picasso paintings were stolen from a Zurich gallery in October. Their estimated value was $44 million. They were recovered, but not until six years later.[14]

1995: TITIAN STOLEN FROM ENGLISH ESTATE

In January burglars using a ladder smashed a third-floor window of Longleat House, a country estate in England, and gained access to Titian's *Rest on the Flight into Egypt* (16th century; valued at between $7.7 million and $12.3 million), as well as two other lesser works while leaving more valuable paintings behind. Police arrived in response to a burglar alarm being activated within eight minutes, but the burglars had departed. The owner of the estate, Lord Bath, was home at the time of the incident. In September 2002 the painting was recovered through the payment of a privately arranged ransom of $150,000, but no arrests were made.[15]

1998: COROT PAINTING STOLEN AT THE LOUVRE

Around noon on May 3, Corot's *Le Chemin de Sèvres* (1855) was removed from its frame at the Louvre by a thief who then managed to escape with it despite police efforts to block exits and search the thousands who were visiting the museum on this busy Sunday. The painting was encased in glass, but this failed to thwart the theft. It was a relatively small painting (about 13-1/4" by 19-1/4") and was valued at $1.3 million. It has never been recovered.[16]

1998: MODERN ART STOLEN IN ROME

In May at the National Gallery of Modern Art in Rome, three thieves stayed behind after the museum closed, overtook three security guards, and turned off the alarm. Within 15 minutes they walked out with two Van Goghs and a Cezanne with a combined value of $34 million.[17]

2000: NEW YEAR'S BURGLARY IN BRITAIN

On New Year's day in Oxford, England, burglars entered the Ashmolean Museum by smashing a rooftop skylight window and then lowered themselves into the gallery using a rope. The fruits of these efforts was the theft of Cézanne's *Near Auvers-sur-Oise* (1879–1882) whose value has been placed between $3 million and $5 million; it remains unrecovered.[18]

2000: FAKE MONET DELAYS THEFT REPORT

Beach at Pourville by Monet (1882; $7 million) was stolen by thieves who cut the painting out of its frame at the Polish National Museum in Poznan and then replaced it with a cardboard copy which delayed reporting the theft.[19]

2000: ARMED ROBBERY AT THE NATIONAL MUSEUM IN STOCKHOLM

In December 2000, three armed and masked men, one of whom was carrying a submachine gun, entered the National Museum in Stockholm shortly before closing in the late afternoon. The guards were ordered to the floor at gunpoint while two of the robbers went to the galleries and returned moments later with three paintings: an eight-inch-by-four-inch Rembrandt *Self-Portrait* on copper that had an estimated value of $36 million; and two Renoirs, *Conversation* and *Young Parisian,* each valued in the $3 million dollar range. As they exited the museum, the robbers threw nails behind them in the roadway in an attempt to disable any responding police vehicles. They then left the vicinity in a motorboat that was waiting for them at the museum's riverfront entrance. During their getaway, confederates set off diversionary car bombs in other parts of the city. The boat was later found abandoned. After a failed attempt by the robbers to ransom the paintings back to the museum, police eventually convicted eight individuals in connection with the thefts. Renoir's *Conversation* was recovered in July 2001 incident to the investigation, but it was not until 2005 that the other works were recovered as a result of international cooperation. The FBI, while investigating a drug-trafficking network in Los Angeles found Renoir's *Young Parisian.* One of the drug-trafficking suspects was discovered to have ties with two suspects in the Stockholm robbery who were originally charged in the case but then avoided conviction. In September 2005, an undercover FBI agent arranged to meet with these two individuals in Stockholm, brothers who were Iraqi nationals, under the guise that he was attempting to broker a deal for the Rembrandt on behalf of a European organized-crime group. Once the terms were agreed upon, the transaction took place in Copenhagen at which point the Rembrandt was secured while the two brothers and two other thugs were arrested by Danish authorities. Thus, all the stolen works in this case were recovered.[20]

2001: $65 MILLION IN ARTWORKS STOLEN FROM HOME OF SPANISH BILLIONAIRE IN MADRID

The Madrid apartment home of Spanish billionaire Esther Koplowitz was burglarized on August 8, 2001, resulting in the theft of $65 million in paintings and sculptures that adorned this residence. Among the items stolen were paintings by Goya (*The Donkey's Fall*), Pissarro (*Child with Hat*), and Pieter Brueghel the Elder (*The Temptation of St. Anthony*). Koplowitz, the owner of Spain's largest construction conglomerate, was on vacation at the time of the burglary. The apartment building's security guard was reportedly overpowered by the thieves in order to gain access to the apartment, and they disarmed the apartment's security system. The Koplowitz's residence was being renovated at that time and the paintings were stacked against walls instead of hanging on display. Police investigation suggested that the burglars were familiar with the premises and spent about an hour selecting certain works to carry off. About a year later, the FBI developed information that the Brueghel was being offered for sale by a Spanish criminal organization that was known for dealing in narcotics, stolen cars, and guns throughout Europe. An undercover FBI agent was introduced to the gang members as a rogue art professor representing Russian buyers who were interested in purchasing the Brueghel. Over the course of two weeks of negotiations in Madrid, the agent gained the gang's confidence, and they solicited him to assist in their next art theft that was planned at the Van Gogh Museum in Amsterdam. In any event, the agreed-upon price for the Brueghel was $1 million, and they offered nine additional paintings for about another $15 million. The transfer of the money for Brueghel was planned at a Madrid hotel room. One of the gang members brought the painting to the room where it was examined by the undercover agent to determine its authenticity. Once satisfied, two Spanish police officers accompanying the undercover agent in the roles of bodyguards placed the gangster under arrest. A second gang member who was waiting in the hotel lobby and who was found to be the capo of the organization was also arrested by Spanish police. The security guard at the apartment building turned out to be an accomplice and he surrendered the following day. Many of the stolen works were subsequently recovered.[21]

2002: FAKE SCULPTURE DELAYS THEFT REPORT

In Hamburg, Germany, a small bronze sculpture by Alberto Giacometti entitled *Figurine (sans bra)* (1956; $500,000) was stolen at the Hamburg Museum. The sculpture was replaced by a wooden copy that delayed identification of the theft until June 3, but it is believed the theft took place on May 25 when 16,000 visitors toured the museum while it was open for a special event until 3:00 AM.[22]

2002: MAJOR THEFTS IN THE NETHERLANDS: VAN GOGH AND HALS MUSEUMS

Two burglars entered the Van Gogh Museum, Amsterdam, through the roof after climbing a ladder and stole Van Gogh's *View of the Sea at Schevegningen* (1882) and *Congregation Leaving the Reformed Church in Nuenen*

(1884–1885), a theft that represents a combined value of $30 million. The burglars were subsequently caught and convicted a year later, but the paintings were not recovered. Stolen from the Frans Hals Museum in Haarlem were five 17th-century paintings, including *The Quack* by Jan Steen. Among the other paintings were one each by Cornelis Bega and Cornelis Dusart and two by Adriaen van Ostade. Their insured value at the time of the theft in 2002 was $4.3 million. Although it took six years, police did recover these paintings in Den Bosch, Holland, three of which were found in damaged condition. Three men were arrested incident to the recovery, one of whom had ties to a major Dutch crime figure.[23]

2003: VIENNA MUSEUM BURGLARIZED
BY BURGLAR ALARM TECHNICIAN

In Spring 2003, Robert Mang, a 50-year-old security-alarm specialist performed work at the Kunsthistorisches Museum in Vienna. While there, he saw the royal saltcellar of King François of France, a work of carved gold with inlaid ebony and enamel by Benvenuto Cellini. It was valued at $60 million. On May 11, 2003, Mang burglarized the museum by scaling exterior scaffolding and breaking a second-floor window. He then stole the saltcellar by breaking its glass encasement and exited, all within 60 seconds. Although the alarm did go off, he was able to get out in time and in fact, the security guard simply reset the alarm and the theft was not found until four hours later. Mang had no prior criminal record or any financial difficulties. He held onto it for two years and then in the fall of 2005 attempted to ransom it for $11.9 million. Police were able to identify him through the cell phone used to make the extortion demand, and they recovered the saltcellar buried in a forest 50 miles north of Vienna. He was sentenced to five years in prison but was released early after serving two years, nine months. He resumed his old profession as an alarm technician.[24]

2003: DA VINCI STOLEN FROM SCOTTISH CASTLE

On August 27 two men dressed as tourists at the Drumlanrig Castle in southern Scotland overpowered a young female guide and staged a daring daylight theft of Leonardo da Vinci's *Madonna with the Yarnwinder* (ca. 1500–1520; 14" x 19"). Valued at $65 million, it was the largest art theft in British history to date. The two men ran out the door to a waiting vehicle in making their getaway. The vehicle, a white Volkswagen Golf, was abandoned not far from the crime scene. Two additional men were believed to have aided the thieves. More than four years later, in October 2007, police arrested four men in Glasgow, Scotland, and recovered the painting incident to the arrest. They were attempting to repatriate the painting to its owners, that is, extort money for its return; and they were charged with robbery and extortion.[25]

2004: VALUABLE PAINTINGS STOLEN FROM
A HOSPITAL IN ROME

A burglary on July 31 from Santo Spirito, a religious complex near the Vatican that was used in the Middle Ages as a hostel and hospital, resulted in the theft of 10 paintings valued collectively at $5 million. Among those stolen included *Flagelliazione* (16th–17th centuries) by Giuseppe Cesari (also known as Cavalier D'Arpino) and *The Holy Family* (16th century), a work that has been attributed to Parmigianino (also known as Francesco Mazzola). The paintings were normally displayed in a room protected by an alarm but had been moved to a nonprotected restoration room a month earlier. In December 2008 the Italian Carabineri paramilitary art squad recovered all 10 paintings from a trailer belonging to a suspected art smuggler. The suspect is not believed to have been involved in the burglary; rather, his role was to take the paintings out of the country in order to sell them.[26]

2005: MUSEUM BURGLARY NETS PAINTINGS
AND SILVER IN HOLLAND

Burglars broke into the Westfries Museum in Hoorn, Netherlands, on the night of Sunday, January 9 and stole paintings and silver-crafted objects totaling $13 million. Twenty-one paintings were stolen including works by Dutch artists Jacob Waben, Matthias Withoos, Jan Clasez Rietschoof, and Herman Henstenburgh. Although it was reportedly checked recently, the museum's alarm system failed to activate and thus the burglary was not discovered until the following morning. Police investigators felt that the thieves had previously surveyed the museum and its contents in preparation for the burglary.[27]

2006: A ROBBERY IN RIO DURING CARNIVAL

In Rio de Janiero four armed men robbed the Chacara do Ceu Museum on February 26 during a Carnival parade, when they overpowered the security guards and forced them to shut down the security cameras. They then proceeded to steal *Luxembourg Gardens* by Matisse, *Marine* by Monet, *Dance* by Picasso, and *Two Balconies* by Dali. The value of the stolen paintings was put at $50 million. They have not been recovered.[28]

2007: PICASSO'S PAINTINGS STOLEN
FROM HIS GRANDDAUGHTER

In February a burglary at the Paris home of Diana Widmaier Picasso netted two of her grandfather's (Pablo Picasso) paintings, *Maya and the Doll* and *Portrait of Jacqueline*, valued at a total of $66 million, and a drawing. Police later recovered these objects when the thieves attempted to sell them.[29]

2007: MASKED GUNMEN STEAL FOUR PAINTINGS
FROM A MUSEUM IN FRANCE

On August 5, 2007, three gunmen stole four paintings from the Musée des Beaux-Arts in Nice. Two of the paintings were by Peter Brueghel the Elder, *Allegory of Earth* and *Allegory of Water;* one was by Claude Monet, *Cliffs Near Dieppe;* and one was by Alfred Sisley, *The Lane of Poplars at Moret.* Soon after the robbery, the gunmen and an accomplice, who acted as a broker, attempted to sell the stolen paintings to undercover officers of the French National Police and the FBI, who were working together on the case. Negotiations between the suspects and the undercover officers continued through the fall of 2007 and into the spring of 2008 in France, Spain, and Florida. These negotiations resulted in an agreed-upon sale price of €3 million and the logistics for the transfer. On June 4, 2008, in Marseille, France, French police arrested the three gunmen and recovered the four paintings while the broker, a French national, was arrested in Florida by FBI and Immigration and Customs Enforcement (ICE) agents. He subsequently pled guilty in the United States to conspiring to transport knowingly stolen property in interstate commerce and he received a prison sentence of over five years.[30]

2007: VALUABLE PICASSO STOLEN IN MUSEUM
BURGLARY IN BRAZIL

Three burglars broke into the Sao Paulo Museum of Art in Brazil on December 20 just before dawn and stole a Picasso painting (*Portrait of Suzanne Bloch*) valued at $50 million along with a painting by Brazilian artist Candido Portinari (valued at between $5 million and $6 million). The burglary occurred during a guard-shift change and involved using a car jack to pry open a metal security gate. The thieves then smashed through two glass doors, ran to the top floor of the museum and stole the paintings, each of which was hanging in a different room. It appeared that the two stolen paintings were targeted since the thieves bypassed other valuable works. The incident was recorded on a security camera, but the museum was not otherwise protected by an alarm system or motion detectors. Moreover, the guards were unarmed. Less than one month later police recovered the paintings and arrested three suspects. One of the suspects was an escaped convict while another had a criminal record. The third suspect, who cooperated with the police, alleged the theft was in fulfillment of an order placed by a Saudi art collector.[31]

2008: A WEEK OF MAJOR THEFTS IN SWITZERLAND

Switzerland was victimized twice within a week by thefts that resulted in a collective loss of over $167 million. On Wednesday, February 6, burglars stole two Picassos worth an estimated $4.4 million that were on display in Pfäffikon. The paintings involved were *Head of Horse* and *Glass and Pitcher*. However, a more dramatic crime occurred on the following Sunday, February 11, when three masked robbers entered Zurich's E. G. Bührle Collection at about 4:30 PM and grabbed four paintings off the wall. This private museum contains the art collection of the late Emil Bührle, a Swiss arms manufacturer who supplied the Nazis and who was also the largest Swiss buyer of art confiscated from the Jews by Hitler's regime.

One of the robbers brandished a pistol and ordered visitors and museum staff to the floor. They made their getaway in a waiting white van. The paintings stolen were *Count Lepic and His Daughters* (1871) by Edgar Degas; *Poppies near Vetheuil* (1879) by Monet, *Boy in the Red Waistcoat* (1888) by Cezanne, and *Blossoming Chestnut Branches* (1890) by Van Gogh. Their estimated value is $163 million. Witnesses described the robbers as speaking German, but with a Slavic accent, raising the concern of the involvement of an international criminal gang. Although the two Swiss thefts were proximate, both temporally and geographically, a connection between them has eluded investigators. Within a week however, the Monet and Van Gogh were recovered in a stolen vehicle found parked at a psychiatric hospital about one quarter mile from the crime scene. Neither the Degas nor the Cezanne from the robbery nor the Picassos from the earlier burglary have been found, and those responsible for these theft have not been apprehended.[32]

2008: ARMED ROBBERY OF SAO PAULO MUSEUM

In June 2008, three armed robbers entered the Pinacoteca do Estado Museum in Sao Paulo, Brazil, as paying visitors. They went immediately to a second-floor gallery where two Picasso prints were on display, *Minotaur, Drinker and Women* (1933) and *The Painter and the Model* (1963). They overpowered unarmed guards who were on duty and grabbed these prints off the wall along with two Brazilian oil paintings: *Couple* by Lasar Segall and *Women in the Window* by Emiliano Di Cavalcanti. The paintings were taken in their frames and they had a combined value of $612,000. The incident occurred at about noon and there were few visitors in the museum at the time. About one month later, police recovered one of the Picasso's, *The Painter and the Model* and arrested one individual. Then in August 2008, a second suspect was arrested and the works by Segall and Di Cavalcanti were recovered, leaving only Picasso's *Minotaur, Drinker and Women* unaccounted for.[33]

2008: DAYTIME RESIDENTIAL BURGLARY IN CALIFORNIA NETS MILLIONS

The residence of an elderly couple in Encino, California, was burglarized during the day in August 2008, with the thieves targeting an art collection worth millions of dollars. The couple was in the residence at the time but did not encounter the intruders. Investigation determined that a housekeeper failed to lock an exterior door, thus permitting easy access to paintings that hung in two adjacent rooms. The stolen paintings included works by Marc Chagall, Hans Hofmann, Chaim Soutine, Arshile Gorky, Emil Nolde, Lyonel Feininger, and Kess van Dongen, and ranged in value between $800,000 and $4 million each.[34]

2008: PRICELESS WORK BY GOYA STOLEN IN COLOMBIA

A Goya engraving entitled *Sad Feelings* (1810–1814), which was part of the Spanish artist's *Disasters of War* series, was stolen in September 2008 from Bogota's Gilberto Alzate Avendano Museum. It was part of a temporary Goya exhibit that that had been on display at the museum since the beginning of the month. The engraving had recently toured France and China and was scheduled to travel to Medellin after Bogota. Museum officials called it a "priceless" piece. It was stolen while the museum was closed for the evening. About one month later, police recovered the work in a Bogota hotel room based on an informant's tip. It was wrapped in a sheet and still encased in its original frame.[35]

2009: CHURCH BURGLARY IN NORWAY NETS CRANACH PAINTING

A church in a small Norwegian town south of Oslo was burglarized on Sunday, March 8 in the early morning. The burglar gained access to the church by breaking a window that was accessed by placing a ladder against an exterior wall after which he removed a Lucas Cranach the Elder painting entitled *Suffer the Little Children to Come Unto Me* (ca. 1540). The painting had an estimated value of $2.1–$2.8 million and had been on display in the church for about 330 years. The burglary was discovered when firefighters responded to an alarm that was triggered by the break-in. A police investigation resulted in the recovery of the painting three days later and the arrest of a 50-year-old male in connection with the burglary. Police believe a second participant was also involved. The painting sustained some damage and required restoration.[36]

2009: THEFT AT PICASSO NATIONAL MUSEUM IN PARIS

In June, 33 pencil drawings by Picasso that were contained in a notebook were stolen from the Picasso National Museum in Paris. The notebook was on display in a locked glass case and was valued at between $8.4 million and $14 million. Details of the theft are unknown, but it is believed it occurred at some point over a two-day period. No recovery has been made.[37]

CHAPTER 4

Art Forgeries and Fakes

While we will revisit the theft of art again in the next two chapters (i.e., when we consider the plunder of art in times of war and civil/religious unrest and thefts of cultural-heritage objects), we will now turn our attention to art forgeries and fakes, that is, objects that falsely portray the work of a particular artist or style, or in the case of unattributed objects such as many antiquities, the timeframe in which they were created.

This form of art crime, in the minds of many, ranks closely behind art theft in terms of concern, familiarity, and severity; and such observations are not unfounded. In fact, Thomas P. Hoving, former director of New York's Metropolitan Museum of Art, called art forgery the "slipperiest game of all and its practitioners the most elusive," noting that art forgers will seldom make a full confession.[1] Once again, however, there is no comprehensive database maintained for forged and/or fake artworks and identifying the frequency of art forgery and fakery, as well as losses that are incurred from it, is even more elusive than it was for art thefts. So, we must rely on estimates or opinions of the magnitude of this problem. First, however, to put these estimates or opinions in perspective let's get a "reality check." Just as we found that art theft needs to be viewed more broadly than just the high-profile, major incidents, likewise art forgery and fakery is not limited simply to attempts to copy and then sell famous works of art (e.g., as some allege was the plan incident to the theft of the Mona Lisa). In fact, the practice of art forgery and fakery is as old as art itself.[2] Thus, when examining this form of art crime, we must not only consider what is really a more modern-day practice of attempts to forge the works of well-known artists but also an age-old and widespread practice of copying un-attributed objects and then falsely representing them as created in the era and/place of their historical origin. Hoving offered a frequency estimate that considers this broad perspective. He stated that in his 15 years at the Metropolitan Museum of Art he examined 50,000 works of art of all categories and found 40 percent of them to be forgeries.[3] When considering just paintings, Robyn Sloggett, an art conservation expert at Australia's Melbourne University, estimated that 10 percent are "misidentified."[4]

Estimates of monetary losses due to forgeries and fakes tend to be even less precise, not only because of the lack of any database but also because of the vagaries of the art market, especially when antiquities are involved. In any event, art investigator Robert Spiel conjectured the value of forged paintings to be at least equal to that of stolen paintings, a figure he placed at $3.1 billion. Again from a broader viewpoint (i.e., beyond just paintings), John Conklin in *Art Crime* (1994) described forged and faked art works as a worldwide problem resulting in annual losses of tens of millions of dollars.[5]

Thus, once again we have evidence that a form of crime is victimizing the art world in what appears to be a substantial manner, both in terms of the number of occurrences and the monetary harm that arises as a result. Numbers aside, however, let's consider how this form of art crime compares to art theft. Recall that when art is stolen, it is not only taken unlawfully from its rightful owner, but in doing so, this act often deprives others (including entire societies) from viewing an important piece of their culture. Moreover, theft itself is a brazen physical act, if not potentially violent, when robberies occur. How do these characteristics compare to conduct associated with forgery and fakery?

THEFT VERSUS FRAUD

From chapter 2 we learned that acts of art theft can be viewed as larceny, burglary, or robbery, depending upon the methodologies employed to steal. However, larceny and burglary are generally differentiated from robbery because the latter is usually considered a crime of violence due to its threat or actual use of force, while larceny and burglary are generally considered property crimes. Clearly, the goal of forgery and fakery is similar to that of theft, that is, the acquisition of money or property to which the offender is not the rightful or lawful owner (although resentment toward the "establishment art world" and its experts is also cited as a motivating factor for some art forgers[6]). However, methodologies associated with forgery and fakery are in stark contrast to the physical acts that earmark the major theft categories. The *Uniform Crime Report* (*UCR*), the primary U.S. compendium of crimes reported to the police, defines forgery (and associates counterfeiting along with it) as:

The altering, copying, or imitating of something, without authority or right, with the intent to deceive or defraud by passing the copy or thing altered or imitated as that which is original or genuine; or the selling, buying, or possession of an altered, copied, or imitated thing with the intent to deceive or defraud.[7]

While forgery and counterfeiting are tracked by the *UCR* because throughout the United States these acts are generally classified as crimes by both the states and the federal government, the term fakery, per se, does not enjoy such legal status. Rather, if one were to look at the *UCR*'s definition for fraud it becomes apparent that this term encompasses the notion of fakery:

The intentional perversion of the truth for inducing another person or other entity in reliance upon it to part with something of value or to surrender a legal right. Fraudulent conversion and obtaining of money or property by false pretenses.[8]

Like property crimes and even robbery, the goal of fraud is to obtain something of value, for example, money or property. However, unlike theft offenses that rely on physical acts of stealing, fraud relies on guile, deception, false pretenses, and/or misrepresentation to cause a person to surrender voluntarily money or property because of being influenced by such untruthful conduct. Thus, with regard to art forgery and fakery, we are not talking about the mere replication of an existing art object; rather, the illegal conduct here is the misrepresentation of its authenticity in an attempt to acquire money or other valuable property.[9] It follows then that forgery and counterfeiting are simply categories that fall within the over-all realm of fraud offenses because the intent of forgery and counterfeiting is to deceive or defraud. In fact, when art forgery is prosecuted, fraud statues are frequently the primary offenses that are charged. The case study, in the form of a U.S. Department of Justice press release, presented in box 4.1 provides an example where fraud violations are charged in connection with art forgery and counterfeiting.

BOX 4.1 FRAUD CHARGED IN ART FORGERY AND COUNTERFEITING SCHEME

Press Release

United States Attorney
Northern District of Illinois
March 19, 2008

Seven Defendants Indicted For Alleged Roles In $5 Million International Fraud Schemes Selling Counterfeit Fine Art Prints

CHICAGO—An international investigation of the production and sale of counterfeit limited edition fine art prints of renowned artists, has resulted in federal criminal charges against seven defendants, including three Europeans

and residents of Florida, New York and Illinois, U.S. and Spanish law enforcement officials announced today. Two separate indictments allege that
the defendants sold thousands of counterfeit prints-at prices well in excess
of their value-to victims in the United States, Canada, Australia, Europe and
Japan. The indictments allege that the defendants together reaped more
than $5 million in illegal proceeds from the separate, but overlapping fraud
schemes. In both cases, investigators tracked the distribution of bogus works,
purportedly by such artists as Pablo Picasso, Marc Chagall, Roy Lichtenstein, Joan Miro, Andy Warhol and others, from counterfeit distributors to an
art dealer in north suburban Northbrook, who allegedly sold the inauthentic
prints to victims, primarily through eBay, an internet auction web site.

The Northbrook dealer, Michael Zabrin, principal in Fineartmasters and
Zfineartmasters, was charged in one indictment, together with the three European alleged counterfeit artwork distributors and a Florida art dealer. A
second Northbrook man, James Kennedy, principal in KFA of Illinois, Inc.,
was charged in the second indictment together with an alleged distributor
of counterfeit artwork based in New York.

"Con artists should not be confused with master artists," said Patrick J.
Fitzgerald, United States Attorney for the Northern District of Illinois. "Buyers of limited edition fine art prints, like all other buyers, are entitled to get
what they pay for. These indictments are significant because they extend
across international borders from one end of the supply chain to the other.
While we urge customers to exercise caution and skepticism of deals that
appear too good to be true, we are determined to preserve the integrity of
an open market."

Mr. Fitzgerald announced the charges together with Thomas P. Brady,
Inspector-in-Charge of the U.S. Postal Inspection Service in Chicago, and
Robert D. Grant, Special Agent-in-Charge of the Chicago Office of the Federal Bureau of Investigation. They were joined by Comissari Antoni Per-
manyer, the investigation commander-in-chief of Mossos d'Esquadra (the
Catalan police), headquartered in Barcelona, Spain. The U.S. Immigration
and Customs Enforcement (ICE) agents and the Northbrook Police Department also assisted in the investigation, which is continuing.

The officials announced that anyone who suspects that they might be
a victim of fraudulent art sales may submit information to law enforcement authorities via a form posted on the U.S. Attorney's web site at www.
usdoj.gov/usao/iln. Persons without internet access may call a toll-free
number-(866) 364-2621-and leave a message with the spelling of their name
and an address, and a form will be mailed to them.

Charged in a 10-count indictment (the "European indictment") were: Os-
waldo Aulestia-Bach, 62, of Barcelona, Spain; Elio Bonfiglioli, 53, of Mon-
summano, Italy; Patrizia Soliani, 56, of Milan, Italy, and Miami Beach, Fla.,
all three of whom allegedly distributed counterfeit artwork; Jerome Bengis,
61, of Coral Springs, Fla., principal in Bengis Fine Art gallery; and Michael
Zabrin, 55, of Northbrook. Aulestia-Bach and Bonfiglioli were each charged
with 10 counts of fraud and the United States intends to seek their extradi-
tion. Soliani, who was released on bond after she was arrested and charged

in a criminal complaint last summer, was charged with four counts of fraud, while Bengis was charged with two counts of fraud and Zabrin is facing six fraud counts. Soliani, Bengis and Zabrin will be arraigned at a later date in U.S. District Court in Chicago.

The indictment also seeks forfeiture of $4 million in addition to more than $125,000 that was seized from bank accounts in San Francisco belonging to Aulestia-Bach and Bonfiglioli.

The second nine-count indictment charged James Kennedy, 55, of Northbrook, with five counts of fraud and one count of obstruction of justice for allegedly threatening injury on January 8, 2008, to an individual who was communicating information to a law enforcement officer in connection with this investigation. Kennedy was arrested on that charge on January 31, 2008, in Jacksonville, Fla., and is being held without bond in federal custody in Chicago. He has a detention hearing scheduled for March 24. Charged with Kennedy was Leon Amiel, Jr., also known as "Leon Glass," 36, of New York City, principal in Glass Inter Corp., who was charged with six counts of fraud. He will be arraigned at a later date in Federal Court in Chicago. The Kennedy-Amiel indictment seeks forfeiture of $1 million.

The European indictment alleges that the five defendants and others participated in a fraud scheme between July 1999 and October 2007 in which Aulestia-Bach and Bonfiglioli caused counterfeit prints of works by such artists as Miro, Warhol, Chagall, Picasso and others to be manufactured in Spain and Italy. The two men allegedly acquired what they knew were counterfeit prints bearing forged signatures of renowned artists to distribute them as limited edition works, and they knew that many of the prints bore false numerical or other markings making them appear as if they had been part of a limited edition or were prepared for the artist's own use. Aulestia-Bach at times allegedly forged the signatures of certain artists, including Chagall, Lichtenstein, Miro and Picasso.

According to the indictment, Aulestia-Bach and Bonfiglioli distributed counterfeit artwork to various dealers, including Soliani, Bengis and Zabrin, who, knowing it was counterfeit, resold the prints to wholesale and retail customers at prices substantially in excess of the market value for inauthentic artwork. It adds that the two European distributors allegedly cautioned Soliani to limit the amount of counterfeit art in the market at one time.

The indictment details specific transactions involving the sale of allegedly counterfeit limited edition art prints, including undercover purchases by law enforcement agents. In one instance alleged in the indictment, Zabrin offered two etchings for sale on eBay, falsely representing that they were 1968 Picasso etchings from the 347 Series, signed by the artist in pencil, and that they were numbered from an edition limited to 50 prints.

Zabrin was also named as co-schemer in the Kennedy-Amiel indictment, which alleges a fraud scheme between 2000 and January 2008 in which the defendants and others acquired counterfeit prints of various artists, including Alexander Calder and Salvador Dali, which they knew bore forged signatures and/or false numbering. Kennedy allegedly forged the signatures of certain artists, including Calder, Chagall, Miro and Picasso.

In one instance, according to the indictment, Amiel distributed to one dealer 2,500 counterfeit Calder prints and 600 counterfeit Chagall "Exodus" prints. Kennedy allegedly traveled to art shows throughout the country where he sold counterfeit artwork of prominent artists as genuine limited edition prints. Between 2005 and 2007, Kennedy received nearly $1.3 million from the sale of art, including 61 successful auctions of counterfeit art on eBay, from which he fraudulently obtained more than $39,000, the indictment alleges.

If convicted, each count of mail and wire fraud in both indictments carries a maximum penalty of 20 years in prison and a $250,000 fine. The obstruction of justice count against Kennedy carries a maximum penalty of 10 years in prison and a $250,000. Restitution is mandatory and the Court would determine the appropriate sentence to be imposed under the advisory United States Sentencing Guidelines.

The public is reminded that an indictment contains only charges and is not evidence of guilt. The defendants are presumed innocent and are entitled to a fair trial at which the United States has the burden of proving guilt beyond a reasonable doubt.

This press release from the United States Attorney's office was accessed at http://www.usdoj.gov/usao/iln/pr/chicago/2008/pr0319_01.pdf

FORGERY, FAKERY, AND ART VALUES

Linking the terms forgery, fakery, and fraud generally with works of art certainly suggests there is something wrong with copying a work that was created by another, and the case study above exemplifies the type of response that law enforcement and legal authorities can put forth when confronted with the sale of counterfeited and forged art objects. Let's look a little closer at why such actions are warranted. Radnóti, in his book, *The Fake: Forgery and Its Place in Art*, defines art forgery as an object falsely purporting to have both the history of production as well as the entire subsequent historical fate requisite for the original work (the latter meaning the aging and accidental wear and tear and natural history). This definition arises from his four-point critical analysis of art forgery that hinges on notions of originality:

- A forged art object pretends to be identical which it is not.
- It expropriates of another personality.
- It expropriates the novelty or problem solution of another person's work.
- It lends historical authenticity to a work that the work is not entitled to, thus claiming a false pedigree and occupying a place in history that it does not deserve.

While clearly portraying forgery as a wrong philosophically, Radnóti nevertheless was also quite aware of the monetary ramifications of art forgery, calling it a function of money and competition. In fact, he contended that art collecting increases demand, which in turn encourages forgery.[10] An economic analysis of the value of paintings concluded that higher prices were associated with more famous artists. Conversely, it also found the most common uncertainty about art is its authorship, an uncertainty that is also most important in determining its value.[11]

The "Areas of Gray"

When considering art authentication issues, there are "gray areas" that should be recognized when dealing with allegations of forgery and fakery. The case study above involved the sale of counterfeit limited edition prints, an illegal practice that unfortunately is not without precedent. This type of scheme has been called the most common present-day form of art forgery and has been responsible for hundreds of millions of dollars in losses dating back to 1980.[12] It may be recalled earlier that limited edition prints are prime targets for theft because if one can be furtively removed from a gallery premises, it will likely not be missed for some time if multiple copies are on hand. Art forgers exploit this multiple edition vulnerability too but in a slightly different manner; that is, without any expectation that the prints they are selling are one of kind, they are able to more easily market counterfeit objects.

Within this context, however, a question of originality can surface. While a recognized practice within the art world, the production of multiple editions of an image raises ambiguity about what constitutes an original artwork, an issue that experts might even differ on.[13] Bear in mind, however, that printmaking as an art form is not new, having evolved in the 1400s incident to the Protestant Reformation. Then, as now, it permits works of art to be replicated and disseminated to a wider audience. Generally, however, prints are considered original artworks when they are produced by and/or under the direction of the artist. Over time, a variety of printmaking processes have been employed beginning with wood blocks. Modern-day processes include lithography and serigraphy. Lithographs are printed from images that are drawn on a greasy wax material that is applied to a smooth polished stone. Serigraph prints are created using a silkscreen process. Following the production process, the artist then signs and numbers each print; and the production materials are destroyed to prevent further duplication. Despite these widely accepted original printmaking practices, it should not be surprising that counterfeiters and forgers easily circumvent these procedures through use of readily available "high-tech" copying and printing equipment, especially in response to market demand for works purportedly by well-known artists.

While the advent of limited edition prints has raised originality questions (or alternatively an excellent opportunity for counterfeiters and
forgers), perhaps a more esoteric, if not perplexing, question has arisen regarding one-of-a-kind works that require restoration. At what point does
an artist/conservator employed to restore a damaged painting, or one that
has suffered the ravages of time, alter the work to the extent that it can no
longer be attributed to the original artist? While current-day restoration
practices are more limited in their approach and scope, greater license was
the norm in the 1930s through 1950s as evidenced by the controversial
Belgian restorer Joseph van der Veken. One of his restorations was that of
Van der Weyden's *Madonna and Child* (ca.1450s), a work that is believed to
have been 75 percent newly painted. The question then becomes should
this work be attributed to the original (and well-known) artist, Van der
Weyden, or to the lesser acclaimed restorer, Van der Veken? Interestingly,
this issue apparently did not dissuade the Nazi leader Hermann Göring
from subsequently buying this painting as a Van der Weyden during
World War II.[14]

But It's Not Just about the Money

While our focus thus far has been on how art forgery and fakery is
tantamount to fraud and its companion, monetary loss, there is another
form of victimization to consider. The expectation of visitors to museums
and other educational custodians of art is that they will be able to view
original and authentic art objects. In educational and research settings, art
objects are studied to learn about the art and artist and/or past eras and
civilizations. Whether for pleasure or as an academic pursuit, those who
unwittingly view and/or study works that are forgeries or fakes are also
victims of these crimes. Moreover, as evidenced by the case studies below,
research findings unknowingly derived from forgeries and fakes can de-
tour our pursuit of truth and knowledge, thus expanding the notion of
victimization exponentially.

FORGERY AND FAKERY: ANTIQUITIES

Various accounts support the ancient origins of art forgery and fakery.
Examples include allegations that one of the earliest artists we know by
name, the Greek sculptor Phidias of the fifth century B.C.E, claimed as his
own (by affixing his signature) the work of his students; and Roman artisans dating back to the reign of Hadrian are believed to have copied the
works of earlier eras in mass quantities.[15] While the popularity of antiquities waned in the Middle Ages, they enjoyed a resurgence in interest beginning in the Renaissance, which spurred Italian forgers to resume mass
production of objects that replicated the works of their forbears.[16] This keen
interest in antiquities has continued unabated to the present day among

collectors, and it has created a market that not only continues to give life to fraudulent pieces that were perhaps even created in ancient times but has also encouraged modern-day forgers to replicate objects from the past. In addition to classic antiquities (i.e., Greek and Roman), ancient works from Asia and Africa have also been subject to present-day fakery (e.g., Buddha statues and African masks).[17] Moreover, a reformed forger of Gothic ivory carvings estimated that 50 percent of all such objects collected after 1890 were made in his and other workshops in France, Italy, and Spain.[18] In fact, one assessment of the overall trade in stolen/smuggled antiquities is that a significant part of it consists of fakes and forgeries.[19] The following case studies (box 4.2 and box 4.3) provide examples of such practices.

BOX 4.2 FAKING A CIVILIZATION: PRE-COLUMBIAN ART FORGERIES[20]

Pre-Columbian art encompasses objects from civilizations in the Americas prior to Columbus's arrival in 1492 and the subsequent European colonization of the Western Hemisphere. Among the most well-known in terms of artistic achievement were the Aztecs who occupied what is now Mexico; the Mayans who were native to modern day Mexico, Belize, and Guatemala; and the Incas located in what is now Peru. According to Conklin, Pre-Columbian art is attractive to forgers for several reasons: it is not attributable to any particular artists; it is not well cataloged so there is no comprehensive record of the known authentic pieces in existence; and scientific tests do not work well with the ceramic material that was used in this type of art. Taking advantage of these characteristics was Brígdo Lara of Mexico, who, according to former Metropolitan Museum of Art Director Thomas Hoving, faked an entire civilization. Lara is believed to have produced thousands of ceramics that were misrepresented as the works of the Totonac Indians of Mexico during the 7th to 10th centuries. While precise numbers are unknown, many of these objects were accorded authenticity including those that were on display at the Dallas Museum of Art and St. Louis Museum of Art. His activities became known in 1974 when he and his two cousins were arrested by Mexican authorities as they attempted to smuggle out of the country what was believed to be archeological items. Sentenced to 10 years, he was released after seven months after he demonstrated to the prison warden his ability to make the objects he was accused of smuggling out of Mexico; thus, his ability to be a forger allowed him to escape confinement as a smuggler.

Lara's success as a forger can be attributed to the fact that he copied only a style and not any specific works. In fact, he created images in this style that are only reflected in literature, hence Hoving's assessment that he created an entire civilization that was assumed authentic. However, Lara claims his works are original interpretations of Pre-Columbian art, and he denies that he was ever in the business of selling fakes. Since his release from prison, Lara has worked for the University of Veracruz in Mexico making copies of archeological finds and restoring authentic pieces; and now with a permit from Mexico's National Institute of Archeology and History, he is back in the retail business making copies of Totonac art (that are stamped as replicas) for a network of vendors throughout Mexico. A four-foot, seven-inch Totonac figure can cost as much as $13,000. Maybe Lara was foremost in Thomas Hoving's mind when he called forgery the "slipperiest game of all and its practitioners the most elusive."

BOX 4.3 BIBLE-ERA RELICS FOUND TO BE FRAUDS IN ISRAEL[21]

In Israel, five men were charged with faking a dozen Bible-era relics including an inscribed stone known as the Yehoash stone from the 3,000-year-old Temple of Solomon and a burial box inscribed with the name of Jesus's brother, James. Experts determined that the entire text (10 lines) on the Yehoash stone inscription was a forgery, as were the words "brother of Jesus" that appeared on the burial box. Both had been accorded high religious significance. Among those charged were Oded Golan, a well-known antiquities collector in Tel Aviv, and Rafael Braun, former head of the antiquities laboratory at the Israel Museum. Also implicated was Egyptian artist Marco Samah Shoukri Ghatas, the confessed inscriber of the Yehoash stone.

Of the five men initially indicted, charges were dropped against two in return for their cooperation and testimony. A third, antiquities trader Faiz al-Amla, entered into a plea agreement and received a six-month jail term. Those who remained under indictment were Golan and Robert Deutsch, another Tel Aviv antiquities trader. The indictment against these individuals laid out a scheme whereby authentic antiquities were altered through false inscriptions and decorations and then an artificial patina was applied, that is, a layer that would naturally accumulate on antiquities. The artificial patina was so cleverly manufactured and applied that even many antiquities experts were misled by it. In fact, the authenticity and importance accorded these objects by experts who examined them resulted in widespread publicity, which in turn inflated their value.

Thus, as illustrated in the case studies, forgeries of antiquities result in twofold harms. One, of course, is that collectors and museums (and thereby the museum-going public) are fooled into believing they are acquiring/viewing authentic objects, and the forgers are unjustly enriched in the process. A second harm is less tangible and is somewhat akin to the intangible harm caused by art theft; that is, it deprives societies of a part of their culture. With regard to false and forged antiquities, our entire sense and understanding of our history can be wrongly altered through these practices.

FORGERY AND FAKERY: FROM THE RENAISSANCE TO MODERN DAY

When we begin to consider art forgery and fakery from the Renaissance forward, an important feature that was not as frequently encountered in ancient or even medieval times was that the identity of the artists began to be associated with their works. Thus, it was no longer sufficient for a forger to copy a general cultural or societal style. Rather unique styles and techniques associated with specific artists or groups of artists (i.e., "schools") had to be mastered and replicated. While modern-day forgers have tackled, and in some instances mastered, the "Old Masters," perhaps more troubling are forgeries that were made closer to the era of the originals. Thomas Hoving in his book *False Impressions: The Hunt for Big-Time Art Fakes* discussed the problem of Renaissance works that were faked in the 16th and 17th centuries using materials similar to those used 300–400 years earlier. Just the mere fact that paintings created in the 1500s or 1600s are likely to display true signs of aging helps to offset suspicions about authenticity. The work of German artist Albrecht Dürer was frequently copied during his lifetime that spanned from 1471 to 1528 and in the years following his death as well. There may be as many as 5,000 fakes of his work, perhaps attributable to the artistic medium that he was so famous for, printmaking (sound familiar?).[22]

More recently, that is, over the past hundred years, we have continued to be fooled by art forgeries all too frequently, but at least we have become acquainted with some of these masters of deceit. The likes of Icilio Frederico Joni of Italy, Elmyr de Hory of Hungary, Englishmen Eric Hebborn, John Myatt, John Drew, brothers Robert and Brian Thwaites, Dutchmen Han van Meegeren and Geert Jan Jansen, and New York City art dealer Ely Sakhai might not be household names, but within the art world they each have established their place in the annals of art forgery and fakery.

The least contemporary of this group were Joni and Van Meegeren. Joni pursued a career as a self-described painter, gilder, and restorer from the late 19th century, until he died in 1946. Like Brígdo Lara from our case study above, Joni was also a highly skilled copier of a style, in this case Italian Renaissance painting. And further like Lara, he was quite prolific in terms of the number of paintings that he produced that reflected this style. Unlike an ancient era that Lara copied, Joni's work reflected a style in which individual artist (or groups of artists) attribution was the norm. However, he avoided any legal entanglements because he simply made his own original work look old, and he then let others decide who the artist was and whether they were authentic Renaissance pieces. Among those fooled was the Cleveland Museum of Art. This institution purchased a painting entitled *Madonna and Child with Angels,* believed to be a 15th-century work by Sano di Pietro. Later, the museum developed suspicions that the fine weblike cracks in the paint that occur naturally with age (i.e., *craquelure*) were really the handiwork of Joni's signature baking process. Then, the discovery of modern-day nails in the frame eliminated any doubts that they had really bought a 20th-century Joni and not a work produced during the Renaissance.[23]

Han van Meegeren was born in the latter part of the 19th-century (1889) and died in 1947, a year after Joni. By some accounts, he is history's premier forger of Vermeer, having created six paintings that were falsely attributed to the great Dutch master; other observers go even further and describe him as the most successful art forger of the 20th century (he also created two paintings in the likeness of another 17th-century Dutch master, Pieter de Hooch). One of his works, entitled *Christ and His Disciples at Emmaus,* was authenticated as a Vermeer in 1937 by a renowned art historian, after which it was acquired by a museum in Rotterdam for $6 million. Interestingly, like Belgian Joseph van der Veken discussed earlier, the infamous Nazi leader Hermann Göring is also connected to Meegeren. Through intermediaries, Meegeren sold Göring one of his Vermeers (*Christ with the Woman Taken in Adultery*), and in return, he received 137 paintings from Göring's illicit collection acquired through theft, confiscation, and extortion. This transaction proved to be Meegeren's undoing as it led to a postwar investigation for collaborating with the Nazis. However, rather than face the far more serious consequences that would have resulted from a collaboration conviction, Meegeren acknowledged his forgery activities. For this, he was sentenced to one year in prison, but he died before ever serving a day.[24]

Elymr de Hory boasted to his biographer, Clifford Irving, that he forged a thousand paintings that purport to be the work of well-known artists including Matisse, Chagall, and Modigliani and sold them for as much as $20,000 each. While no one disputes that De Hory was an art forger, whether he produced 1,000 fake works might be open to question, however. Consider the scenario where this information came from: an art forger made this statement to an author who served a prison sentence for writing a fake autobiography of the reclusive Howard Hughes! Credibility problems, anyone? Nevertheless, film director Orson Welles then produced a movie entitled *F is for Fake* in 1975, one year before De Hory's death.[25]

Eric Hebborn was so brash that he wrote a book that purportedly disclosed his forgery techniques (some of which we will cover later in this chapter). He was also killed in 1996 under mysterious circumstances in Rome, one week after the book's publication. Hebborn copied the styles of the Old Masters and created original works in these styles as opposed to producing counterfeits of existing paintings. He claimed that between 1963 and 1978, he produced 500 such paintings and although he was exposed in 1978, he faced no criminal charges.[26]

Geert Jan Jansen fed the Dutch market with forgeries of such artists as Picasso and Chagall until 1988 when he moved to France to escape suspicions of his activities. However, by the mid-1990s he came under investigation by the French police because he continued to market his forgeries to auction houses. In May 1994, police found him living in Poitiers in possession of 700 fake drawings and gouaches and 1,500 forged certificates of authenticity. Jansen acknowledged this was less than 5 percent of his total production. He subsequently served prison time in France.[27]

From 1987 to 1994 John Myatt produced in the vicinity of 200 paintings that copied the styles of such well-known artists as Marc Chagall, Georges Braque, Joan Miro, Pablo Picasso, Vincent van Gogh, Alberto Giacometti, and Claude Monet. His work was so convincing that many were auctioned off as authentic pieces by leading auction houses including Sotheby's and Christie's. However, as skilled as Myatt was, the commercial success of his paintings can actually be attributed to a customer turned coconspirator, John Drewe. Drewe's scheme was to create catalogs of the artists' works that included Myatt's forgeries, and he planted these doctored catalogs in libraries utilized by art dealers and experts to authenticate Myatt's fakes. Thus, he could offer Myatt's works to reputable art dealers and auction houses, and then point to their authenticity in catalogs that he manufactured. Drewe netted nearly $2 million in this manner, some of which he shared with Myatt, who became a knowing participant in the scheme. However, Myatt was the first to be apprehended by Scotland Yard detectives in 1995 for this fraud. He was convicted and served less than a year in prison, in part because of his assistance to police in making a case against Drewe. Subsequently, Drewe was also convicted, but he received a six-year prison term.[28]

Ely Sakhai, a New York City art dealer, operated a forgery scheme in a different manner. He bought little known and relatively inexpensive (e.g., around $300,000) works of Cézanne, Chagall, Renoir, Gauguin, Paul Klee, and Amedeo Modigliani and then he commissioned forgers to make copies of them. After waiting a period of years, he sold the forgeries along with false documents of authentication that conveyed the provenance of the real work. Over the course of 15 years, he sold a dozen or more forgeries, often targeting Asian customers, who he felt would not complain if they found they had been duped, in order to avoid humiliation. His scheme was exposed by a chance coincidence, although in retrospect one that grew more likely as an increasing number of his forgeries was sold. His practice was to eventually sell the original and in the spring of 2000, he placed a Gauguin, *Vase de fleurs (Lilas)*, with Sotheby's in New York City for auction. However, up for auction at the same time at Christie's, also in New York City, was one of the forgeries of this work, which was unwittingly being presented as authentic. An investigation ensued that brought the entire scheme to light and Sakhai received a prison term of 41 months and was ordered to pay $12.5 million in restitution to those who purchased the forgeries.[29]

In 2006, 54-year-old Robert Thwaites was sentenced to two years in prison while his brother received a one-year suspended term for forging and selling two Victorian-era oil paintings. These paintings were sold to local art dealers for a total of $229,000, money that Robert Thwaites reportedly was to use to finance his son's education. When British police searched his home, they found an invoice for Hebborn's *The Art Forger's Handbook*, original Victorian era newspapers that were applied as backing to the forged paintings to enhance their authenticity, and another completed forgery still on an easel.[30]

HOW DO THEY DO IT? AN OVERVIEW OF ART FORGERY TECHNIQUES

Art investigator Spiel found those who engage in art forgery first consider how difficult a piece will be to fake and how much money a forgery will bring. As evidenced by the earlier case studies and other examples that have been discussed, many art forgers create original works but copy in a very detailed way the unique style of a specific artist (and, of course, do not place their own signature on it nor provide any type of disclaimer as to authenticity). Moreover, they will attempt to use materials that mimic those of the era they are copying. Then, they let art dealers (who are sometimes unscrupulous), art experts, and/or the art-buying public determine whether the work is genuine. However, art forgery can take on other forms as well, not the least of which would be the copying of existing works. Other variations include creating a preliminary study and then falsely attributing it to a well-known artist; an unfinished painting can be completed by a forger and then be represented as a genuine work of the originating artist; and works completed by students or assistants of a famous artist can be falsely attributed to the master. In each of these scenarios, the forgery of an artist's signature may also play a role in misrepresenting authenticity.[31]

However, those who monitor the world of fraud and swindles know that these types of crimes have a way of mutating much like viruses do; that is, they adapt to changing conditions that present new opportunities for victimization. Art forgery/fakery is no exception as evidenced by counterfeiters using modern technology to reproduce limited edition prints. In another example, burgeoning wealth among some of the populace in Russia has created a strong demand for art, and art forgers have responded to this market in a unique manner. Landscape paintings by little-known 19th-century Scandinavian, German, Austrian, English, and Dutch artists have been bought at auction and in galleries throughout Western Europe by forgers at relatively inexpensive prices (i.e., ranging from a few thousand dollars to $50,000–$60,000). The forgers then modified these paintings in ways that resembled the works of revered 19th-century Russian landscape artists. For instance, vestiges of Western clothing on human figures and architecture would be removed while Russian peasant girls might be added, as would Russian flora and fauna, and farmhouses. When the purported

Russian artist customarily applied a signature to a painting, a forged signature would be added. These works have been resold as originals for prices ranging from $100,000 to over $1 million, and some have moved out of Russia to major Western art auctions. One Russian art expert places the number of these phony Russian pieces in circulation to be well over 100.[32]

Art forgers recognize that higher prices will bring more scrutiny. Forgeries of oil paintings tend to command the highest prices while counterfeit prints are at the low end of the pricing scale for fake works. Falling in between in descending order are unique sculptures, watercolor paintings, and cast sculptures. Within this scale, the identity of the purported artist and the technical/artistic difficulty that the piece presents are then factored in to determine final pricing.[33]

Make no mistake: many art forgers are very talented artists. However, they use their talents to recreate the styles of other artists and, in doing so, they often employ methods and techniques to date their work to the era it purports to represent. These methods and techniques fall into two general categories. First, for objects that represent art that is hundreds or even thousands of years old, the forger must find ways to recreate the natural aging process that would occur over time. Paper and canvas must show age-related signs of discoloration, brittleness, and fading. Paint must also present signs of age to include fading and, as discussed earlier, *craquelure*, or fine, weblike cracks. Wood frames also need to present evidence of age that could include damage from worms or insects or other types of damage such as scrapes and gouges that inevitably occur to objects with a long history. Wood also tends to darken over time.

The second consideration for a forger is to obtain and utilize materials that are consistent with the era that the object purports to represent. Acquiring pieces of canvas, paper, and wood frames from the era being forged, when possible, would be considered a best practice and in doing so, the need to apply artificial aging techniques would be offset. Forgers must also be familiar with, and be able to create, the paints and/or inks that were used in the era they are replicating. As will be covered in the final chapter, scientific analysis can identify the chemical composition of the paints used in a work. Thus, to be successful, forgers must recreate paints from bygone years.

We have already learned about one trick used by a famous forger, Icilio Joni, that is, the baking process to which he subjected his paintings to cause paint to crack in a manner consistent with age-related *craquelure*. He also bragged that realistic-looking glaze on gold frames of his works was really a solution of water and cigar stumps. John Myatt was known to mix K-Y Jelly to household paint to add body to his brushstrokes. Another forger disclosed that baking a canvas makes it brittle and that applying urine to it will hasten its deterioration.[34]

Eric Hebborn authored *The Art Forger's Handbook*, in which he provides how-to instructions for those who wish to create paintings of earlier times.

While some of his techniques are disputed, much of what he recommends follows the consensus that the work must exhibit appropriate age and wear and tear; and the extent to which materials used are actually from the era being copied, the more likely the work will be viewed as authentic. He specifically mentioned the need to use glues that would be traceable to the era of the painting as well as brushes that resemble those used during that period. He noted that while acquiring old mounting material and frames is desirable, many works are remounted over time; and thus having on hand authentic frames and mounting material might not be an absolute necessity. In executing the painting, Hebborn recommended to would-be forgers that they emulate artists they admire, keeping in mind their skill level or lack thereof. He further recommended copying lesser known artists rather than major figures in the art world. Even better, he suggested emulating the school or workshop of a famous master because a heretofore-unknown work would have greater credibility if it can simply be attributed to a student or assistant working under the master. Moreover, he saw the need to understand the artist's thought process in creating work that is to be copied, a sentiment that was also echoed by Elmyr de Hory. Hebborn concluded his book with marketing advice. He rightfully stated that simply copying a style is not illegal, as long as no representations are made about a work's authenticity, including providing any fictitious documentation that attests to its provenance. Finally, he viewed art experts as an ally because if they found a work he created to be authentic, then it was to his advantage.[35]

DISTRIBUTION NETWORKS: MARKETING FORGERIES AND FAKES

When we begin to consider how forged, faked, and counterfeit art objects reach the art market, that is, get into the hands of dealers and auction houses and then on to consumers, we must recall two underlying concepts. It is not illegal to merely copy an existing work of art or a style associated with a particular era or group of artists. However, what becomes problematic is when an existing work is copied or an original work is created that reflects a particular style or group of artists and this object is then misrepresented not to be a recreation, but rather genuine with regard to the associated artist or time period it represents. The harm this situation presents is twofold. First, fictitious art objects distort our view and understanding of art history and, in some cases, the history of humankind generally (e.g., recall the case studies above involving Pre-Columbian and biblical objects). From this perspective, we are defrauded in a cultural/societal sense.

The second harm is the fraud that occurs in perhaps the more familiar sense; that is, purchasers of forged, faked, and counterfeit art objects part with their money based on a false representation of authenticity; and this problem brings us back to the other underlying concept we need to review. Conklin observed that just as high prices for art propelled the incidence of art theft, these high prices encouraged some to engage in art forgery and counterfeiting.[36]

Again following in the footsteps of what we learned about stolen pieces of art, the role of the intermediary, or "fence," can come into play in the distribution of forged/fake art objects. Art investigator Spiel found that forged art can be brought to the art market by the forger or through a fence or forgery distributor. He further noted that fences who deal in stolen art and forged art might be one in the same although this is seldom true with regard to art thieves and art forgers. He observed that the ease with which false documentation of authenticity can be created, combined with customarily poor record keeping and a tendency toward secrecy among many in the art world, facilitates the entry of forged objects into the legitimate market. A supporting sentiment was expressed by a prominent museum curator when he remarked that provenance is often difficult to establish and nobody checks it out.[37]

Thomas Hoving (the former director of the Metropolitan Museum of Art in New York) added another necessary element when attempting to introduce a fake object into the legitimate art market, that is, the role of the "con." He stated, "You can have the best looking Vermeer or Greek kouros, but without the right scam artist to pawn it off on vulnerable suckers, then even the most brilliant fakes can't be sold."[38]

In addition to providing instruction on how to create a fake painting, Eric Hebborn offered some insight into a forger's marketing techniques. He identified four outlets that he would consider depending upon the quality of the object he wished to market and the types of relationships he could establish at these outlets: the junk dealer, the antique dealer, the picture dealer, and the auctioneer. Perhaps surprisingly, he favored dealing with auction houses (at least for his better works) because terms of auction sales often exclude errors in authenticity or do so for only a specified period of time. Of course, regardless of the outlet chosen, the origin of the painting was always introduced as an inheritance, a family heirloom, or in some other vague terms; and he only sought what he considered a fair price for it. Beyond that, he allowed the market and its experts to judge the genuineness of his work and he avoided providing any false authentication documents.[39]

If we consider only the distribution networks for fake art discussed above, images that arise would range from dealing with shady characters who engage in fencing and cons to sometimes duped and sometimes unscrupulous art dealers and auctioneers. However, before we leave this subject we must revisit the marketing technique described above in the case study involving the sale of counterfeit limited edition prints (box 4.1), that is, the Internet. Recall in this case, counterfeit limited edition prints were auctioned online. Rather than being a unique scenario, the use, or more appropriately the abuse, of popular online auction sites to mass-market bogus art appears to be a growing phenomenon. In fact, this sales methodology would seem to be tailor-made for the limited edition print medium that has already been too frequently exploited by counterfeiters. Internet art sales and auctions have the potential to reach a broader and sometimes less knowledgeable group of art buyers, thus enhancing the likelihood of success for those engaging in bogus art-sales schemes. Rather than dealing with reputable and knowledgeable art dealers and auction houses that can often provide needed education and guidance in making an art purchase, those who purchase art over the Internet can be victimized by false representations followed by layers of impenetrable anonymity. Moreover, these schemes need not be as elaborate as the one detailed in the box 4.1. For example, shortly before the Chicago indictments, a one-man operation in Florida defrauded 40 people nationwide over a 12-month period through the sale of fraudulent works by Picasso and Chagall for $1,500 to $2,000 each through Internet auctions.[40]

Notwithstanding these high-tech approaches to art forgery and distribution, the tried and true methods of handcrafting art works and antiquities and then distributing them through the use of false provenance continues. Our final case study (box 4.4) provides a recent, but sure-to-be-enduring example.

BOX 4.4 THE GREENHALGHS OF GREAT BRITAIN[41]

In 2002, The Art Institute of Chicago hosted the major exhibition "Van Gogh and Gauguin: The Studio of the South." Appearing in this exhibition was a sculpture attributed to Paul Gauguin entitled *The Faun*. The Institute had bought the work in 1997 for a reported $125,000 from a London art dealer/collector who had acquired it through Sotheby's at auction for about $32,500 three years earlier. The Institute's art historians had found a reference to a ceramic faun in a catalog from a 1906 Gauguin exhibition and a tiny drawing of this figure in a Gauguin sketchbook from 1887. At 18-1/2-inches tall, *The Faun* depicted a half-man, half-goat figure. The work was described in the exhibition's catalog as symbolic of Gauguin's failing marriage since it lacked a penis. The catalog also noted that the facial features of the figure were similar to Gauguin himself, although it also speculated that the face could be that of a prominent Danish writer of the late 19th-century who was to become the brother-in-law of Gauguin's ex-wife. The only problem with all of this serious art scholarship and theorizing was that *The Faun* was a fake.

Shaun Greenhalgh of Bolton, England, a town near Manchester, was a self-taught painter and stone sculptor. He dropped out of high school at age 16 and then failed to qualify for the British Marines because he could not swim. He continued to live with his mother and father into adulthood. While the family subsisted on government-provided subsidies and displayed a life-style consistent with low income earners, Shaun perfected his artistic skills although he recognized that there was little likelihood that he would reap financial reward in producing works bearing his own name. Beginning in the mid-1980s, he began to create various art objects ranging from antiquities to 19th-century works such as Gauguin's *The Faun* and landscapes in the style of American watercolorist Thomas Moran. Not only was his work, for the most part, artistically sound, but as evidenced by *The Faun,* through careful research he created objects that had some basis for existence, but whose whereabouts were unknown. He then enlisted the help of his mother and father to peddle his works to galleries and museums, occupations they took on as senior citizens. For instance, it was Mrs. Greenhalgh using her maiden name of Roscoe as an alias who approached Sotheby's in London in 1994 with the fake Gauguin *The Faun*. She presented a false invoice from a Paris art gallery that purportedly showed the piece was sold by the gallery in 1917 to Roderick O'Connor, a known artist friend of Gauguin and an alleged forbear of "Mrs. Roscoe." Thus, when Sotheby's subsequently sold *The Faun,* it was the Greenhalghs who profited through forgery, a scenario that repeated itself time and again over a 17-year period. In fact, it is estimated that they sold at least 120 fake works of art that netted them about $3 million. Another of their major successes was the sale of a purported 3,000-year-old Egyptian statue known as the "Amarna Princess" to their local museum in Bolton in 2003 for $706,400. In reality, Shaun Greenhalgh had carved the statue in just over three weeks, but his father convinced museum officials that his great-grandfather purchased the statue at an auction in 1892 and produced an auction catalog to support his story. While this auction catalog was authentic, it was not acquired incident to a purchase of the statue by any Greenhalgh relative. Instead, Shaun used the information in the catalog about this piece as a blueprint to recreate it and then his father presented the catalog to support his story about his great-grandfather's purchase. In 1994, the Greenhalghs also sold the Bolton Museum a watercolor painting by the Bolton-born American artist Thomas Moran, which was again really the handiwork of Shaun Greenhalgh. The museum paid $15,400 for this fake.

The scheme began to unravel in 2005 when George Greenhalgh, Shaun's father, now in his eighties, approached the British Museum in a quizzical manner with three Assyrian stone reliefs that he alleged were part of an inheritance. After some initial euphoria over this potentially significant acquisition, experts at the museum recognized technical inconsistencies in how the depicted horse harnesses were carved and also found errors in the ancient script that was carved into the stone. They reported their suspicions to Scotland Yard and an investigation soon resulted in the execution of a search warrant at the Greenhalgh residence in Bolton. Found at this location were the various materials Shaun Greenhalgh used in crafting his forgeries, documents from which false provenance was created, and works completed, but not yet distributed. The investigation continued through the following year and in late 2007, Shaun Greenhalgh, now 47; mother Olive, 83; and father George, 84; were convicted for their roles in the forgery scheme along with

brother George, Jr., age 51, who was charged with benefitting from some
of the scheme's proceeds. Shaun was sentenced to prison for four years,
eight months, while his parents received suspended prison terms, in part
due to their advanced ages. George, Jr., also received a suspended sentence.
As the Scotland Yard investigation unfolded, the misdeeds of the Greenhalghs were shared with the likes of the Art Institute of Chicago, the Bolton
Museum, and others who were unfortunate enough to have these works in
their collections. Art and Antiques Squad Detective Sergeant Vernon Rapley,
who headed the investigation, called Shaun Greenhalgh the world's most
diverse forger, in recognition of the range of styles he so convincingly was
able to copy.

ART FORGERY AND FAKERY—IN SUMMARY

While widely recognized, the extent to which forgery and fakery plague
the art world is uncertain, once again due to the absence of any comprehensive data or monitoring. Knowledgeable observers see it as a pervasive problem, especially when viewed from the broad spectrum ranging
from antiquities to limited edition prints. Forged and fake works of art can
distort or alter our knowledge of the history of art and, at times, human
history in the more general sense. Moreover, those who purchase forged
or fake works of art can be defrauded of substantial amounts of money,
and the collective monetary loss through such schemes has been estimated
to be in the tens of millions of dollars annually. However, it should be re-
membered that the mere creation of an object that resembles another work
or style is usually not unlawful; rather, illegalities come into play when
false representations of authenticity are made, especially when these false
representations are the basis for the sale of a fictitious object.

While some forgery schemes attempt to duplicate specific works of art
(e.g., Ely Sakhai), the more common practice appears to be creating arguably original works, but in the style of a particular era or a specific artist. In
this latter scenario, the creation of false documentation to accompany the
work is a common method employed to falsely link it to a purported artist or otherwise substantiate its authenticity. Some forgers, however, have
been successful in simply placing their work into the art market and then
letting the experts decide whether it is real, thus avoiding responsibility
for making any affirmative representations about a fake work's authenticity. While traditionally, successful art forgers have taken meticulous care
to simulate the materials and methods used by artists hundreds, if not
thousands of years ago, recent forgery practices rely on high-tech copying
and duplicating processes to exploit the vulnerabilities of limited edition
prints, which are then mass-marketed, often through online auctions.

CHAPTER 5

Art Theft and Destruction: The Perils of Wars and Civil/ Religious Unrest

So far, we have examined crimes related to art that can be attributed to individuals or groups of individuals acting in concert. We view these individuals as criminals and deal with them (hopefully) in criminal-justice settings. Regrettably, art has also been victimized by criminal-like activity that has been much broader in scope. Human history has been littered far too frequently with episodes of wars between nation-states or other organized social groups linked through geography, politics, ethnicity, race, religion, and so forth. Episodes of violent hostilities between social groups that fall short of the scope and perhaps severity of war, referred to here as civil and religious unrest, have also interrupted periods of peaceful coexistence. It is well established that wars and other forms of social unrest inflict a horrible toll on humankind in terms of death, injury, sickness, destruction, and economic devastation. These forms of organized hostilities have been no less kind to the preservation and propagation of human cultural activities and achievements either. With regard to the latter, art objects have been particularly vulnerable. Clearly, as physical objects, artworks can suffer damage or complete destruction incident to violent attacks especially when explosive weaponry and firearms are in play. Often damage to artwork in these situations is collateral or unintended by the combatants; although as will be documented later, at times artwork has been purposely targeted for destruction. And if such destruction is a disturbing scenario, consider another common outcome of war: the traditional custom of the victors seizing the art and other cultural valuables of the vanquished as booty. Bringing home vestiges of an opponent's cultural valuables has provided tangible proof of victory and has helped to engender support for a government/army among the populace. Looting a defeated opponent's cultural valuables also serves as another form of denigration and humiliation. Evidence of this practice can be traced back to wars conducted in ancient times, and to this day, it retains a certain level of acceptance among warriors and combatants. For instance, civil wars in such countries as Lebanon, Cambodia, Vietnam, Congo, Nigeria, Colombia, and Nicaragua have resulted in the looting of cultural-heritage sites; the proceeds of which have gone to finance the warring parties and/or for the personal enrichment of individuals who were involved in the fighting.[1]

While some hostilities that have resulted in art and cultural-heritage looting may not be widely known, others have been well documented, especially in more recent times because of the modern world's pervasive media coverage. Readers of ancient literature know that Greek and Roman writers make frequent references to looting by conquerors. In the annals of more modern history, one of the better-chronicled episodes of war-related art looting are the exploits of the French emperor, Napoleon Bonaparte. In the latter part of the 18th-century, Napoleon's army rampaged through Italy and stripped Rome and Venice of many of their cultural and artistic treasures. As a victor, Napoleon felt entitled to bring back to Paris and parade before the masses such famed pieces as the classical sculptures *Laocoon Struggling with Sea Snakes* and *Apollo Belvedere* taken from the papal collection at the Vatican and *The Dying Gaul* from Rome's Capitol Museum, along with great masterpieces by Raphael, Titian, and Tintoretto. Napoleon reportedly stated, "Rome is no longer in Rome, the whole of Rome is in Paris," and many of these works are still on display at the Louvre. From Venice, he stole four gilded bronze horses from the San Marco Cathedral, which 600 years earlier were brought back from Constantinople by marauding Crusaders. The Louvre was also the beneficiary of Napoleon's pillaging in Germany. In 1807 he brought back from a museum in Kassel, Germany, 299 paintings including 16 Rembrandts, 4 Rubens, and 1 painting by Titian.[2]

Napoleon set a dubious standard for widespread looting of art and cultural-heritage incident to wars. Unfortunately, this standard was far surpassed by the greatest villains the art world, and arguably the world as a whole, has ever encountered: Adolf Hitler and his Nazi regime. In this respect, one comparison described the art looting by Napoleon as "planned" while Hitler and his Nazi henchmen "industrialized" this concept. For the Nazis, stealing art was institutional policy.[3]

WORLD WAR II: THE NAZI PLUNDER OF ART

Understanding the looting of art by Hitler and his Nazi regime before and during World War II goes beyond simply quantifying the extent of their plunder. For the record, numbers in this regard have been put forth. For example, one report places the losses suffered in France at 60,000 pieces, a figure that accounts for one-third of all art in private hands in that country. A Polish database of artworks stolen or missing incident to World War II contains 59,000 pieces and this number might only represent 10 percent of the artworks destroyed or stolen during that period (as will be discussed below, the Nazis pursued a much different war strategy in Poland than in France, which resulted in far greater devastation generally and thus widespread destruction of art). To be clear, the Nazis stole art from every country they conquered.[4] Their motivations to do so were fueled not just by desires to enhance the status of the regime and the Germanic people (and for top-level Nazi leaders, personal enrichment), but they also stole and destroyed art as part of their ethnic genocide programs. The origins of these motivations can be traced to Hitler himself.

Those who rise to national leadership positions do so by virtue of a number of different pathways, often depending upon the nature of the national government. In traditional monarchies, royalty status was a certain pathway to leadership regardless of talent, experience, education, or achievement. These latter characteristics, however, have tended to play a greater role in attaining national leadership positions in most modern-day nation-states (and even in modern-day monarchies as the royalty positions are often little more than ceremonial in nature). Common backgrounds of national leaders include training, experience, and achievement in such fields as the military, law, business, education, and the clergy. Curiously, Adolf Hitler's background was that of an artist, and a not very successful one. In fact, as a youth in 1907, he applied to become a student at Vienna's Academy of Fine Arts, but he was rejected. Ironically, contemporaries who were studying at the Academy at that time included Egon Schiele and Oskar Kokoschka, both of whom became major figures in the modern art movement, an art form despised by Hitler, but one that found acceptance at the Academy. Moreover, in the early 1900s there was a strong Jewish influence at the Academy of Fine Arts. Hitler was embittered by his rejection, and it has been suggested that the circumstances under which it occurred fueled his anti-Semitism and his disdain for modern art. When he rose to power as chancellor of Germany in 1933, he gained a platform to take these views to an extreme. Art became very fashionable under his regime, but Hitler dictated what was acceptable in this respect; that is, Nordic and classical images were considered ideal forms of beauty (e.g., paintings by Vermeer, Cranach, Holbein, Rembrandt, and Da Vinci), while modern art was labeled as "unfinished" or worse yet, "degenerate." Even more disturbing was that his tastes in art reflected his views on the people and cultures that produced it. Those of Germanic or Nordic origins were looked upon with favor while Jews and Slavic peoples were considered racially inferior, a view that eventually led to genocide programs that targeted these groups.[5]

World War II officially began on September 1, 1939, with the German invasion of Poland. However, Germany placed Austria under its control in 1938 when its troops crossed the border in March of that year. A year earlier Hitler began his campaign to cleanse German museums of art he found distasteful, that is, modern art that destroyed the classical concept of beauty and replaced it with interpretative works that were incomprehensible. These included works by 20th-century German Expressionist and Fauvist artists (Schiele and Kokoschka among them); others of that period such as Picasso, Leger, Matisse, and Chagall; as well as late 19th-century Impressionists such as Van Gogh, Degas, and Gauguin. This cleansing campaign resulted in the confiscation of over 16,000 artworks, compensation for which was barred by legislation passed by the German government in 1938. Nevertheless, this same government did not hesitate from profiting from the sale of these works at art auctions in Switzerland. However, nearly 4,000 paintings, sculptures, drawings, watercolors, and graphics branded as "degenerate" were burned by the Nazis in March 1939. Others were put up for ridicule in Berlin in a display entitled the "Degenerate Art Exhibition."[6]

As Hitler was attempting to rid Germany of art he disliked, he simultaneously cataloged works of art he sought for repatriation. These were works that had been removed from Germany over the preceding 400 years, but with his war machine in place they could now be targeted for seizure upon conquest.[7] Thus, as World War II commenced the Nazi motivation for art pillage was driven by a vile combination of ethnic hatred and racist nationalism. The art and culture of Jews and Slavs were to be destroyed (or sold to profit the Nazi regime) whereas Germanic/Nordic and classical art was to be seized for the benefit of the regime and the German people, including the establishment of what Hitler planned as the world's greatest art museum in his hometown of Linz, Austria. And there was one final ingredient in this vile motivation mix, that is, personal ambition and greed. As we shall see, some art, even "degenerate art," was acquired by Nazi leaders when a profit potential was recognized through resale on the open market.

Wreaking Havoc in the East

Thus, Hitler's military objectives and strategies carefully considered the value of art and culture (at least by Nazi standards) of each nation targeted for invasion. As Hitler viewed the Polish people and culture as inferior, he ordered the complete destruction of that nation, its people, and its art. Although Poland and the Polish people managed to survive the Nazi onslaught, they suffered a horrific toll in terms of loss of life and property, including an untold number of art objects. However, certain artworks in Poland were identified by Hitler for "repatriation," or otherwise fit the Nazi standards. In these instances, he ordered his troops to locate and seize them for safe return to Germany. Most notable among the works confiscated from Poland was the altarpiece at the Church of Our Lady in

Cracow, created by the 15th-century German artist Viet Stoss. Hitler also sought out and found the private art collection of the Czartoryski family of Cracow. This collection contained coveted works by the likes of Da Vinci, Raphael, and Rembrandt.

The Soviet Union was similarly targeted for destruction by the Nazis because of its Slavic population and culture. Their goal here was to cleanse and germanize through genocide and decimation. They invaded the Soviet Union on June 22, 1941, and within days were in the outskirts of Leningrad (now St. Petersburg). However, as in Poland, they looted valuable works of art and antique furniture for shipment back to Germany before attempting to demolish this city and its residents. An estimated 5,000 pieces of antique furniture were seized along with 35,000 other works of art, including the gilded fountains at the Peterhof Palace, which required dismantling before shipment. From the Catherine Palace at Tsarskoye Selo the Nazis seized for repatriation to Germany panels from the Amber Room. These panels crafted from amber were a gift to the Russian leader, Peter the Great, in 1716 from the King of Prussia and, thus, of Germanic origin. The fact was, however, the Nazi's never did overrun Leningrad though the siege lasted 900 days. Moreover, the Russian people managed to protect their great museum, The Hermitage, and its impressive collection during this long ordeal. Throughout the Soviet Union during the three years of Nazi occupation, no less than 427 museums, 1,670 Russian Orthodox churches, 237 Catholic churches, and 532 synagogues were looted or destroyed.[8]

A Different Plan for the West

Non-Slavic, European nations invaded by the Nazis fared somewhat better if only because Hitler's goal in these countries was to conquer and bring them within his realm, although demonically, sans a Jewish population. Nevertheless, even in these countries, works of art remained a primary target for the invaders, either because of their value to the Nazi regime or because they were classified as "degenerate" works and/or owned by Jews. And as suggested above, some Nazi leaders acquired art for their personal enrichment including pieces that were categorized as "degenerate." Following time-honored tradition, much of the artwork they acquired in the conquered Western European nations was through theft and looting/confiscation. However, the tenor of the times also gave rise to a variety of purported arms-length business transactions between some art owners and Hitler and his top aides, most notably Hermann Göring. Typically, these transactions involved Jewish art owners who were fearful of losing their collections through confiscation, if not their lives as well. As a result, many of these owners entered into coerced sales at less than market prices with the hope of salvaging some value from their collections and/or gaining some benefit that might help them survive the Nazi occupation. Such transactions were usually mediated by representatives of Hitler and Göring and these representatives were not always Germans; rather, some local art dealers in the Western countries collaborated with the Nazis in this respect.[9]

Countries with Germanic origins such as Holland and Belgium were destined to be incorporated into Germany. Nevertheless, these nations suffered heavy losses of their artistic patrimony. For instance, among the significant works of art taken by the Nazis in Belgium was the *Ghent Altarpiece* by Hubert and Jan van Eyck, as this work fit into Hitler's notion of the ideal art genre.[10] Sought from Holland was the art collection of Jacques Goudstikker, a wealthy Jewish art dealer. The Nazis succeeded in acquiring this collection, but as outlined in the following case study (box 5.1), they relied more on subtle tactics such as greed, betrayal, and fear.

BOX 5.1 THE LONG JOURNEY OF THE ART OF JACQUES GOUDSTIKKER[11]

Jacques Goudstikker took over his family's art gallery in Amsterdam at the age of 21 in 1919. In the years that followed and leading up to World War II, his gallery enjoyed considerable success and he became very wealthy. However, by May 1940 it became apparent to him that as a Jew he had to flee Amsterdam in order to avoid the imminent takeover of Holland by the Nazis. Thus, on May 14, 1940, he boarded a ship bound for England along with his wife and infant son; and he left behind in his gallery at least 1,113 paintings, most of which were by 16th-century Italian artists and 17th-century Dutch artists. Unfortunately, Goudstikker never made it to England as he died on board the ship incident to an accidental fall. Nevertheless, the collection of art he left behind in Amsterdam was of a genre favored by the Nazis, and it became an acquisition target soon after they occupied the city. Although Goudstikker's mother refused to leave Amsterdam, the gallery business was left in the hands of the family lawyer, but he died in a bicycle accident about the same time Jacques departed. Two employees of the gallery then convinced Goudstikker's mother that they should become trustees of the family holdings, and they soon entered into negotiations for the sale of the collection with Alois Miedl, a German banker headquartered in Amsterdam who was fronting for the number two man in the Nazi regime, Hermann Göring. Acting under the premise that it would be better to sell the collection than to have the Nazis confiscate it, a deal was made for the paintings with 800 acquired by Göring while Miedl retained the rest. Whether the trustees were acting solely in good faith on behalf of the Goudstikkers in negotiating this transaction, or whether self-interest and/or collusion with Miedl played a role is uncertain. However, the threat of confiscation without any compensation was very real, in light of the value of this collection to the Nazis combined with its Jewish ownership. At the conclusion of the war, about 400 of these paintings were recovered by Allied Forces and returned to the Dutch government. Goudstikker's widow litigated with the Dutch government for seven years over the return of the recovered paintings. Dutch officials contended that the Goudstikkers relinquished their rights to the paintings incident to the sale and eventually reached a settlement wherein she bought back 165 paintings. The Dutch government then sold some of the remaining works while the majority was incorporated into its national art holdings. Thus, pieces from this collection were on display at Dutch embassies and museums including the Rijksmuseum in Amsterdam. In 1998, however, a Goudstikker family heir living in the United States filed a claim with the Dutch government for the remaining paintings based on the renewed argument that the family only parted with the collection under forced circumstances arising from the imminent Nazi occupation in 1940. After a lengthy review, this time the Dutch government agreed that the original sale was, in fact, involuntary and returned over 200 paintings to the Goudstikker heirs.

The Favored French?

Different plans were in store for France, however. French culture was admired by the Nazis, and it was to be left intact. Nevertheless, French art losses were the greatest of any of the Western European countries that were conquered by the Nazis. While the extent of these losses was a function of the abundance of works of art in France, it was also attributable to a very systematic approach the Germans organized to facilitate their pillage. In September 1940, Hitler established a specialized unit known as the Einsatzstab Reichsleiter Rosenberg (ERR) whose mission was to seize those works that were in concert with the cultural ideals of the Nazi regime and confiscate for sale or destruction degenerate objects. This unit was headed by the long-time Nazi loyalist and anti-Semite, Alfred Rosenberg. Rosenberg's credentials in these respects can be traced back to at least 1930 when his dubious contribution to the art-history literature, *Myth of the Twentieth Century,* was published. In it, he characterized German Expressionist art as "syphilitic, infantile and mestizo." He also somehow credited the Aryan Nordic peoples with producing Greek sculpture and the masterpieces of the Italian Renaissance. Rosenberg eagerly assumed his task, one that was made easier with the Nazi decree that Jews in France no longer had any rights of citizenship and thus could no longer own property. As a result, over 16,000 paintings were stolen from Jews in Paris alone, while the total haul from all of France was 21,000 pieces from 203 collections. Then beginning in January 1942, the Nazis undertook house-to-house searches throughout Paris and seized whatever property they deemed desirable. This practice continued until August 1944 when Allied Forces began making headway in their fight to rid the Nazis from France. By that time, however, over 71,000 homes were searched and property filling over 29,000 rail cars was confiscated.[12]

Artworks seized by the Nazis in Paris and vicinity were concentrated and inventoried at the Jeu de Paume, a small museum near the Louvre. Hitler, of course, had first choice on any works seized through this confiscation program with many designated for the collection at his proposed Linz museum. Next in line was Hermann Göring, Hitler's second in command and a self-styled art aficionado. Over the period of the German occupation of France, Göring made 20 visits to the Jeu de Paume during which he took for himself and/or for future sale over 700 paintings, many of which were classified as "degenerate" pieces by the ERR staff and, thus, were technically forbidden imports into Germany. However, as no one in the Nazi regime other than Hitler could challenge his authority, Göring's only limitation was to avoid taking possession of works that were prized by the Fuhrer. Many of the "degenerate" works he left behind at the Jeu de Paume were eventually burned by Nazi SS officers in July 1943. However, art that fit into the Nazi ideal was shipped to Germany beginning in April 1941, and this continued until the summer of 1944 as Allied Forces advanced on Paris. Unbeknownst, however, to the ERR was that one of their French employees involved in the inventory process at the Jeu de Paume was actually a member of the French Resistance. Rose Valland maintained separate records at her home of the artworks she was inventorying at the Jeu de Paume, which in many cases included their eventual disposition and relocation by the Nazis. Her records were helpful in efforts to track down their subsequent whereabouts, a subject that will be addressed in more detail later.[13]

Among the most coveted artworks by Hitler were paintings in a private collection held by a wealthy Jewish family, the Rothschilds. Included in this collection was Vermeer's *The Astronomer;* Boucher's *Portrait of Marquise de Pompadour;* Memling's *Virgin and Child;* Hals's *Portrait of Isabella Coymans; Phillip II, King of Spain,* believed at the time to be a work of Velázquez; Van Dyck's *Portrait of Henriette of France as a Child; Woman with a Cat* by a painter of the Flemish school; several works by Rubens, a Titian; two works by Watteau, *Standing Guitar Player* and *Minuet;* two portraits by Goya; a portrait by Ingres; and several by Joshua Reynolds. When the German invasion of France became imminent, museums as well as private holders of art took steps to protect, if not secrete, their collections, against damage and theft. In the case of the Rothschilds, they placed some of their works in the care of the Louvre while others were stored at their chateaux in the French countryside. The family members then fled France to safe havens in an effort to avoid the Nazi onslaught of the Jewish people. Their art collection, however, was tracked down by the Nazis and by February 1941, Hitler took possession of the major works in this collection including

Vermeer's *The Astronomer,* Boucher's *Portrait of Marquise de Pompadour,* and Hals's *Portrait of Isabella Coymans.*[14]

The Nazi Defeat and the Recovery of Stolen Art

As the Allied Forces began to make headway against the Nazi war machine, German troops made a final grab for art in Italy under the guise of protecting this country's many treasures. In October 1943, German troops in Naples under the direction of Hermann Göring removed 187 cases of art to their headquarters in Spoleto for safekeeping and eventually to the Vatican after Italian officials protested their removal from Naples. However, during these relocations the Nazis stole the most valuable paintings and shipped them to Germany. Likewise, in Florence, German troops took for safekeeping over 500 paintings from this art-rich city as they retreated northward to their homeland. These were works by the likes of Donatello, Botticelli, Michelangelo, and Titian. As the Allied Forces commenced aerial bombardments of Germany and with their troops advancing toward German soil in February 1944, Hitler ordered all his confiscated art to be moved to safe locations. A salt mine near Salzburg, Austria, Alt Aussee, became the depository for the most valuable of these objects. Here the humidity and temperature were constant, the storage chambers were more than a mile inside the mountain and could be reached only by tiny trains. By spring 1945 with the Nazi defeat imminent, German officials planned to blow up the salt mine and thus destroy all the artwork stored therein. However, Austrian Resistance forces managed to deter this plan by redistributing the artworks to other chambers in the mine. Although the mine was blasted on May 5, 1945, their efforts paid off as the artworks were undamaged.[15]

The Allied Forces were not unaware of the Nazi plunder of art, nor were they insensitive to the many cultural icons that were part of the Western European landscape (e.g., cathedrals and other architectural masterpieces, religious shrines and structures, sculptures displayed in outdoor locations, and museums that housed irreplaceable works of art). Both the American and British armies established specialized units to recover artworks stolen by the Nazis, and although not always successful, to guide combat operations around areas of cultural importance. In fact, it was the American unit, known as the Monuments, Fine Arts and Archives (MFAA) officers, that recovered over 6,500 paintings, 2,300 drawings and watercolors, 954 prints, and 137 pieces of sculpture hidden in the salt mine at Alt Aussee in May 1945 after the Nazis' unsuccessful attempt to destroy this treasure-trove. These were the works of such artists as Michelangelo, Vermeer, Titian, Tintoretto, Rubens, and Rembrandt. The *Ghent Altar Piece* by Hubert and Jan van Eyck that was earlier confiscated from Belgium at Hitler's direction was found here along with paintings from the Rothschild and Goudstikker collections and works taken by Göring from his safekeeping pillage in Naples.[16]

Policies set forth by American and British officials regarding artwork recovered from the Nazis were for its return to the countries from where it was stolen with the understanding that these nations would restitute these pieces to individual owners. The Russians were also involved in recovering art in the hands of Nazis through its specialized unit, the Red Army Brigades. Their approach, however, differed markedly from the American and British policies as their recoveries were more akin to the tradition of seizure of a conquering army. The Russians felt entitled to compensation for losses sustained at the hands of the Germans, and as they occupied German territory, they shipped back to the Soviet Union hundreds of thousands of pieces of art and cultural artifacts. While more than 60 years have passed, both these policies have left unresolved legacies.[17]

WORLD WAR II (CONTINUED): REPATRIATING THE NAZI PLUNDER

Despite well-intentioned, and in many ways, successful efforts by American and British forces to return recovered works of art stolen by the Nazis back to their countries of origin, placing these works in the hands of rightful individual owners has proved problematic in numerous instances. Even more troublesome in this respect has been the art taken by the Soviet Army.

The Russians

As discussed earlier, unlike their Western Allies, the Soviets viewed art held by the Nazis as an opportunity for compensation for the losses they sustained in fighting the war, including art losses of their own. Thus, artworks seized in Germany by the Red Army trophy brigades were brought back to the Soviet Union, now Russia, for inclusion in its national holdings. Some of these pieces were subsequently released to its Iron Curtain surrogate, East Germany, in the 1950s, but now part of the Federal Republic of Germany. However, as many as 400,000 artworks taken from Nazi Germany remain as government property and are in the collections of various Russian museums and libraries including the Pushkin Museum in Moscow and the Hermitage in St. Petersburg. In fact, Russia's legislative body, the Duma, as recently as 1998 formally nationalized these holdings. No known comprehensive inventory of objects seized by the Red Army trophy brigades exists, but among those seized were private holdings that were first confiscated by the Nazis. Thus, many of the war trophies now in Russian custody were not the rightful property of the Nazi regime but rather were the fruits of Nazi thefts from Jews and other persecuted groups and/or were of genres that were out of favor. If in fact there were any valid arguments justifying one nation-state seizing the property of another as compensation for war losses, retaining property that had been previously stolen from private individuals would seem only to weaken such rationales. Nevertheless, the Russians have shown only fleeting and limited interest in identifying and making efforts to return these works, many of which are believed to be Impressionist and Post-Impressionist masterpieces, to the rightful owners or their heirs. Clearly, the Russian people suffered horribly at the hands of the Nazis during World War II and their suffering in the form of lost lives, injuries, sickness, and destruction of property and other hardships continues to haunt them. One Russian official has suggested that only with the passage of time and the emergence of generations unaffected by the ravages of World War II will there be any interest in repatriation.[18]

Struggles in the West as Well

Considering the Soviet's starkly different policy from the Western Allies at the outset regarding seized art and the totalitarian nature of that regime, it is perhaps not surprising that relatively little progress has been made in repatriating art now in Russian hands back to individual owners who were victims of Nazi theft and persecution. What is more surprising however has been the slow and tortuous process engaged in by Western nations to fulfill promises made to return art stolen by the Nazis to the rightful individuals or their heirs. In summary, when a clear ownership trail existed back to original owners, Western nations tended to return recovered artworks to them. However, many owners of these recovered works perished during World War II as a result of the Holocaust, other war-related hostilities, or through natural causes. In these instances, Western governments tended to retain the works in their national collections until, and if, claims were made by the owners' surviving heirs. A complicating feature in many of these claims has been the manner in which the piece(s) came into Nazi hands. With the Goudstikker case (see box 5.1) being a prime example, the Nazis purchased many works of art under the threat that they would be confiscated if the owners failed to part with them. Whether claimants have been able to make a convincing argument that any transaction with the Nazis was not arms-length in nature, but rather a forced sale, has been a pivotal issue, and one where the facts surrounding the transaction have tended to become clouded with the passage of time.[19]

Another part of this complicated scenario has involved the many works that were acquired by the Nazis and then sold through auctions or art galleries, with Switzerland being a favored outlet. Under Swiss law, good ownership title vests even in stolen property after five years incident to a good faith purchase. The only way a theft victim can reacquire his/her stolen property at that point is to purchase it back from the new owner.[20]

In both of the above scenarios, the longer pieces of art from the Nazi plunder have remained out of the hands of rightful owners or their heirs, the more reluctant some current custodians have been to relinquish them.

As suggested earlier, this reluctance, in part, can be attributed to unclear facts surrounding the ownership claim, which can be a result of the passage of time. However, in many instances these works have become prominent parts of museum collections and, thus, requests for their return have been evaluated in terms of not only the merits of the ownership claim but also in terms of the institution's self-interest.

After the mid-1950s, interest in placing recovered but unclaimed artwork into the hands of rightful owners or heirs began to fade. In fact, it was not until the 1990s that this issue regained some level of public concern and prominence, a reemergence that can be attributable in part to two important books on the subject: *The Rape of Europa: The Fate of Europe's Treasures in the Third Reich and the Second World War* by Lynn Nicholas in 1994 and, a year later, *The Lost Museum: The Nazi Conspiracy to Steal the World's Greatest Works of Art* by Hector Feliciano.[21]

Nicholas presented a detailed history of World War II as it relates to the plunder of art by the Nazis and subsequent attempts to recover and repatriate their pillage. Feliciano's focus is narrower, that is, the Nazi art confiscation program in France, the country that suffered the greatest losses among the Western European nations invaded and occupied by the Nazis. According to his research, over 61,000 pieces of Nazi-looted art were returned to France and over 45,000 pieces had been returned to the victimized owners at the time of his research. His concern was the 15,000 (or so) pieces that remained under the guardianship of the French government and that little has been done to identify their ownership. In fact, he contended that no complete inventory of these unclaimed works had been undertaken by French officials and that they were scattered among various French museums including the Louvre, the Musée d'Orsay, and the Pompidou Center, and even government office buildings. In his book, Feliciano called for active research on these pieces to identify rightful ownership. Aside from this research being laborious and time-consuming, another factor that has dampened the will to move in this direction has stemmed from fears of uncovering embarrassing art-market collaboration between some French citizens and the Nazis during World War II. Accordingly, even more recent updates have labeled France's efforts in identifying and restituting to rightful owners Nazi-plundered artworks now in its possession as not a high priority.[22]

In 1998, the United States hosted an international conference in Washington, DC, from which evolved a declaration that committed the 44 nations in attendance to make proactive efforts to return Nazi-looted art in their possessions to rightful individual owners. Like the circumstances Feliciano found in France, some European nations received recovered artworks through the work of Allied military forces at the conclusion of the war, but pieces not claimed by individual owners were placed in museum collections or placed in government office buildings for safekeeping. In other instances, both in Europe and beyond, some museums have unwittingly acquired artwork through donations or purchases that were the fruits of the Nazi pillage. The principles agreed upon by the nations in attendance committed them to (1) undertake provenance research of unclaimed works in order to return them to rightful owners and (2) develop mechanisms to facilitate the resolution of ownership disputes when claims are filed. Although the results of the Washington conference held out hope for final disposition of the Nazi war plunder, effective implementation of the agreed-upon principles has been uneven, thus bringing into question to what extent meaningful progress has been made. Implementation obstacles have been twofold: (1) the lack of "frontline" resources, that is, staffing sufficient researchers at museums where artwork in question is on hand; and (2) a varying array of rules and regulations that govern ownership claims among the countries that participated in the conference.[23]

As evidenced by the Goudstikker case (see box 5.1), the Netherlands has been among the leaders in taking more progressive steps in restituting unclaimed Nazi artwork. These steps have included revising their criteria that eliminates an earlier requirement for exhaustive proof that the claimant is a rightful heir. Now an applicant must make a plausible case that the artwork in question belonged to his or her family in May 1940; and if there was an alleged sale to the Nazis, it must have been involuntary and connected to the Nazi occupation of Holland. The Dutch received in excess of 50 claims and have returned over 500 pieces of art.[24]

Germany, on the other hand, falls into the camp where halting progress has been made in returning artworks that were stolen by the Nazi regime to the rightful owners. To its credit, Germany was one of 44 signatories at the Washington conference notwithstanding the difficult experience in dealing with its Nazi past. This latter encumbrance combined with museums that are purportedly unable to support adequate research efforts (which in some cases might be related to their reluctance to part with valued pieces in their collections) have been contributing factors to a less than stellar restitution record. Moreover, it must be recognized that prior to the reunification of Germany following the fall of the Iron Curtain in 1989, there was little likelihood of the return of Nazi-seized artworks located in East Germany to the rightful owners. By 2006, however, German officials began to acknowledge a lack of progress in complying with the Washington conference principles and pledged a renewed effort in that direction.[25]

Ironically, while the United States played a primary role in recovering the Nazi art plunder during World War II and then years later hosting the conference that revived a commitment to the ultimate return of these objects, it too has not been free from Nazi-tainted artwork. Here, of course, the situation differs from European countries that received quantities of recovered stolen artwork for redistribution to its owners. The concern in America has been that museums have acquired pieces through art-market channels and/or donations that were originally stolen by the

Nazis. Following the Washington conference in 1998 and at the behest of a commission appointed by President Clinton in 2000, U.S. museums were asked to disclose provenance information on their collections in an effort to identify any unlawful appropriations of Holocaust-era artwork. Objects of special concern were those involved in transfers of ownership over a broad period of Nazi art acquisition, spanning from January 1, 1933, to December 31, 1945. The American Association of Museums has established a Web site (www.nepip.org) where objects in American museum collections that show changes in ownership during this period are to be posted to solicit proactively ownership claims by aggrieved parties. From the Web site's inception in 2003 through 2008, over 27,000 qualifying pieces of art located in 163 museums are listed. Nevertheless, relatively few works from American museums have been returned to Holocaust survivors or their heirs. For example, just 22 settlements between Holocaust survivors/heirs and American museums were reported for the 10-year period ending in December 2006 with six cases still in a pending status in 2006. More disturbing, however, were the results of an inquiry with 332 American museums in 2006 into the status of their provenance research efforts. First, only about two-thirds of the museums queried responded to this survey. Of those that did respond, 52 percent acknowledged that provenance research had been completed on less than one-half of their collections. As in Europe, the time-consuming nature of provenance research, combined with a lack of staff to conduct it, has been cited as the major limitation to completing this task. Thus, to what extent American museums hold objects derived from the Nazi art plunder is not yet fully understood, nor is their exposure to potential claims from rightful owners or their heirs.[26]

Austria has also struggled with restitution issues arising from Nazi seized artwork although it has managed to compile a creditable record of returning over 5,000 pieces.[27] A high-profile restitution case involving a painting in Austria is detailed in box 5.2. This case study provides an example of the intricacies and complexities that can be involved in restitution claims and the lengthy litigation that can arise in efforts to resolve them.

BOX 5.2 THE TRIALS AND TRIBULATIONS OF REPATRIATION: KLIMT'S PORTRAIT OF ADELE BLOCH-BAUER[28]

In 1907, the Austrian Modernist painter Gustav Klimt completed a portrait of Adele Bloch-Bauer, the wife of a wealthy Jewish Austrian business executive, Ferdinand Bloch-Bauer, and Klimt's rumored mistress. Tragically, in 1925 at the age of 43, Adele died of meningitis (seven years after Klimt himself died). Prior to her death, she reportedly willed this portrait along with four other works by Klimt she owned to her native Austria, although these paintings were to pass first to her husband in the event she predeceased him. The other paintings included another portrait of her painted in 1911 and three landscapes. Ferdinand did survive his wife but fled to Switzerland in 1938 once the Nazis took over Austria. He left behind all his property including the five paintings by Klimt, which were then confiscated by the Nazis. Thereafter, Adele's 1907 portrait, the most acclaimed of the five works, was prominently displayed in the Austrian Gallery in Vienna, near another of Klimt's famed paintings, *The Kiss.* Ferdinand died in 1945, but not before revoking earlier wills that addressed the disposition of the Klimt paintings. Instead, he left his entire estate to the three children of his brother as he and Adele had no children of their own. One of these designated heirs, Maria Altman, fled Austria in 1942 and settled in Los Angeles. After the war, Altman attempted to recover the Klimt paintings from Austria but was rebuffed based on the argument that Adele's original will gave them to the people of Austria. It was not until 1998 that Adele's will was finally located and it was determined that she expressed the wish, but did not *require,* that the paintings become the property of Austria. Based on this finding, Altman filed suit in the United States against the Austrian government in 2000, the legality of which was eventually approved by the U.S. Supreme Court in 2004. This ruling forced the Austrian government to reconsider its position, and in 2006, all five paintings were awarded to Altman, by then the only surviving heir and 90 years of age. Soon after finally acquiring the 1907 Klimt portrait of her aunt Adele, Maria Altman sold it for a reported $135 million to Ronald S. Lauder, owner of the cosmetics conglomerate that bears his name, who then placed it in the Neue Galerie, a small New York museum devoted to German and Austrian fine and decorative arts which he founded in 2001.

ART PLUNDER IN TIMES OF WAR AND CIVIL/RELIGIOUS UNREST: THE DAWN OF THE 21ST CENTURY

To reiterate, the plunder of art during World War II by the Nazis is without parallel, both in terms of the vast quantities seized and the systematic nature in which this occurred. While there are other examples of conquering armies seizing art for trophy purposes in an organized manner (including the Soviet Red Army once it subdued the Nazis), the chaotic environments created by wars and civil/religious unrest have provided even more frequent opportunities for art theft by individuals or groups of individuals and, unfortunately, examples abound. For illustrative purposes, we will limit our discussion here to two major conflicts that arose at the outset of the 21st century: Afghanistan and Iraq.

Afghanistan

The people of Afghanistan have long endured wars, foreign invaders and occupiers, and civil/unreligious unrest. Like other peoples whose origins extend far back in time, Afghanis also have a rich cultural history that is reflected in the art and artifacts of the past civilizations that once flourished within their present-day borders. In recent history, the Afghani people, its infrastructure and its cultural heritage, have suffered from an invasion by the Soviet Union in the 1980s, occupiers who were eventually repelled and replaced in the early 1990s by the Taliban, a brutal fundamentalist Islamic regime. Under their brand of Islam, the Taliban ordered the destruction of depictions of the human figure and symbols of non-Islamic beliefs. As a result, the National Museum of Afghanistan in Kabul was fair game for fire, bombing, and looting, resulting in the disappearance or destruction of about two-thirds of its 100,000-piece collection of art and artifacts. Many archeological sites in Afghanistan, which are estimated to total about 3,000, have also been destroyed and/or looted. The most highly publicized event in this regard was the Taliban's deliberate demolition in March 2001 of two giant Buddhas in the Bamiyan Valley, carvings in facing rock formations that date back over 1,500 years. These carvings were designated by UNESCO as a world-heritage site. One report claimed that Al Qaeda leader Osama bin Laden ordered their demolition.

As with the Nazis, however, there have been those in Afghanistan who saw profit potential in works of art that were politically out of favor. Rather than destroying these objects, art and artifacts looted from the National Museum and archeological sites throughout the country have been trafficked in the world antiquities market. In contrast to well-heeled Nazi art aficionados, here those who have sought profit in banned objects have more frequently been peasants eking out a daily survival, although warlords from neighboring Pakistan are believed to be providing the smuggling network out of the country. The U.S.-led military offensive to rid Afghanistan of the Taliban regime and the Al Qaeda terrorists that it hosted is only the latest in a seemingly unending series of hostilities that have provided the chaos and cover that enable this type of activity to continue.[29]

Iraq

Iraq is referred to by many historians as the cradle of civilization. Under Saddam Hussein's reign, Iraq's record of protecting its rich cultural heritage was markedly better than that of Afghanistan and many other nations in the Middle East and Central and Southeast Asia. Saddam took interest in his nation's archeological resources and tightly controlled the access to these sites, thus limiting the potential for looting. The National Museum in Baghdad was the primary beneficiary of objects unearthed at these sites and, as a result, its collections of the Sumerian, Assyrian, Mesopotamian, Babylonian, and Islamic objects were the envy of museums worldwide. Its holdings reportedly totaled about one-half million (although an antiquated and less than up-to-date inventory system precluded an accurate assessment in this regard). Saddam treated this museum as his private preserve and access to the museum was limited to both scholars and tourists alike. As with Iraqi society in general, the U.S.-led invasion in April 2003 upset the status quo at the museum as well as at the estimated 10,000 archeological sites throughout the country. In fact, as U.S. troops began to enter Baghdad, the museum was ransacked by thieves and looters who are believed to have stolen about 15,000 objects. In addition, the chaos and instability created by the war provided opportunities for untold looting at the nation's archeological sites. U.S. coalition forces were not insensitive to these events and extended efforts to recover stolen objects and protect the museum and archeological sites (with the protection of archeological sites being a less successful undertaking than safeguarding the museum). Through liaison with the reestablished Iraqi museum as well as archeological and police authorities, and with worldwide law-enforcement cooperation, somewhere between 4,000 and 5,400 objects stolen from the National Museum have been recovered in the five years following the looting incident. In addition, another 17,000 objects looted from Iraq's archeological sites have also been recovered over this period, although to what extent this figure represents the total number of objects stolen is unknown. The good news here is that among the works recovered have been some of the museum's most cherished pieces, including one of the earliest known depictions of the human face, the *Mask of Warka,* a product of the Sumerians in 3,100 B.C.E., and a ninth-century B.C.E. Assyrian ivory headboard from Nimrud. The bad news is that five years after the National Museum was ransacked many thousands of objects from it collection are still missing, including the museum's most noted holding, an eighth-century B.C.E. ivory carving known as the *Lioness Attacking a Nubian.* Whether the missing pieces have survived the turmoil in Iraq or have perished is unknown. Some reports indicate that warring militia groups and even terrorist organizations like Al Qaeda have profited from black market sales of looted Iraqi antiquities. Many nations have barred the import of Iraqi antiquities recognizing that they are the fruits of theft and looting. Whether these formal barriers will prevent these objects from reaching the hands of unscrupulous dealers and private collectors is uncertain. As will be explored in the next chapter, networks throughout the world that traffic in looted cultural-heritage objects have been quite successful in not only satisfying the demands of private collectors for these objects, but many museums as well.[30]

CHAPTER 6

Stealing the Past: The Looting of Cultural-Heritage Objects

In setting the stage for our exploration of art crime in chapter 1, a broad, inclusive definition of the types of objects that fall into the realm of "art" was adopted. However, rather than reinventing the wheel with regard to a unique, broad, and inclusive definition, typologies of art objects developed by three organizations were presented (see table 1.1) to demonstrate the breadth of the objects to be considered here as "art." While there is variation in the descriptive labels attached to categories in these typologies, there are common themes; and the variations may have more to do with the missions of the organizations that formulated them. Among the common themes is recognition of the artistic achievements of earlier civilizations. The Metropolitan Museum of Art typology is very detailed in this respect as it includes such categories as ancient Near Eastern art, Egyptian art, Greek and Roman art, and medieval art. Categories such as the arts of Africa, Oceania, and America; Asian art; arms and armor; and Islamic art also bring within their focus the achievements of earlier civilizations. The IFAR and FBI art categories are generally broader, but in one important way even more inclusive with regard to objects from past civilizations; that is, they reflect the categories of ethnographic objects and/or archeological material. If one were to associate these latter categories with the more traditional art forms reflected in the Metropolitan Museum of art typology, an arguably fair way to describe this broad range of material would be as cultural-heritage objects, the primary label we will adopt for our discussions here, although at times terms such as antiquities, ancient art, and archeological material or objects will be used interchangeably. Again, for purposes here they can be considered largely synonymous with our primary term, "cultural-heritage objects."

Turning our attention to cultural-heritage objects marks an important transition in the way we have approached art crime so far. Although we have not ignored the art of earlier civilizations (for example, we learned in chapter 4 about the prevalence of forgeries of cultural-heritage objects and, in chapter 5, about the looting of cultural-heritage objects in Iraq and Afghanistan incident to war and civil/religious unrest), we have largely focused on crime that has affected works of art created since the Renaissance. Many of these works can be attributed to known (if not widely acclaimed) painters and sculptors, and some have achieved great value both as cultural icons and monetarily. In this chapter, we shift our attention to the broad range of art we refer to here as cultural-heritage objects, a category that is worldwide in scope and covers objects created by past civilizations extending back to earliest human beings. Unlike more modern-day works of art, we rarely know the identities of the creators of these objects; but these largely unknown artisans were no less capable of producing beauty than their more modern, sometimes famous counterparts. Perhaps more importantly, these objects provide one of the only ways we can learn about many ancient civilizations. Thus, cultural-heritage objects have value arising from two dimensions. Even without famous creator names attached to them, cultural-heritage objects have value arising from their beauty and the skill that created them. And perhaps even more so than art created in recent eras, these objects have value because of the insights they provide into civilizations where there are little or no written records available. Unfortunately, however, like their more modern counterparts, the value of art objects from the past has attracted an unscrupulous following, ranging from those who excavate and/or tear them from their places of origin, to those who smuggle them into the world's art markets, and finally to those who buy them with little concern about their provenance, or lack thereof. Essentially, we are again talking about the theft of art and the networks that enable this type of stolen art to reach the legitimate art market. Sound familiar? Only here we often replace the term, "theft" with "looting," a term the renowned British archeologist Colin Renfrew defined as the excavation of sites without maintenance of a competent record for publication and with the subsequent sale of the finds for commercial gain.[1] In fact, aside from questions about the legality of unearthing or otherwise removing cultural-heritage objects from within any national jurisdiction, and then covertly transporting them across national boundaries to avoid export laws against such activity, is the concern over the often crude and careless methods used to gather these objects. As Renfrew suggests, those who loot are not scientists studying the context in which objects are found, nor do they carefully remove and document their finds. Rather, looters use the most expedient methods available to rip objects from the ground or other settings with little regard for any collateral damage that they might cause, and even to the objects they seek to recover as well. Thus, through looting, valuable archeological knowledge can be lost forever.

THE THEFT OF CULTURAL-HERITAGE OBJECTS:
THE SCOPE OF THE PROBLEM

A theme that seems to be recurring in our exploration of art crime is one of magnitude. The dollar values of many pieces of stolen art discussed in chapters 2 and 3 are huge; forgery of art as described in chapter 4 is pervasive; and as most recently demonstrated in chapter 5, the Nazis stole art as part of their war strategy on an unprecedented scale. In attempting to describe the scope of theft of cultural-heritage objects, one is again struck by the magnitude of the problem and in a multidimensional manner. One of the ways the scope of this problem can be viewed is from a historical perspective. To be clear, the theft of cultural-heritage objects is not a recent phenomenon brought on by a modern-day curiosity about the past. Just as forgery and pillaging incident to conquest have ancient roots, so does grave robbing, a common way for thieves to steal valuable cultural objects that were customarily buried with the dead. In fact, Karl Meyer, whose book, *The Plundered Past* (1973), ignited renewed interest in the looting of cultural-heritage objects, called grave robbing the "second oldest profession." He cited evidence of tomb robbing in ancient Egypt as far back as 1134–1117 b.c.e. and noted that the ancient Greeks referred to grave robbers as *tymborychoi*.[2] However, it was not until centuries later with the advent of early archeologists/adventurers and colonial occupation forces, that in some instances we have more detailed accounts of the acquisition/ removal of cultural-heritage objects from their lands of origin. Ironically, while the documentation of these acquisitions provides a form of provenance, this information has also been used as evidence by countries of origin in their efforts to repatriate objects they contend were illegally removed from their soil. Perhaps the cause célèbre of such repatriation efforts are those by Greece, which for about 200 years has sought the return from Great Britain of what has become known as the Elgin Marbles. In the early 1800s, the British ambassador to the Ottoman Empire, Lord Elgin, acquired portions of the marble carvings from the Parthenon that depict mythical battle scenes and a procession in honor of the goddess Athena. He eventually sold them to the British government and they are in the British Museum in London. Thus far, the British have resisted the overtures for their return. Initially, they contended that the Parthenon was being destroyed by the Turks and neglected by the Greeks. With the departure of the Turks, their argument shifted to Greece's failure to protect and maintain their cultural treasures generally, and their lack of a suitable facility to display the Marbles to the public. The British cite the excellent care they have given to these pieces and their public display at one of the world's great museums (arguments that are being subjected to renewed challenges with the opening of a new Acropolis Museum in Athens).[3]

Egypt has also contested the acquisition and removal of certain high-profile antiquities between the late 18th century and early 20th century.

Unlike the Greeks' long saga, their protests have been put forth in only more recent years. In 1799, what has become known as the Rosetta Stone was seized in Egypt by a member of Napoleon's occupation forces. This is a stone tablet inscribed with ancient Egyptian hieroglyphics that is dated at 196 B.C.E. In ancient Egypt, such tablets were akin to modern-day billboards and in this instance, the Rosetta Stone published a decree made by a council of priests. By 1801, British forces seized control of Egypt from the French and gained possession of the Rosetta Stone, and since 1802, it has also been housed in the British Museum in London (although the French were permitted to make a wax impression of it and a French Egyptologist worked diligently for 20 years thereafter and finally deciphered the hieroglyphic code). In the early 1820s, another French collector of ancient Egyptian artifacts managed to dislodge the Zodiac ceiling from the Temple of Denderah and then sold it to King Louis XVIII of France. The Zodiac ceiling has been on display in the Louvre since 1919. A purported 3000-year-old bust of Nefertiti was taken from Egypt by a German researcher in 1912, and it is now part of the collection in Berlin's Egyptian Museum. Unlike the Greek's long saga in seeking return of the Elgin Marbles, Egyptian protests have evolved only in recent years; but like the Greeks, they have been unable to convince the current custodians of these objects to part with them thus far.[4]

The Americas have not escaped the imbroglio of repatriation controversies arising from long-past archeological expeditions. Beginning around 1911 and continuing to about 1916, Hiram Bingham, a Yale historian, Connecticut political figure, and adventurer, undertook a series of expeditions to Machu Picchu, Peru, to research Incan civilization. During this period, he brought back to Yale nearly 5,000 Incan artifacts, 380 of which Yale has described as museum-quality pieces. At issue has been whether these artifacts were loaned to Bingham/Yale with the understanding that they would be returned to Peru upon request, a contention that is supported by correspondence that documents that all parties involved—Bingham, the Peruvian authorities, and Yale—knew the terms under which these artifacts were permitted to leave Peru. With the dawn of the 21st century and the ascendancy of Alejandro Toledo as Peru's first president of indigenous descent, what had been sporadic attempts for repatriation over the years became a much more aggressive undertaking by the new Peruvian government. Initially Yale balked, arguing that, in fact, it did have good title to the objects in its possession, having returned those on loan in the 1920s. However, in 2007, Yale agreed to the return of most of the objects, including most of the museum-quality pieces, while it was to retain certain research-quality objects for 99 years. Although both sides hailed the agreement at the time, it later faltered in the face of Peruvian opposition at home. The political winds in Peru demanded no less than the return of all objects from Yale and a lawsuit seeking this remedy was subsequently filed in the United States that sought this remedy, litigation that is still pending.[5]

The Scope of the Problem: Geographic Magnitude

While the problem of theft of cultural-heritage objects extends far back in time, its magnitude can also be characterized in terms of geography: it is a worldwide problem. Examples of stealing cultural artifacts from earlier civilizations have been documented in just about every corner of the globe. Countries whose earlier civilizations provided the roots from which the modern Western world evolved have long been favored targets of those who have sought to acquire, legally or illegally, the cultural-heritage objects of these ancient peoples. Largely, this group of countries consists of those that border the Mediterranean Sea; whether European, Middle Eastern, or North African, all have long been ravaged by the theft of antiquities. The looting of cultural-heritage objects has also been pervasive throughout the Middle East in general, with the widespread thefts in Iraq following America's 2003 invasion being just one (documented) example of this activity in this part of the world. Elsewhere in Europe, a byproduct of the fall of the Soviet regime in the late 1980s and early 1990s has been widespread looting of cultural-heritage objects in many of the newly freed lands of Eastern Europe. For example, from the breakup of Yugoslavia in 1991 emerged the tiny nation of Macedonia, which nevertheless has 4,000 archeological sites, most of which are unprotected. These sites contain a treasure trove of artifacts from a variety of cultures that have influenced this land throughout the ages, including ancient Macedonian, Roman, Byzantine, medieval Bulgar, and Ottoman.[6]

In the Americas, early civilization sites in Central and South America including those of the Mayans, Incans, and Aztecs have long suffered from widespread looting. Even in the United States, Native American artifacts have been targeted by thieves. Perhaps less well known in the Western world has been the looting of cultural-heritage objects in China, India, Southeast Asia (especially Cambodia), and throughout Africa. In some countries of Southeast Asia and Africa where there is little written history of the ancient peoples who occupied these lands, cultural-heritage objects provide one of the only (if not *the* only) knowledge sources available about these civilizations. Sadly, one observer likened the vast commercialized enterprise that looting cultural-heritage objects has become in Africa to a form of cultural genocide.[7]

The Scope of the Problem: Describing the Magnitude Quantitatively?

Historically, we have evidence that the looting of cultural-heritage objects as a practice has ancient roots. In addition, we have evidence that this problem is worldwide in scope. The available evidence also suggests that the problem of looting cultural-heritage objects is huge in quantitative terms, whether measured by the frequency of occurrence, the number of objects involved, and/or the value of the looted objects. One rule of thumb used to describe the quantitative magnitude of cultural-heritage looting is known as Chippendale's Law (named after Christopher Chippendale, the distinguished archeologist based at the Museum of Archeology and Anthropology in Cambridge, England): "However bad you feared it would be (so far as antiquities looting and smuggling are concerned), it always turns out to be worse."[8] As discussed earlier, the absence of any comprehensive, routinely collected and/or standardized data with regard to art crimes of all types precludes definitive quantitative assessment; and this limitation hinders our ability to describe accurately the magnitude of cultural-heritage looting numerically. Thus, we tend to rely on estimates from informed sources.

A popular notion is that art theft generally ranks just behind drug trafficking and arms smuggling as leading international crimes and that sales from this stolen property account for billions of dollars annually. Interpol, however, can endorse neither this ranking nor the dollar loss attributed to art theft based on a lack of supporting data, even though it attempts to solicit information from its members on this type of activity, an effort that is supported by only about one third of its membership. Moreover, the data it does compile combines art theft arising from traditional crime scenarios (larceny, burglary, and robbery as discussed in chapter 2) and looting/smuggling of cultural-heritage objects.[9] Thus, Interpol data does not permit us to focus solely on the latter in terms of any type of quantitative assessment, and this is frequently a limitation we have with other available art-theft data sets.

However, when we examine informed estimates of cultural-heritage looting, they are curiously similar to estimates reported in chapters 1 and 2 that place a monetary value on art theft in general, that is, between $1 billion and $6 billion annually. For instance, Roger Atwood in his book *Stealing History: Tomb Raiders, Smugglers, and the Looting of the Ancient World* (2004) cited estimates of the value of looted cultural-heritage objects that range from $300 million to $6 billion annually. Likewise, La Font in *Pillaging Cambodia: The Illicit Traffic in Khmer Art* (2004) also talked in terms of billions of dollars when attaching an annual value to cultural-heritage looting. Absent estimates that specifically focus on art theft arising from traditional crime scenarios (i.e., larceny, burglary, and robbery), it would appear that most attempts to place a monetary value on worldwide art theft are inclusive of looted cultural-heritage objects; and that the latter contributes substantially to this estimated value. Based on this premise alone, it could be argued that the magnitude of cultural-heritage looting measured quantitatively is huge.

This argument, however, can be augmented by examining available data that reports the number of objects that have been looted. For instance, in Italy, a major source country of antiquities, the Carabinieri (the Italian paramilitary police force) claims that a half million artifacts have been stolen from its archeological sites since the 1970s, although they believe this figure might only represent a fraction of the actual volume of thefts since so much looting goes undetected. They have recovered about 350,000 looted objects. Another assessment of the number of looted objects from Italy, and one that tries to deal more in "hard numbers" than estimates, is offered in a study entitled "Analysis of the Looting, Selling and Collecting of Apulian Red-Figure Vases: A Quantitative Approach" by Elia (2004). Focusing only on one type of Italian cultural heritage object, that is, Apulian red-figure vases, Elia found that about 13,600 such objects are known to exist throughout the world, the majority of which are located in the United States and Great Britain. Less than 12 percent of these objects have any type of provenance attached to them, including about one-half of this total that was recovered incident to archeological excavation, the implication being that the vast majority without a recorded history were looted.[10]

LOOTING AND SMUGGLING NETWORKS

The contested acquisitions of the Elgin Marbles in Greece, the Rosetta Stone and other objects from Egypt, and remnants of the Inca civilization in Peru can be looked upon as a starting place (at least for the purposes of relatively modern history) to examine the networks that engage in the looting and smuggling of cultural-heritage objects. On the one hand, these examples reflect parts of the world that have continued to be primary sources of looted cultural-heritage objects, that is, the lands bordering the Mediterranean Sea and Central and South America. On the other hand, however, these examples reflect a simpler time as the contested issues have more to do with whether there was appropriate authority to remove the objects from the countries of origin and less so with clandestine looting and smuggling operations, as is the more current concern. Unlike these simpler days where the removal of cultural-heritage objects from a source country was either not regulated at all or authority was granted locally and/or informally, most modern-day nations now specifically prohibit the removal of such objects, absent special export permission which provides a limited, legal supply of these objects to the remainder of the world. In response, clandestine looting and smuggling networks have arisen to meet a demand for these objects that exceeds the legal supply.

Moreover, these clandestine looting and smuggling operations have not been confined just to the Mediterranean and Central and South America but rather have evolved throughout the world wherever cultural-heritage objects can be found. For instance, La Font found that hundreds of Khmer antiquities are smuggled out of Cambodia daily into Thailand through a network that involves organized gangs and Cambodian military and administrative officials. Bangkok, Thailand, in fact, has earned a reputation as a clearinghouse for looted cultural-heritage objects from throughout

Southeast Asia including Vietnam, Myanmar, Laos, as well as Cambodia, and from there find their way to the United States, Europe, and Japan where there is a great market demand. La Font estimated that 80 percent of the Southeast Asian antiquities that are sold in the United States entered illegally, primarily through Los Angeles, San Francisco, and New York.[11] One report out of India described the looting of antiquities as "unchecked" and credited this level of activity to the work of criminal gangs who coordinate with local art dealers and even international smugglers. Brazen thefts of religious idols that were under the protection of the government's archeological authority have served to highlight the reality that India's cultural heritage is being stripped away by thieves.[12] As suggested earlier, this same reality is shared by observers of the looting activity in Africa, one described as a "vast commercial enterprise" that has arisen to meet market demand. This market is very much international in nature with the primary dealers in African artifacts located in London, Brussels, Paris, and several cities in Switzerland. Those who deal in looted objects reportedly facilitate this trade by providing false documentation to create legitimate provenance.[13]

The Chinese claim the loss of 10 million cultural-heritage objects, most of which were removed prior to the advent of the People's Republic of China in 1949. However, a growing awareness among rural Chinese residents of the monetary opportunities that lie beneath their soil has been the impetus for a continued supply of antiquities from China. While the Chinese government has banned the export of such items, they are easily smuggled into Hong Kong where there remains a separate customs authority; and they are readily available for sale.[14]

Looting and Smuggling in the Americas

While resolving the disposition of Hiram Bingham's cache of Inca objects from Machu Picchu has occupied the attention of diplomats and academics for years (at least intermittently, anyway) and sometimes grabbed news headlines as well, other more sinister characters have continued to loot and pillage the cultural heritage of Peru. Local police officials have characterized the level of this activity as exceeding that found in Bolivia and Mexico, two other primary sources of pre-Columbian artworks. Organized criminal gangs are believed to be responsible for the looting and smuggling, and the objects eventually find their way to markets in the United States and Europe. One estimate placed the annual value of the illegal trafficking in Peruvian artifacts at $18 million, a figure that might be on the low side when considering the circumstances that unfolded during an investigation in Miami, Florida, in 2006. In this case alone, $2 million was sought by smugglers who attempted to sell American undercover agents 150 pre-Columbian art objects dating back to 3,000 B.C.E. not from Peru, but from Ecuador, a neighboring country that heretofore had not been known to rival Peru as a major source of illicit cultural-heritage ob-jects.[15] To be clear, however, the illicit flow of cultural-heritage objects out of Central and South America is not limited to just pre-Columbian objects; rather, it also includes artworks from the Spanish Colonial era, pieces that frequently adorn unprotected churches. Mexico, for example, estimated it has lost at least 1,000 such artworks since 1999.[16]

"Classic" Looting and Smuggling Networks

The terms "classics" or "classical" are commonly used references to the histories and cultures of ancient Greece and Rome. While it cannot be overemphasized that no part of the world has been immune from loot-ing of cultural-heritage objects, Greece and particularly Italy have perhaps suffered longest from this plunder. In the Western world, a renewed ap-preciation for classical art and architecture evolved with the Renaissance, and antiquities from these eras have been actively sought and collected since then, initially throughout Europe and then later in the United States. This interest in classical antiquities has created a demand for these objects from both museums and individual collectors, a demand that has been met through the evolution of supply networks that can also be described as "classic" but not in the context of ancient Greece or Rome. Rather, these networks, like those elsewhere in the world that illicitly traffic in cultural-heritage objects, can be described as "classic" or typical criminal organiza-tions, that is, networks of individuals that are multilayered by functional responsibility to facilitate criminal activity, in this case the looting and smuggling of Greek and Roman antiquities. A prime example of such a network is detailed in the case study in box 6.1.

BOX 6.1 ITALIAN CARABINIERI DISMANTLE THE MEDICI NETWORK[17]

A January 1994 armed robbery of eight ancient vases at a museum housed in a medieval castle in Melfi, Italy, set the stage for one of the great law-enforcement successes in the fight against illicit antiquities trafficking. Three men, one of whom was armed, tied up the lone guard on duty, smashed a glass case housing the vases, and made off with them in an auto bearing a Swiss license plate. While art-squad officers from the Carabinieri, Italy's paramilitary police, pursued leads and suspected international implica-tions due to the sighting of the Swiss license plate, it was not until Octo-ber 1994 that further developments occurred. An Italian national living in Munich, Germany, came under suspicion by Greek authorities for traffick-ing antiquities out of Greece and Cyprus, and German police were asked

by the Greeks to execute a search warrant on his home. An invitation to
participate was extended to the Carabinieri. Information provided by the
Greek authorities proved correct, as found on the premises was a treasure
trove of antiquities mostly Italian in origin, but also objects from Greece and
Bulgaria. The objects ranged from ancient vases and jars (many just in fragments) to bronze figures, statues, mosaics, jewelry, and stelae (stone slabs
bearing inscriptions). Moreover, the residence also housed a laboratory/
workshop where these objects were cleaned and restored. Most important
to the Italian officers, however, was the discovery of the eight vases stolen from Melfi earlier in the year. After examining business records at the
search premises, they were able to identify a connection between the Italian
national in Munich and individuals in Italy who were suspected of violat-
ing Italian laws that control the export of cultural-heritage objects out of
Italy. Ironically, one of those identified was subsequently killed in an auto
accident and in his car were found photographs of antiquities. Combined
with the information gathered from Munich along with recorded telephone
conversations through wiretaps, art-squad officers obtained a search warrant for the deceased's apartment in Rome. Documents recovered at this
location led to numerous other investigations that resulted in the recovery
of looted antiquities, the conviction of those involved in these activities, and
most importantly, an organizational chart of a major antiquities-trafficking
network that stretched throughout Italy, into Switzerland and beyond, including an American contact, Robert Hecht, a known antiquities dealer who
had been under suspicion for illicit trafficking in the past. The kingpin was
identified as Giacomo Medici, an Italian who operated out of a warehouse
in Geneva, Switzerland. His network included looters in Italy, or *tombaroli,*
who illicitly unearthed or otherwise stole antiquities and then sold them to
regional "middlemen," the *capa zona;* they, in turn, arranged for these objects
to be transported to Medici's warehouse in Geneva where he was able to
peddle them in the legitimate worldwide art market, sometimes employing
third parties to mask his involvement. In 1995, the Carabinieri art squad,
working in conjunction with Swiss authorities, obtained a search warrant
for Medici's Geneva warehouse and they were not disappointed with what
they found: about 4,000 suspected looted antiquities including vases, fres-
cos, and marble and bronze statues and figures along with thousands of
documents and photographs of antiquities encrusted in dirt. Some of these
photos depicted objects that passed through Medici's hands and into museums and other collections. However, a long and detailed examination of the
records recovered at this site showed Medici to exercise the care of a skilled
smuggler and launderer of stolen goods or monies derived there from to
disguise the origin of his product and often his direct involvement. Among
the photos was one of Medici and the American antiquities dealer Robert
Hecht standing in front of cases of looted antiquities; and in fact, the Italian
investigation shifted its focus to Hecht in 2001, when working with French
law enforcement they were able to secure a search warrant for Hecht's Paris
apartment. This search resulted in the recovery of an unpublished memoir
that detailed Hecht's involvement in the unprovenanced antiquities trade

(more on that later). Meanwhile, the wheels of justice ground slowly but surely in Italy and the authorities there built a sound case against Medici for dealing in stolen artifacts. He was convicted in 2004, after which he was sentenced to 10 years in prison and fined €10 million (about $13 million). The Italian authorities followed up Medici's prosecution by charging one of his customers, Robert Hecht, and Marion True, the former curator of Greek and Roman art at Los Angeles's Getty Museum with receiving stolen antiquities and conspiring to traffic illegally acquired artifacts (a set of events with regard to True that will be detailed more fully in chapter 7).

THE MARKET FOR LOOTED CULTURAL-HERITAGE OBJECTS: MUSEUMS AND COLLECTORS

Our journey through the world of art crime thus far has a recurring theme: the value of art, whether measured in aesthetic and/or monetary terms, creates a demand because the supply of these objects is limited. At times, that demand is met through providing artworks acquired through criminal means, although not without difficulty. As we have seen, stealing well-known artworks carries with it a tremendous limitation: who but perhaps a reclusive, wealthy art connoisseur would buy such a work only for his/her personal viewing? Moreover, the advent of stolen art databases has made peddling an even lesser known art object a risky proposition, both for dealers and for purchasers. Looted cultural-heritage objects, however, are less problematic. They were not stolen from museums, residences, or galleries, events that are usually reported to authorities. In fact, most of these objects were not even known to exist; there is no catalogue raisonné (i.e., a complete, scholarly compilation of the works attributed to a particular artist) available, especially since the identities of ancient artists, with few exceptions, are unknown. Typically looted cultural-heritage objects have been unearthed from previously unknown ancient sites or surreptitiously removed from known, but poorly guarded, archeological sites (often uninventoried as well), and then smuggled out of their countries of origin in contravention of prevailing laws and into the waiting arms of the legitimate art market. At least until recent years, otherwise law-abiding museum curators, dealers, and individual collectors asked few, if any, questions about provenance when acquiring cultural-heritage objects. Thus, unlike the smaller, underground market that deals in artworks stolen from museums, galleries, and residences, and populated by unsavory thieves and fences, looted cultural-heritage objects have been openly marketed in the well-funded legitimate art world populated by respected art institutions, art professionals, and art aficionados. Thus, the looting and smuggling of cultural-heritage objects have been directly financed by the legitimate art world. Collectors generally have been roundly criticized for creating the demand for cultural-heritage objects. One Thai archeologist in commenting on the illicit flow of cultural-heritage objects out of Asia was quoted as stating, "The main problem is the demand; rich people want to buy and collect these antiques."[18] Matthew Bogdanos, author of *Thieves of Baghdad: One Marine's Passion for Ancient Civilizations and the Journey to Recover the World's Greatest Stolen Treasures* (2005), echoed a similar sentiment, but his comments were specifically aimed at the U.S. market which he described using terms such as "well-placed individuals" from "the Upper East Side, Georgetown and Pacific Heights" and "genteel money."[19]

While in the past the shroud of "high society" protected collectors of undocumented antiquities, in recent years their activities have been called into question. For instance, in January 2008, New York City philanthropist and member of the Metropolitan Museum of Art Board of Directors Shelby White agreed to return 11 objects from her antiquities collection to Italy, based on Italian assertions that they were looted from that country. Evidence presented by Italian authorities included photographs recovered from the Geneva warehouse maintained by Giacomo Medici (see box 6.1) that depicted some of the antiquities that became part of White's collection. White maintained that she and her late husband, Wall Street financier Leon Levy, bought the objects in good faith from Robin Symes, a London antiquities dealer that Italian authorities have linked to Medici. White's philanthropic largesse has included a $20 million gift to the Metropolitan Museum of Art to finance the expansion of a wing that houses Greek and Roman art; and her late husband's foundation, The Leon Levy Foundation, provided $200 million to New York University to establish the Institute for the Study of the Ancient World. The media reported that White felt unfairly targeted by Italian authorities because she placed her objects on public display at the Metropolitan Museum of Art instead of in the privacy of her home, as is more common among other collectors.[20]

Also in 2008, diamond importer and one-time companion of the late Jackie Kennedy, Maurice Tempelsman, returned two 6th-century B.C.E. marble statues to Italy that authorities there maintained were unearthed by tomb robbers in Sicily and then smuggled out of the country. Tempelsman purchased them in 1980 for $1 million and, once again, the London antiquities dealer Robin Symes was the seller. Immediately prior to their repatriation to Italy, the statues were on loan to the University of Virginia and Tempelsman had plans to gift them permanently to the University. He too contended that his purchase was made in good faith.[21]

While these examples illustrate the role of those in society's upper echelons as passionate collectors who fuel the demand for antiquities, they also provide evidence of the central role that dealers play as intermediaries in bringing looted objects into the legitimate market. Evidence from the Medici investigation brought the scruples of dealers such as Robin Symes and the American Robert Hecht into question. Recall from chapter 2 the critique of the art world as being "secretive." That assessment certainly applies to dealers in the antiquities trade and perhaps for very self-serving reasons. In fact, it has been opined that any unprovenanced antiquity on the market should be assumed to be looted and smuggled.[22] Moreover, as discussed earlier, looting and smuggling networks are not limited to those trafficking in classical antiquities. Rather, they exist in response to the market demand for cultural objects from all sectors of the world; and dealers, whether knowingly or unknowingly, are at the transition point where illicit goods become legitimatized through public sale. For example, in 2009 both China and India aggressively challenged sales at auction houses of objects each country contended were looted from their soil. In an effort to disrupt an auction at Christie's of two Chinese bronze figures that the Chinese government alleged were looted, a Chinese art dealer submitted the successful bid of $40 million and then stated he had no intention of paying for it. While this art dealer claimed he was acting independently of the government, an Indian business executive assisted by the Indian government paid $1.8 million at auction to secure Gandhi artifacts.[23]

Museums, too, have fueled the market demand for antiquities; and in their quests to enhance their collections, many have been patrons of illegal looting and smuggling networks, wittingly or unwittingly, directly and indirectly. With regard to the latter, it should be explained that in the United States, the tax laws provide for charitable donation deductions, which can include donating artwork to nonprofit organizations such as museums. Thus, it has been an all too frequent practice for individual antiquities collectors to purchase unprovenanced objects and then donate them to their favorite museums.[24] In return, they receive a tax deduction as well as recognition from the recipient museum for their good works.

To be clear, many of the antiquities that are on display in the world's great museums have been part of those collections for a century or more. Although there are instances such as those reviewed at the outset of this chapter, where repatriation is being sought for long-held objects, for the most part objects acquired since 1970 have received the most scrutiny. The United Nations Educational, Scientific and Cultural Organization (UNESCO) in 1970 passed a convention that called on governments to make it illegal to import, export, or transfer ownership of cultural property without permission from the country of origin. While it took years for some governments to ratify this convention (e.g., Italy in 1979; the United States in 1983; France in 1997; along with Great Britain in 2002; and to date, some nations including Germany and the Netherlands have not done so), it nevertheless represented an international statement that sought to bring to an end unregulated trafficking in cultural-heritage objects.[25] Thus, the year 1970 is a frequently used marker by which to judge the legitimacy of a cultural-heritage object, that is, from 1970 forward if there is no record of an object's legal export from its country of origin, then it can be assumed to have been looted and smuggled out.

Among major American museums that have faced allegations of acquiring looted antiquities are the Getty Museum in Los Angeles, the Museum of Fine Arts in Boston, the Cleveland Museum, and Metropolitan Museum of Art in New York City. The Getty is a relatively new institution, having first opened its doors in 1954, and has been in a particularly vulnerable position with regard to developing its collection of Greek and Roman art. Not only is this an area of emphasis at the museum, but it is also amply endowed too, thus enabling it to aggressively pursue acquisitions. However, this aggressive, well-funded pursuit has occurred during an era of scrutiny not faced by its older, more established counterparts when much of their collections were accumulated. The Getty curator of Greek and Roman art from 1986 to 2005 was Marion True, a well-respected art historian who was also considered a leading advocate for the ethical acquisition of antiquities. However, evidence developed in the Medici investigation suggested that while she "talked the talk," she did not "walk the walk." In fact, photographs and records recovered incident to this investigation documented that 42 objects which had been in Medici's possession were acquired by the Getty through the complicity of Robert Hecht and Marion True. In September 2007, after protracted negotiations between the Getty and Italian authorities, the museum agreed to the return of 40 objects in return for long-term loans from Italy of objects of similar value. However, criminal charges against True and Hecht, as reported in box 6.1, remained in effect despite this settlement.[26]

Through the Medici investigation, Italian authorities also identified 30 objects at the Museum of Fine Arts in Boston as looted from Italy and requested their return. The Boston museum acknowledged it had previous dealings with Robert Hecht in acquiring antiquities as well as Swiss antiquities restorer Fritz Burki, an admitted confederate of both Medici and Hecht. The museum reached a negotiated settlement in September 2006, which required them to turn over 13 of the objects in question.[27] The Cleveland Museum of Art was approached by Italian authorities in 2007 with evidence from the Medici investigation that it possessed 42 looted objects. By the end of 2008, the museum agreed to the return of 14 of the contested objects with the stipulation it nevertheless acquired these pieces in good faith.[28] Even the venerable Princeton University in New Jersey became enmeshed in the Medici investigation when photographs from this case depicted objects that had been in Medici's possession and were now held by the university's art museum. After talks that spanned a year and a half, in October 2007 Princeton agreed to return 8 of 15 objects that were contested by the Italians.[29]

American antiquities dealer Robert Hecht also figured prominently in a high-profile acquisition by New York's Metropolitan Museum of Art and its subsequent repatriation to Italy, as detailed in the case study in box 6.2.

BOX 6.2 THE MET'S EUPHRONIUS KRATER[30]

In June 1970, Thomas Hoving, then director of the Metropolitan Museum of Art in New York City, voiced support for the recently passed UNESCO convention that called for governments to make it illegal to import, export, or transfer ownership of cultural property without permission from the country of origin. Although the U.S. government would not ratify this convention until years later, Hoving stated it would be the museum's policy to respect the export laws of pillaged countries and would cooperate with authorities whenever there was a question about provenance. Nevertheless, a little over one year later, the Met was presented a rare acquisition opportunity and, in retrospect, one that seemed to call into question Hoving's commitment to support the UNESCO convention. In fact, the prevailing sentiments and practices within the museum community at this time ran counter to such a commitment. The attitude among curators was (and perhaps to a lesser extent, still is; more on that later) that for the most part, antiquities-rich countries tend to do a poor job in protecting and studying their own cultural-heritage objects; and regardless of how they might be acquired, they fare far better and are more accessible to scholars and the interested public in a museum setting. This type of sentiment lessened concerns about provenance and perpetuated a "don't ask, don't tell" culture within the museum community.

The rare acquisition presented to the Met was a 2,500-year-old Greek bowl known as a krater that was believed to be the work of one of few named artisans of that era, Euphronius. The antiquities dealer making the offer was none other than Robert Hecht. Hecht represented to the Met that he obtained the krater through a Lebanese source who provided a letter claiming family ownership since 1920, and thus falling far outside of the prohibitions set forth in the 1970 UNESCO convention and even Italy's 1939 law that prohibited the export of antiquities from their soil. This documentation apparently eased the consciences of Met officials who agreed to a then unprecedented price for an antiquity of $1 million, a transaction that was completed in 1972. However, not long after the purchase, information began to surface that the krater had actually been looted from Italy in December 1971. Hecht's Lebanese source did have a krater attributed to Euphronius, and Hecht apparently played shell game with the Met; that is, he provided the letter of family ownership from the Lebanese source in support of another krater attributed to Euphronius that was only recently looted and smuggled out of Italy. This set of events was initially documented in 1972 by a *New York Times* reporter who located and interviewed an Italian *tombaroli* who claimed responsibility for unearthing what became the Met's $1 million prize possession. The immediate aftermath of these news stories was an internal museum investigation that concluded that their krater was not smuggled out of Italy and a federal grand jury investigation in New York City that failed to develop sufficient evidence of any wrongdoing by Director Hoving and his curator of Greek and Roman Art, Dietrich von Bothmer.

However, the Medici investigation proved once again to be the undoing of Hecht and his customer, this time the venerable Metropolitan Museum of Art. French and Italian authorities executed a search warrant in 2001 at Hecht's Paris apartment that was triggered by evidence of Hecht's collaboration with Medici in trafficking looted Italian antiquities uncovered at the Geneva warehouse. Here they found Hecht's memoirs of his colorful, if not unscrupulous, antiquities-trading career, which included notations that he purchased the Met's Euphronius from Medici in 1971. Armed with this new information, Italian authorities resasserted their claim on the Met's Euphronius krater although it took until the end of 2006 before an agreement was reached for its return. Under the terms of this agreement, the Met was able to continue to display the Euphronius for almost two additional years, but by November 2008, Italy finally regained custody and it was placed on display in Rome.

CONTROLLING THE LOOTING OF THE WORLD'S CULTURAL HERITAGE: ISSUES AND POLICIES

While the looting of cultural objects thus far has been cast as a form of art theft (with associated clandestine smuggling), there is another side of this story that must be told, a not uncommon scenario when considering many types of illegal conduct. For instance, there has been an ongoing debate for years about whether drugs that are widely banned for use and possession should, in fact, be legalized. One of the arguments for doing so would be that criminal organizations that trafficked these drugs would no longer be needed, thus eliminating smuggling and money laundering networks that currently consume a great deal of time and money by the world's law-enforcement agencies and governments in general, not to mention a reduction in the violence that is affiliated with the illicit drug trade. Another example of viewing differently a widely accepted form of wrongdoing is captured in the by now well-worn statement, "a terrorist to one person is a freedom fighter to another." The fact is, human conduct is not inherently illegal or criminal. Rather these labels are attached to some forms of human conduct by those in a given society who control the apparatus for doing so, usually because a particular type of conduct is viewed as detrimental to the society as a whole and/or its individual members, or in some instances because it challenges the power of those in charge.

Just what is the alternative position with regard to the looting of cultural-heritage objects? To be clear, any such position does not condone the all-too-often crude and reckless methods used to unearth and remove culture heritage from their settings. Such methods result in the loss of knowledge because looters are not concerned about historic context; rather, their goal is tantamount to archeological rape. Furthermore, their methods are destructive, resulting in collateral damage to other objects and archeological sites in general.

However, as suggested in the Euphronius krater case study (see box 6.2), there exists a sentiment in the museum community that cultural-heritage objects fare better in terms of survival and accessibility when in the hands of those who value them, admire them, and want to learn from them. While there are merits to this argument, it is a sentiment that perhaps has been tinged with an air of arrogance and disdain toward the underdeveloped world. In recent years, this air of superiority may have given way to a focus on the real deficits this part of the world has had in terms of caring for and making available for study remnants of ancient civilizations, civilizations that many scholars would argue have influenced humankind in general and therefore are of worldwide interest. Much of the underdeveloped world lacks the resources (and in some cases the expertise) to properly preserve and guard archeological sites, to conduct archeological research, and to make their cultural-heritage treasures available for study and viewing to the rest of the world.[31]

At the same time, emerging within the underdeveloped world has been a host of newly independent nation-states that for political reasons have sought to control access to and possession of cultural-heritage objects within their boundaries. These political reasons typically turn on the notion that the current inhabitants of a given nation-state are blood relatives of the great ancient civilization(s) that previously resided within their borders, and their achievements (including works of art) are sources of national pride. In addition, some of these nations see the remnants of ancient civilizations within their borders as a tourist opportunity on which they can capitalize as well. As a result, these newly independent nations have been fervent supporters of national retentionist policies that forbid the export of cultural-heritage objects from their boundaries, to include international agreements such as the 1970 UNESCO convention. To be clear, neither Italy nor Greece can be considered underdeveloped or newly independent, and yet they are strong advocates of national retentionist policies, which is perhaps an outcome of being antiquities-rich combined with a long history of being victimized by looting. Ironically, while the governments of many antiquities-rich nations have enacted retentionist policies as part of an effort to foster a sense of national identity, segments of their own populations have not fully bought into these efforts, if only because there is money to be made by those who otherwise struggle on a subsistence level of existence. Quite literally at the ground level of the illicit antiquities trade, it has been largely poor people who have been looting, unearthing, and removing cultural-heritage objects in order to survive. Another irony when considering retentionist policies is tendencies within some portions of the Islamic world to frown upon the ancient civilizations that occupied these lands and the works of art they produced, on religious grounds, with Egypt and Turkey being examples of where there has been, at the very least, disinterest in the past among large portions of the modern-day populations while their respective governments have sought to control and preserve vast treasures of the ancient civilizations that once occupied what is now their lands.[32]

Within this milieu have arisen tensions between the two professional groups whose members have devoted their lives to studying and preserving the remaining vestiges of the ancient world: archeologists and museum curators and associated professionals. Archeology tends to be a field-level endeavor; that is, the remains of ancient civilizations are studied on site. The unearthing of ancient sites is a painstaking, methodical task to ensure a complete record of the findings, that is, what was found, where it was found, what was found along with it, and so forth. Archeologists maintain that objects found during this process can only be fully appreciated when they are understood in the full context of the ancient site from where they originate. Thus, for archeology an object has more than artistic value. In order to gain knowledge of the past, archeologists contend that it important to understand the role of the object in an ancient society, and many in this field would argue for not removing objects from the settings in which are they found. Without questioning the primacy of the field of archeology in providing knowledge and understanding of the ancient civilizations, its in situ approach has played into the hands of national retentionist governments, who have taken measures to keep national-heritage objects from leaving their countries for largely political reasons.[33]

The museum community, on the other hand, has a different orientation. Museums exist to educate the public and provide opportunities for research and study of objects within their collections. It is perhaps not surprising then that a common attitude in the museum community has been that many cultural-heritage objects would be under better care and more accessible to those who appreciate them by being placed in a museum than by being left in an unprotected, remote environment. While this argument has merit, some attitudes and practices have been observed in the museum community that have detracted from the good work that these institutions have rendered to their communities. Museums compete for dollars from the public and from funding sources. In order to thrive, they must seek to acquire and build attractive collections. As we have seen already, to meet these demands, some museums have ignored issues of provenance when making acquisitions and continued a policy of "don't ask, don't tell" with regard to the origins of antiquities. In turn, such practices have perpetuated the stereotype of arrogance on the part of museum officials from the developed world among politicians and perhaps others in antiquities-rich countries, many of which are now reveling in heightened feelings of nationalism.[34]

So, therein lies the divide between the two professional groups we most depend upon to learn about our past as humans. Is there common ground that will permit us to enjoy the tremendous contributions of both fields?

James Cuno addressed this subject in his book, *Who Owns Antiquity?: Museums and the Battle Over Our Ancient Heritage* (2008). As director of the Chicago Institute of Art, Cuno wrote from the perspective of the museum community. Although he addressed the schism between the museum community and the field of archeology, his major thesis was the need to establish better working relationships with the governments of antiquities-rich countries that would allow these nations to enjoy the benefits of scholarly expertise in archeology and museology from abroad, as needed, and in return, a sharing of recovered artifacts with those institutions that have contributed the expert personnel and resources. As he was quick to point out, this concept is by no means new or innovative. Rather it is known within the archeological and museum communities as *partage,* a common practice from the years that predated the proliferation of newly independent nations when the trading of expertise for a share of the recovered objects was negotiated with local governments. In fact, the university museums at Chicago, Pennsylvania, Yale, and Harvard built their collections through such arrangements, as did the British Museum in London and the Metropolitan Museum of Art in New York City. As well, museums in source countries including Egypt, Iraq, Afghanistan, and Turkey also benefited from the cooperative arrangements under the concept of *partage.* Cuno also argued that the current array of national laws and international conventions that limit the export of antiquities from source countries has hindered the ability of museums to share the world's cultures with their communities while doing little to halt illicit trade in cultural-heritage objects.[35]

While returning to the practice of *partage* could be viewed as a multilateral approach and, at best, one that is a work in progress, in the summer of 2008 the U.S. museum community, unilaterally, published best practices for the acquisition of antiquities. Two umbrella groups, American Association of Museums (AAM) and the Association of Art Museum Directors (AAMD), issued separate but similar guidelines that called for greater scrutiny and transparency with regard to ancient art and archeological artifacts. The AAM called for its member institutions to make ownership history records publicly available for all ancient art and archaeological artifacts in their collections and rigorously research new acquisitions. AAMD guidelines specifically state that its members should not acquire any such work unless it can be substantiated through research that its discovery predated the 1970 UNESCO convention or was legally exported from its country of origin after that date.[36]

These guidelines enhance the integrity of the U.S. museum community and to some extent might even dampen the enthusiasm of many individual collectors who would purchase unprovenanced antiquities from dealers for the purpose of donating the object(s) to their favorite museum for a federal tax deduction. Proposed donations should now come under greater scrutiny. However, whether this greater scrutiny will result in a decrease in demand by individual American collectors is open to speculation. While museums have contributed to the demand for cultural-heritage objects, which in turn has fueled the illicit trade, also part of this equation has been the individual collector market, a market serviced by dealers and other forms of middlemen. Controlling the activities of the latter has remained an elusive goal. At the retail level, dealers have been known to rationalize that regardless of its origins, an object is better off in the hands of those who will appreciate and care for it than left to the vagaries of risky parts of the world. Sound familiar? Recall that some members of the museum community have expressed similar sentiments when not wanting to explore the origins of a desirable acquisition. Some dealers have also been known to refute the archeological position that knowledge is lost when an object is taken out of its context. One safeguard against such slick salesmanship has always been an informed consumer. Esteemed British archeologist Colin Renfrew has called for efforts to persuade private collectors to shun purchases of unprovenanced antiquities as a way to shut down the illicit market. Developing this idea further was Roderick J. McIntosh in *Plundering Africa's Past* (1996), where he advocated that a "Just Say No" campaign might be more successful when applied to the acquisition of undocumented cultural-heritage objects because the individuals who populate this type of market actually do have reputations to consider, unlike many of those involved in the illegal drug trade. At the other end of the illicit antiquities continuum, that is, in the source countries, Renfrew has called for educational efforts directed at the populace about the value of their cultural heritage and the economic opportunities that can ensue if their archeological sites are developed for tourism. The goal of these ideas is to put the middlemen out of business, or at least out of the business of handling looted material. If buyers won't purchase unprovenanced antiquities, combined with whatever progress can be made in source countries to divert would-be looters to other forms of employment, the illicit role of the middlemen should shrivel.[37]

Thus, the alternative view of the looting of cultural-heritage objects as a form of art crime revolves around questions of how to make this type of material more readily available for a world that is eager to enjoy and learn from these objects. Unlike the harms associated with the two other major forms of international crime, narcotics trafficking and arms smuggling, the commodity being criminalized here is art. Thus, its proliferation poses no danger to the world; on the contrary, such proliferation will only expand knowledge and foster good will and better cultural understanding in a world that suffers from too many frayed international relationships. Cooperative relationships between source nations and those countries that can assist them in developing their knowledge and preservation of their cultural-heritage riches in return for some legal export of recovered objects would seem to be a win-win situation for all concerned. And from a crime perspective, with an increase in legally exported material there should be a corresponding reduction in illegal looting and its accompanying damage and destruction, along with a reduction in clandestine smuggling networks, organizations that rival those found in narcotics and arms trafficking in terms of complexity and the involvement of unsavory characters. Combined with campaigns that urge scrutiny and avoidance of undocumented antiquities at the end-user level (e.g., museums, individual collectors), these efforts could result in the removal of illicit trafficking of cultural-heritage objects from the list of the top international crimes, a goal that would certainly be a worthy endeavor.

CHAPTER 7

White-Collar Crime in the Art World

So far, the misconduct we have examined as art crime has been largely comprised of various manifestations of theft (e.g., those that arise in traditional crime contexts such as larceny, burglary, and robbery; stealing art incident to wars and civil/religious unrest; and the looting of cultural-heritage objects) and the forgery and counterfeiting of artwork. Think back, however, and recall that intertwined in many of the scenarios that have been discussed have been efforts to bring artworks tainted by illegal activity into the legitimate marketplace. To reiterate an obvious but important point from chapter 6, art per se is not contraband in contrast, for example, to narcotics or war materiel (weapons, explosives, etc.), both of which are widely proscribed and/or controlled. Thus, if evidence of the illicit origins of an art object can be disguised or manipulated (or as we have seen earlier, ignored through a convenient rationalization), it is usually welcomed into the legitimate art market and subsequently into the hands of consumers with the (often substantial) financial resources to acquire it. Sometimes the steps associated with the introduction of illicit art into the legitimate art market/art world constitute a separate form of art crime, that is, white-collar crime. Unfortunately, however, white-collar crime in the art world is not just limited to this type of scenario. Rather, it is the appropriate umbrella term under which to discuss such misconduct as art dealers and gallery owners defrauding their customers and consignors, art related tax and investment schemes, and even antitrust violations in the art-auction industry.

WHITE-COLLAR CRIME: WHAT IS IT?

In chapter 2, we viewed art theft in terms of larceny, burglary, and robbery in an effort to understand more fully the methodologies and circumstances under which art thefts occurred. As may be recalled, there tends to be universal agreement about the specific misconduct associated with each term. Larceny refers generally to the unlawful taking of another's property without that person's consent; burglary refers to unlawfully breaking into a structure for the purpose of committing a theft or other crime; and robbery involves the threat or actual use of force to steal the property in the custody of another person. Likewise, there is widespread agreement on the misconduct associated with many other crime labels as well, for example, assault, rape, and murder.

In contrast, attaching a generally accepted definition to the term "white-collar crime" has proved elusive. In fact, as may be recalled from chapter 1, white-collar crime as a unified crime category has relatively recent origins, notwithstanding the fact that some of the misconduct that could be placed within this category has ancient origins. The chapter 1 discussion on white-collar crime served to draw an analogy with art crime that both forms of misconduct have suffered from a lack of recognition and study. It is timely to review that discussion again from a different perspective, that is, linking white-collar crime to the art world.

In 1940, American criminologist Edwin Sutherland introduced the term "white-collar crime" in an article entitled "White-Collar Criminality," which appeared in *American Sociological Review* 5 (1), pp.1–12. In this article, Sutherland argued for recognition of crimes committed by the upper classes in connection with their business activities and suggested that the term "white-collar crime" be the umbrella crime category for this type of misconduct. Sutherland felt that the field of criminology was too oriented toward offending that typically occurred within the lower socioeconomic classes and ignored crimes that were committed by upper-class individuals, thus skewing crime statistics and unfairly associating crime with those in the lower socioeconomic groups. He saw upper-class offending as a serious crime problem and one that arose from the unique occupational opportunities associated with higher socioeconomic status. Sutherland also put forth the concept that white-collar crime had to be inclusive of conduct that violated both criminal laws as well as civil/administrative laws. His argument was that the type of misconduct that often arose out of upper-class business activities was addressed not by traditional law enforcement in criminal courts but rather by regulatory agencies in civil/administrative forums. Nevertheless, the actual misconduct addressed in these civil/administrative cases was not unlike that proscribed under criminal laws, for example, criminal fraud; and he offered the analogy that juvenile delinquency is not adjudicated in the criminal courts, but there is little public debate over whether this type of conduct is, in actuality, a criminal concern. He followed up these initial arguments with a book entitled *White Collar Crime* (1949) in which he examined the offending activities of the then 70 largest U.S. corporations in an effort to prove his thesis of widespread and repeated offending in the business world. The offenses he focused on in this study help to provide a framework to his general white-collar crime concept, that is, "crimes committed by the upper classes in connection with their business activities":

1. Restraint of Trade (e.g., antitrust violations)
2. Rebates (i.e., kickbacks)
3. Patents, Trademarks, and Copyrights Violations
4. Misrepresentation in Advertising
5. Unfair Labor Practices
6. Financial Manipulations (e.g., embezzlements, stock fraud, false financial statements)
7. War Crimes (violations of emergency wartime regulations affecting corporations)
8. Miscellaneous (includes Food and Drug Act violations)

Perhaps not surprisingly, Sutherland's treatise on white-collar crime drew a fair amount of criticism, not the least of which was from the business community that was offended by the innuendo of criminal activity within its ranks. Others questioned whether it was fair to bring non-criminal wrongdoing such as regulatory violations under an umbrella crime category since, legally, such conduct is not criminal, per se. Another area of debate centered on whether only those individuals in the upper classes should qualify as white-collar crime offenders or whether the nature of the misconduct should be the primary qualifying criteria. While few today may associate these issues with Edwin Sutherland, they continue to cause controversy within business, academic, and government circles. The business community remains unhappy with any type of government oversight or academic focus on it activities. The issues of whether noncriminal violations may be brought under the white-collar crime umbrella and whether only upper-class individuals qualify as white-collar crime offenders have hindered the development of a generally accepted definition of white-collar crime. However, at least within government ranks, policy and enforcement initiatives have tended to ignore the socioeconomic status of the offender. Rather, typically included under the banner of white-collar crime is a wide range of fraudulent and deceptive conduct that runs the gamut from antitrust violations, corporate malfeasance, and conflicts of interest on one end of the socioeconomic spectrum to credit card, check, and welfare fraud on the other. The FBI's definition of white-collar crime, while not universally

accepted in either government or academic circles, reflects this broad
category of misconduct which spans the socioeconomic spectrum:

White collar crimes are categorized by deceit, concealment, or violation of trust
and are not dependent upon the application or threat of physical force or violence. Individuals and organizations commit these acts to obtain money, property
or services; to avoid payment or loss of money or services; or to secure personal or
business advantage.[1]

   Academics are somewhat split on the issue of whether the characteristics
of the offender or the nature of the misconduct should be determinative
in attaching the white-collar crime label. Many would argue that conduct
rather than class status should be the defining criteria, an argument that
is augmented by the reality of the much wider spectrum of white-collar
offenses addressed by government policy-making and enforcement agencies. This academic trend is reflected in the topical coverage in some of the
white-collar crime literature, as summarized in table 7.1. Note that these
typologies also help to provide a further framework to the otherwise elusive definition of white-collar crime.
   While many of the offenses listed in the typologies presented in table 7.1
could be associated with upper-socioeconomic-class individuals, in today's society (perhaps unlike Sutherland's early- to mid-20th-century
America), opportunities to participate in many of these categories of misconduct also extend far down the socioeconomic spectrum. In fact, some
studies have shown that white-collar crime enforcement actions have
shied away from targeting upper-class individuals.[2] Such findings fuel
the fears of some academics that by removing the upper-socioeconomic-class criterion from any definition of white-collar crime, government
policy and enforcement initiatives will focus on less complicated cases
typically committed by lower socioeconomic individuals and avoid the
often more complex, costly litigation that tends to be encountered when
dealing with upper-class offenders. In any event, with our lack of a universal definition and ongoing debates about social-class connections and
criminal versus noncriminal offending, perhaps Hazel Croall's summa-
tion in her book, *White Collar Crime* (1992), is one we need to remember
when we are struggling to explain what we mean by white-collar crime:
"However defined, white collar crime encompasses an enormous range
of activities . . ."[3]
   As identified at the beginning of this chapter, the types of misconduct
that will be considered here include a broad spectrum of deceptive and
fraudulent practices on the part of museum officials, art dealers, gallery
owners, private collectors, and auction-house executives in the course of
their business activities within the art world, most of which fall into the various typological categories discussed above. Moreover, whether through

Table 7.1
Topics Addressed in Selected White-Collar Crime Literature

Trusted Criminals: White Collar Crime in Contemporary Society (2007) by Friedrichs	*The Criminal Elite: Understanding White Collar Crime* (2006) by Coleman	*Profit Without Honor: White-Collar Crime and the Looting of America* (2007) by Rosoff, Pontell & Tillman	*White Collar Crime* (1992) by Croall
Crimes by corporations	Larceny and embezzlement	Crimes against consumers	Employee theft
Crimes within occupations	Violating intellectual property	Unsafe products	Computer crime
Crimes by governments	Computer crimes	Environmental crimes	Tax fraud
Crimes arising from "state/corporate relationships" and "globalization"	Identity theft	Institutional corruption, e.g., media, religion	Crimes against consumers
Crimes within the financial industry	False advertising	Securities fraud	Employee and public safety violations
Crimes arising from technology (e.g., computers)	Consumer fraud	Corporate fraud	Pollution violations
Corrupt/Illegal business practices	Fraud in professions	Fiduciary fraud (e.g., banking, insurance, pension funds)	Fraud
Illegal individual practices (e.g., insurance fraud, tax fraud)	Financial fraud	Crimes by governments	
	Tax evasion	Public corruption	
	Bribery/Corruption	Medical crime	
	Conflicts of interest	Computer crime	
	Manipulating the marketplace		
	Civil liberties violations		
	Political violence		
	Unsafe products		
	Unsafe working conditions		
	Environmental crimes		

professional status, financial prowess, or some combination thereof, individuals occupying these positions arguably fit Sutherland's profile as members of the upper classes. Thus, a strict application of Sutherland's view of white-collar crime seems to fit in the art world quite nicely. The case study presented in box 7.1 serves further to illustrate this point, as it details a saga of upper-class individuals engaged in questionable, if not improper, transactions in the course of their business activities.

BOX 7.1 WHITE-COLLAR CRIME AT THE GETTY: MARION TRUE ET AL.[4]

Marion True was introduced in chapter 6 as a defendant in a criminal case in Italy for receiving stolen antiquities and conspiring to traffic illegally acquired artifacts along with her codefendant, Robert Hecht, an American antiquities dealer with at best, a checkered reputation and known associate of convicted antiquities trafficker, Giacomo Medici. True was also introduced as the *former* curator of Greek and Roman art at Los Angeles's Getty Museum. Her spiral from the top ranks of her profession to that of criminal defendant is a tragic story in itself, but one that cannot be told in isolation from the freewheeling culture that pervaded her place of employment, the Getty Museum.

Marion True became curator of Greek and Roman art at the Getty in 1986, assuming this position after her predecessor left two years earlier amidst allegations of involvement in a charitable donation tax fraud that lured antiquities to the Getty based on inflated appraisals. She had been working at the Getty since 1982 as a curatorial assistant but did not complete her PhD at Harvard until 1986, the same year she was elevated to curator. With Bachelor's and Master's degrees from New York University to go along with her Harvard PhD, her academic credentials were impeccable although she was exposed to the prevailing attitudes of that era with regard to museum acquisitions; that is, it was impolite to inquire about an object's origins and there was nothing unethical associated with museums' building their collections. Early in her career as Getty's curator, True voiced concern over the antiquities trade being corrupt, that is, objects being removed illegally from countries of origin, but she also feared that if museums did not take possession of important objects that lacked provenance, they would disappear forever into the hands of private collectors. For these situations, she implemented guidelines at the Getty that permitted such acquisitions under the condition that these pieces would be promptly acknowledged and exhibited. The countries of origin would be notified before the acquisition and if they could present evidence of illegal removal, the object would be returned. These guidelines were in contrast to some museum practices whereby objects lacking provenance were acquired without fanfare and then after a period of time in storage, quietly exhibited. Proceeding in this manner eased True's primary concern, that is, an ethical balance between acquiring antiquities that were likely looted and smuggled from their countries of origins versus the value of making important objects available to the public and for scholarly study. For her, concerns of illegality were not paramount; she dismissed enforcement and repatriation efforts by source nations as ineffective. Moreover, she was publicly critical of Greece and Italy for blaming the destruction of archeological sites on the demand created by institutional and individual collectors when well-known sites were poorly maintained and inaccessible to visitors. She also chided these nations for not cataloging and making available for study thousands of recovered objects.

When viewing Marion True retrospectively, it could be argued that she comes across as a person of contradictions, a characterization that can be applied to many white-collar offenders who might represent the *ideal* in terms of family commitment and community standing, but who leave their sense of right and wrong at home when they go to work. As a student at prominent art history graduate programs, she was influenced by "old school" acquisition philosophies and practices, which in the name of preserving *antiquity* were "don't ask, don't tell," in nature. Yet in her professional career, perhaps the social-justice influences so prevalent on college campuses during her student days in the 1960s (and for a while in the 1970s) might have had a voice in her positions on ethical acquisition policies. Nevertheless, Marion True worked for the Getty, a wealthy institution that sought preeminence in Greek and Roman art; and in pursuing this goal as its curator of Greek and Roman art, she aligned herself with the likes of the now infamous antiquities dealers Robert Hecht and Giacomo Medici to assist her. The case against her in Rome was brought in April 2005 and alleged conspiracy to traffic in millions of dollars worth of Greek and Etruscan antiquities through her alliance with her codefendant Hecht and the convicted Medici. Photographs of antiquities recovered incident to the Medici investigation depicted objects that were subsequently acquired by the Getty. Italian authorities also recovered letters True wrote to Medici in which she expressed interest in some of these pieces that eventually made their way into the Getty collection. However, their route to the Getty was circuitous in that acquisition records show Robert Hecht as the source, with no mention of Medici's involvement, keeping in mind that Medici was previously convicted of antiquities trafficking in which he employed laundering methods that shielded him as the source of looted objects. In this sense, True's activities as an alleged coconspirator placed her more within the realm of a white-collar crime offender than that of a looter, fence, or smuggler. The Italian case against her and Hecht was built on a repeated pattern of alleged fraudulent behavior that suggested they participated in a scheme to bring to the Getty antiquities that were removed from Italy contrary to Italian law, thereby providing these objects false legitimacy. Thus, whether viewing True's conduct within the parameters of definitions for white-collar crime offered by Sutherland or the FBI, or within certain categories of white-collar crime listed in table 7.1 (e.g., crimes within occupations or professions or fraud generally), her alleged role in the Italian case arguably places her under the white-collar crime umbrella.

The Italian judicial process is slow and intermittent; and to date, no disposition has been rendered. However, while these proceedings were underway Italian law enforcement provided information to Greek authorities, which resulted in True's indictment in Greece as well for trafficking in three Greek antiquities. Moreover, as reported in chapter 6, True's former employer, the Getty Museum, agreed to the repatriation of 40 objects that were acquired through True's association with Medici and Hecht, as well as the three objects contested in the Greek indictment against True. Throughout her legal imbroglio, True has limited her comments about the charges on advice of legal counsel although she denied any wrongdoing. She has publicly stated that if she had any wrongful intent, she never would have written letters to Medici expressing interest in certain objects. Moreover, she has denied knowing anything about Medici's involvement in antiquities trafficking prior to the onset of the charges leveled against him by Italian authorities. However, these denials need to be balanced against her well-established position that it is better for unprovenanced objects to be in the hands of museums for study and public display than to disappear forever in the hands of private collectors, and her reported dismissive attitude toward enforcement efforts.

In any event, regardless of the outcome of the case against True in Italy, it was her conduct in another scenario related to her professional role that resulted in her ouster from the Getty, that is, engaging in conflicts of interest, a form of misconduct specifically identified as white-collar crime in table 7.1. Her position as curator of Greek and Roman art at the Getty enabled her to travel abroad to seek out new acquisitions and to establish relationships with those who could facilitate such acquisitions, that is, dealers, other institutions and/or governments; hence, association with Robert Hecht and Giacomo Medici. These travels enabled her to visit the Greek isles and in 1995, she became particularly enamored with a vacation home on Paros. However, she needed financing in the amount of $360,000 to purchase the property and encountered difficulty in attempts to borrow money for this transaction. Greek banks did not want to lend to a foreigner and American banks did not want to finance a property located offshore. She discussed her dilemma with the Greek antiquities dealer, Christos Michaelides, and his British companion Robin Symes, also an antiquities dealer, notwithstanding their history of business transactions with the Getty involving the sale of objects that totaled $30 million. True was directly involved in at least one of these transactions, a 1988 purchase that totaled $18–$20 million. Michaelides directed her to a Greek lawyer who arranged loans for shipping companies and he quickly secured a four-year balloon loan at 18 percent interest so that she could move forward with her home purchase. Whether using her professional connections to locate financing for a personal residence constituted a conflict of interest for True is perhaps debatable to some and de minimis to others. On the one hand, after being unsuccessful in securing financing through traditional sources, True reached out to those she was involved with in often high-value business transactions for other funding connections. Would the fact that she secured financing through Michaelides's assistance for a personal purchase improperly influence her decision making as a representative of the Getty on future antiquities transactions with him and/ or Symes? Or at the very least, would True's mix of personal/professional business relationships create an appearance of impropriety? Given her intellect and educational level attainments, why did she not foresee that taking this path might be viewed as a conflict of interest and seek counsel about it, through her employer or privately? On the other hand, a four-year balloon loan at 18 percent hardly seemed liked a "sweetheart" arrangement in 1995 (or in most other years) for True. However, it did enable her to make the purchase of her home, a transaction that might not have occurred without

Michaelides's intervention. And to be clear, some sources have indicated that the Greek lawyer she was sent to was, in fact, a Michaelides family attorney and the loan she received was actually funded by Christos Michaelides under a subterfuge established by the attorney. Even if this information is true, however, there is no evidence that Marion True was aware of it; and Christos Michaelides is now deceased.

Perhaps if the story of Marion True purchasing a home on Paros ended at this point, so too would the debate on whether her financing arrangements constituted a conflict of interest; but it did not end here. True soon found the 18 percent interest rate burdensome and in 1996, she paid off the Greek loan with private, *unsecured* financing she obtained at 8.25 percent through Lawrence and Barbara Fleischman. The Fleischmans were wealthy art collectors who had been negotiating with True (on behalf of the Getty) over the purchase of their 300-piece collection of Greek, Roman, and Etruscan artifacts. In the spring of 1996, an agreement was reached between the Fleischmans and the Getty (True, herself, was not a final decision maker in this transaction) whereby the Getty purchased 32 objects from the collection for $20 million, and the Fleischmans donated the remainder of the collection to the museum with the understanding they would take a $40 million charitable-donation deduction on their income taxes. The personal loan True received from the Fleischmans was finalized three days after the Getty approved the $20 million purchase from the Fleischmans and the associated donation arrangements. True never reported entering into this relationship with the Fleischmans to her employer, perhaps because the Getty's ethics policy prohibited employees from borrowing money from individuals or entities with whom the museum does business. Then four years later, in 2000, Barbara Fleischman was appointed to the Board of Trustees of the Getty and she never reported loaning any money to True on financial disclosure statements she was required to file in order to hold this position. Nevertheless, it took until 2005, shortly following True's indictment in Italy, for information about the loan arrangement with the Fleischmans to surface, a revelation that led to her resignation as curator of Greek and Roman art at the Getty because of the apparent conflict of interest involved in that arrangement.

As the events surrounding Marion True drew unwanted, negative attention to the Getty, questions began to arise about the overall management of this wealthy, high-profile institution. Barbara Fleischman submitted her resignation from the Getty's Board of Trustees without explanation, within months following True's departure. There was also concern over the proprieties of certain expenditures approved by the then museum director, Barry Munitz. As museum director, Munitz was not only responsible to his institution for prudent financial management, but as the director of a nonprofit organization under California law, he was also barred from using tax-exempt charitable assets for personal use. Among the questionable expenditures was the payment of legal fees for Barbara Fleischman, who was questioned by Italian prosecutors prior to the True indictment about the suspicious origins of her private antiquities collection that she eventually sold and donated to the Getty. He also approved a $300,000 payment to a retired chairman of the Getty Museum Board of Trustees as compensation to write a coffee-table style book months after this person, while in the position as chairman, intervened on Munitz's behalf to award him a five-year contract as director; and four other departing trustees each received gifts valued at $20,000 on earlier occasions. Another questionable transaction involved his approval of the sale of a piece of property owned by the museum to a friend and business associate for $700,000 under its appraised value. And perhaps not surprisingly, Mr. Munitz traveled regularly and lavishly at the museum's expense. In 2005, both the Board of Trustees and the California Attorney General's Office launched investigations that examined Munitz's activities at the Getty and, by February 2006, Munitz resigned his position. He left without a contractually negotiated severance package of $2 million. Rather, he paid the Getty $250,000 to settle any outstanding balance he might owe. As for the attorney general's investigation, the outcome was all too "Sutherland-esque"; that is, in October 2006, he was cleared of any criminal wrongdoing, but his expenditures for first-class travel and luxury dining and lodging were found to be an improper use of charitable funds, thus perhaps explaining the $250,000 payment he made on his way out the door eight months earlier.

WHITE-COLLAR CRIME IN THE ART WORLD: HOW BIG OF A PROBLEM?

The saga of Marion True and her colleagues at the Getty Museum was a high-profile example of white-collar crime in the art world, misconduct that involved pervasive conflicts of interest and an alleged fraudulent conspiracy in the acquisition of art objects. Is this case an anomaly? And if not, how much white-collar crime victimizes the art world and in what forms does it present itself?

In chapter 2, we reviewed U.S. and international statistics for the crimes of larceny/theft, burglary, and robbery. These statistics did not identify cases in which art was stolen through these three means of theft; rather, they reflected frequencies, loss data, and offender characteristics attributable to these crimes generally. Absent comprehensive data on art theft, these general crime statistics allowed some rough comparisons with the limited, consolidated information we have on larcenies, burglaries, and robberies in which art was stolen. For instance, while in the United States and elsewhere in the world larceny/theft is the most frequently occurring form of theft, the consensus is that most art theft is attributed to burglary.

With regard to evaluating frequencies and losses attributable to white-collar crime, however, we do not have any comprehensive data available generally, let alone data on such victimization in the art world. In the United States, the major nationwide crime data-gathering program, the *Uniform Crime Report (UCR)*, focuses primary attention on crimes including larceny, burglary, robbery, assault, rape, murder, arson, and auto theft. On a secondary level, it collects data on other types of crime occurrence but only three categories would fall under the white-collar crime umbrella: fraud, embezzlement, and forgery/counterfeiting. The proposed/still emerging successor to the *UCR*, the *National Incident-Based Reporting System (NIBRS)*, expands data collection on white-collar crime to some extent but still will not capture the full scope of this type of offending. Moreover, as Sutherland observed 70 years ago, much white-collar offending is adjudicated in noncriminal agency/regulatory forums and the outcomes of these adjudications are not reflected in any consolidated database. Thus, only by accessing each of the myriad agencies of the federal government involved in white-collar crime enforcement (both criminal agencies and regulatory agencies) could a comprehensive picture be developed of the amount of white-collar offending and the federal government's responses to it. For the ambitious soul who attempts such a project, he/she will likely find a lack of continuity in the types of data maintained from one agency to another that will hinder the development of the elusive "big picture" of white-collar crime. And that "big picture" of white-collar crime would not be complete without taking into consideration actions by state-level agencies, an undertaking whose difficulty might be likened to multiplying the problems encountered in developing such a data set at the federal level by 50.

Thus, without a universally agreed-upon definition for white-collar crime nor a comprehensive data set on this type of offending, it should not be surprising that we gauge how much white-collar crime there is and how much it costs us in terms of estimates, a scenario that harks back to how we try to understand the amount of art crime. One attempt to arrive at an estimated annual loss attributable to white-collar crime in the United States was made by the Senate Judiciary Committee in 1986, a figure the committee calculated to be $250 billion.[5] White-collar crime scholar David Friedrichs once estimated white-collar crime losses to be 10 times greater than losses from traditional crimes on a yearly basis.[6] Based on 2007 data from the *Sourcebook of Criminal Justice Statistics* for dollar losses arising from robberies, burglaries, larcenies, and motor vehicle theft (based on an average loss figure per incident), the total losses attributable to these crimes was a little over $13 billion.[7] Thus, based on Friedrichs's formula the white-collar crime loss estimate for 2007 would be about $130 billion. Surely, the 1986 estimate from the Senate Judiciary Committee is by now dated and others might put forth loss estimates that differ from those of Friedrichs both in terms of methodology and result. However, with regard to this elusive figure there tends to be consensus in one important respect: losses caused by white-collar crime dwarf those resulting from traditional criminal activity.

The point to this discussion is that without any type of comprehensive white-collar crime data, we know even less about the scope of this form of victimization in the art world than we do when considering other forms of criminal victimization such as those arising from the various manifestations of art theft. Added to this uncertainty is that while dollar losses arising from white- collar crime are believed to exceed those associated with crimes such as larceny, burglary, and robbery, that "rule of thumb" might not be as applicable to the unique circumstances of the art world. Here, on the one hand, the values of some pieces of stolen art are quite substantial while, on the other hand, as evidenced in the case study in box 7.1, it can be difficult to place a dollar loss value on some white-collar offending. Clearly, conflict of interest policies, laws, and regulations are developed to prohibit individuals from using their professional positions to realize personal gain at the expense of and/or to the detriment of their employer. While Marion True's ouster from her position arose from a conflict of interest violation, it is unclear what dollar loss, if any, can be attached to her misconduct. In fact, notwithstanding the huge losses associated with white-collar crime generally, the violation and/or loss of trust between offender and victim is often viewed as part of the injury or harm arising from this form of misconduct, a concept that readily applies when evaluating losses suffered by the Getty vis-à-vis Marion True.

Thus, while perhaps difficult to quantify, anecdotal evidence suggests that white-collar crime must be considered if the full scope of misconduct in the art world is to be explored. In fact, failing to do so could reignite criticisms levied long ago by Sutherland that the focus on criminal offending is too oriented toward conventional crimes, which are usually associated with the lower socioeconomic groups while ignoring offenses committed in society's upper echelons. Clearly, the case study in box 7.1 that details alleged fraudulent conduct in the acquisition of artworks, conflicts of interest, and financial improprieties by art professionals and museum executives shifts our focus on misconduct in the art world away from the thieves, fences, smugglers and forgers that have occupied much of our attention so far. Moreover, for the first time in our discussion of crime in the art world, females (as opposed to males) rose to prominence as offenders, an ascendancy that will also be apparent in other cases discussed below.

Earlier, in chapter 6, we already discussed another form of white-collar crime in the art world, that is, tax fraud related to donations of objects to museums, a subject that will be further addressed in chapter 9. The nature of the art gallery/art dealer business has also provided fertile ground for white-collar offending. Consider for instance, some of the services that art dealers/gallery owners can offer: they can take artworks on consignment from collectors who wish to sell certain pieces they currently own or sell artists' works on consignment. In another variation, dealers/gallery owners have been known to offer art-investment opportunities using art as an investment commodity; that is, investors place money with a dealer/gallery owner under the representation he/she will buy artworks that will then be sold at a profit in which the investors will share. Given that the art world works on the basis of secrecy and handshakes involving goods that defy precise evaluation, tales of the lack of scruples and integrity among some gallery owners and art dealers should not be surprising.

A high-profile case that typifies the schemes dealers can orchestrate involved Lawrence Salander, the chief executive officer of Salander-O'Reilly Galleries in New York City. In March 2009, Salander was indicted on charges that he stole $88 million from collectors and artists who consigned artworks to him for sale. He had a wealthy clientele that included highly successful Wall Street financiers who invested millions with him for the purchase of artworks that he represented he would then sell at a profit, with the investors sharing in those proceeds. A month later, his gallery director pled guilty to a lesser charge of falsifying business records, circumstances that would suggest that he cooperated with investigators against his former boss. Salander and his gallery had long been on the New York City art scene and both he, personally, and his gallery were well regarded. However, by 2004 signs of financial troubles began to evolve, that is, paying bills and consignors for sales proceeds. Lawsuits began to be filed, including one by tennis great John McEnroe over a $325,000 payout he was promised after investing $162,500 with Salander. To avoid the onslaught of lawsuits, he filed for bankruptcy in 2007. Two more years passed until criminal charges were filed in what some liken to a giant Ponzi scheme; that is, he paid off early investors and consignors with monies he collected from later customers rather than from sales and investment proceeds; and as is inevitable in such schemes, the demand for payouts began to exceed his incoming cash flow.[8]

While the Salander case represents high-profile gallery/dealer malfeasance in terms of dollar loss, wealthy victims, and perhaps complexity, other cases of this genre, but on a lesser scale, have been reported from one end of the United States to the other. In October 2007, a Seattle gallery owner was sentenced to 40 months in prison for stealing $435,000 from victims who entrusted him with painting consignments. The victims received neither proceeds from the sales of their paintings nor their return. In May 2006, a Milwaukee gallery owner was sentenced to 14 months in prison for defrauding customers of $634,750 by not remitting any monies from the sales he made of their artworks. In a civil trial in Chicago, a judge ruled that a prominent art gallery sold more than $1 million in paintings on consignment but largely failed to pay consignors any proceeds.[9]

A further variation of gallery/dealer fraud is illustrated in another New York City case, and again, one involving high-profile victims. The late William Ziff, who headed the Ziff-Davis publishing house, and his wife paid out $63 million between 1989 and 1999 to New York antiquities dealers Edward and Samuel Merrin, father and son, for the purchase of hundreds of ancient objects including those of Syrian and pre-Columbian origins. The scheme involved the Merrins inflating the prices of the objects they purchased on the Ziffs' behalf, which in turn, inflated the commission to which they were entitled for acquiring the objects. The Merrins were successfully prosecuted although they suffered little consequences. In 2007, Edward Merrin was sentenced to probation for one year, eight months, which consisted of home confinement. He was fined $3,000 and ordered to make restitution to the Ziffs in the amount of $44,455, a figure which reflected the loss suffered on only 11 fraudulent transactions that he was specifically charged with. Son Samuel Merrin entered into a deferred prosecution agreement with the government, a program for first-time offenders that allows for the dismissal of charges once the terms of a probationary period are completed.[10]

The buying and selling of art is also accomplished through the auction process, a forum that, at times, has also been manipulated to the disadvantage of its customers. In its simplest form, auction house manipulation can resemble the consignment schemes operated by gallery owners and art dealers; that is, individuals place art objects for sale at auction with an auction house, but the auction house fails to remit the proceeds from any auction sale that takes place. A Houston couple operated such a scheme from at least 2003 to 2006 when they filed for bankruptcy, but not before defrauding hundreds of victims of $3.5 million. They were eventually convicted.[11]

Just as white-collar crime has been found at the most prominent levels of the museum community (e.g., Los Angeles's Getty Museum), so too has it pervaded the elites of the art-auction industry. Likewise, the complexities of the schemes involved in these settings go beyond the mere failure to remit sales proceeds. Our final case study in this chapter (box 7.2) provides the details.

BOX 7.2 WHITE-COLLAR CRIME AT THE TOP OF THE ART-AUCTION INDUSTRY: SOTHEBY'S AND CHRISTIE'S[12]

While some variations exist in the white-collar crime typologies that are generated within government and academic circles, among the consensus selections is antitrust violations. After the Civil War, as America began the transition from an agrarian to an industrial society, it became apparent that some of the growing industries were being controlled by a few wealthy, influential individuals/corporate entities. Such control negated the advantages of the free market to consumers in that prices were being set collectively by those who controlled these industries and it tended to deny newcomers a level playing field in terms of competing for market share. While America from its outset was committed to a capitalist economy, its traditions have also valued the notion of providing opportunities to prosper to those willing to work hard and take risks. In 1890, Congress passed legislation to combat the control and manipulation of any given market in the form of the Sherman Antitrust Act. Among the practices outlawed were those in which companies colluded to set prices in a given market and conspired to agree which company would win a competitive bid contract. Especially within the context of this case study, it is important to recognize that the Sherman Antitrust Act carries both civil and criminal penalties, meaning that, potentially, offenders can be imprisoned. Criminalizing antitrust violations in a free market, capitalist nation has not been without controversy and the criminal enforcement provisions of the Sherman Antitrust Act have been somewhat selectively applied, decisions that usually reflect the prevailing political climate. Other industrialized, free market nations have also found the need to limit consolidation of market control in a given industry, but it is rare to find this type of misconduct labeled as criminal as it is in the United States. Great Britain falls into the camp where antitrust offending is a civil violation.

A common feature that does tend to be shared across the range of nations that proscribe antitrust activity is that the offenders are typically upper-socioeconomic-class corporate executives, thus placing this type of misconduct clearly within Sutherland's concept of white-collar crime (in fact, it was one of the offenses that formed the basis for Sutherland's study of the offending activities of America's 70 largest corporations; see above, *White Collar Crime*, 1949).

As suggested above, criminal prosecutions of antitrust violations in the United States are infrequent, but they do occur; and importantly for our concerns, a case of this type targeted the business activities at the world's best-known art-auction houses, Sotheby's and Christie's, beginning in the 1990s and continuing into 2002. One does not have to be an artist, art professional/executive, or art aficionado to be familiar with these names as arguably the world's leaders in this industry. As discussed in chapter 1, the auction process is a well-established forum for selling and buying works of art because their unique qualities defy the application of conventional pricing protocols. Although minimum prices for artworks at auction are established through appraisals, the auction process arrives at the market prices through a competitive bidding process among interested buyers. Some of the highest prices paid for works of art have been achieved through the auction process; and the two auction houses most frequently associated with record sales, both in terms of volume and prices, have been Sotheby's and Christie's. Both firms operate on a worldwide basis, although Sotheby's is headquartered in the United States while Christie's is in Great Britain—a crucial geographic difference when engaging in a scheme to control pricing in the art-auction industry. Christopher Mason provides a primary source for this story in his book, *The Art of the Steal: Inside the Sotheby's-Christie's Auction House Scandal* (2004).

How did the world's two leading art-auction houses find themselves in the crosshairs of a criminal antitrust investigation by the U.S. Department of Justice? First, it should be pointed out that the chairmen at both Sotheby's and Christie's were not art professionals by education/training, but corporate executives for whom art was an avocation. Sotheby's chair was Alfred Taubman, a retail mall developer by trade; while Anthony Tennant, who formerly headed Guinness Breweries, was Christie's chair for most of the period that this investigation focused on. The orientation and approaches employed by both men were that they were running businesses and profit was the bottom line indicator of success. Taubman was particularly motivated to establish Sotheby's as the world's preeminent art-auction house and he sought to expand Sotheby's customer base by retailing art to the tens of thousands of newly enriched stock investors from the soaring markets of the late 1980s and early 1990s. Under his leadership, Sotheby's also extended credit services to its buyers. Christie's began to find it difficult to compete against Sotheby's aggressive marketing practices. In September 1992, Tennant approached Taubman while both were attending a social event in London and asked for a meeting. This overture resulted first in a meeting in New York City on April 1, 1993, and then another in London on April 30, 1993. At the first meeting Taubman warned Tennant that he would not discuss pricing as such discussions would violate U.S. antitrust laws, but by the second meeting Tennant told Taubman that the auction business must become more profitable and that it was time to raise prices, to which Taubman replied that Christie's would have to go first in this direction because Sotheby's was the first to raise the buyer's premium (a fee that a buyer at an art auction pays to the auction house that is in addition to the cost of the artwork).

The only other parties who were privy to these initial meetings and who had ongoing involvement in the cooperation between the two auction giants were the respective CEOs, Dede Brooks of Sotheby's and Christopher Davidge of Christie's. By November 1993, the two CEOs had met in London to discuss a cooperative pricing arrangement. Davidge claimed that they both knew it was unlawful to have this meeting, and he portrayed Brooks as being particularly eager in coming to an agreement on this issue. Brooks was a banker by profession and shared Taubman's vision that Sotheby's must be operated in an aggressive businesslike manner. They agreed to cease providing worldwide market share figures and agreed to a sliding scale for guarantees on artwork consigned for auction; that is, the greater the sales risk at the price guaranteed to a consignor, the greater the percentage on any overage earned by the auction house. They also agreed to stop providing interest-free advances to buyers and advances to consignors. They further agreed not to meet in public in order not to raise any suspicions about their activities. In fact, one of their later meetings took place in the backseat of an automobile at New York's Kennedy airport. Subsequent meetings in the summer of 1994 and the winter of 1995 resulted in an agreement that both firms would offer only nonegotiable sales commissions. Then in the summer of 1995 Brooks met with Davidge in London to exchange lists of customers that each had preexisting sales contracts with, which would not be affected by the new pricing arrangements they had agreed upon.

In February 1996, Brooks certified Sotheby's 1995 financial statement in which it declared there were no violations of law or regulations to report, a year that saw Sotheby's profits increase by 25 percent over 1994. However, information about the collusive activities between Sotheby's and Christie's, described as coming from "disgruntled sources," was provided to the U.S. Department of Justice (DOJ) and based on this information, an antitrust investigation was launched. Successful prosecutions in white-collar crime cases are often dependent upon the cooperation of insiders, that is, participants in the scheme who are viewed as being more valuable as cooperating witnesses than as criminal defendants. These types of decisions are often the subject of debate and controversy because they sometimes afford fully culpable individuals immunity from prosecution or at least much more lenient treatment. In this case, an assessment of this type was made early on by the government and while some might question it, it made sense from a prosecutorial perspective.

When Christie's became aware of the investigation, it retained legal counsel who eventually advised the firm to apply for amnesty that was available under DOJ guidelines. The government had received via subpoena a volume of records from Christie's, and many of the documents required interpretation and deciphering, particularly notes authored by Christopher Davidge. The scenario that evolved was that if the government was to pursue this investigation, it needed to understand these records, and Christopher Davidge could provide the necessary insight. He was also a British citizen who was not subject to criminal penalties in Great Britain for antitrust activity, nor could he be compelled to return to America to stand trial for any charges brought here. Thus, for the government there was much to gain and little to lose by granting him immunity even though he and Chairman Anthony Tennant played primary roles in the scheme. The government needed Christie's assistance, however, to convince him to come to America and cooperate and testify, if necessary, in the case. As Christie's was seeking acceptance into the amnesty program, it seized the opportunity to ingratiate itself with DOJ by producing Davidge.

Once amnesty was granted and Davidge began cooperating, the investigation moved ahead against the other parties involved in the collusive arrangements, Anthony Tennant of Christie's and Alfred Taubman and Dede Brooks of Sotheby's. Tennant enjoyed the same protection as Davidge in that he was a British citizen and could not be compelled to face antitrust charges in the United States. However, granting him immunity was not an attractive option for two reasons. First, as much of the documentary evidence turned over by Christie's was generated/authored by Davidge, Tennant was not as valuable in providing the necessary interpretation. Second, as the evidence suggested the chairmen of both Sotheby's and Christie's were responsible for their respective firms unlawfully working together, charging Taubman and not Tennant would provide an appearance of unequal treatment by the prosecutors. Thus, prosecutors proceeded to put together a case in which both would be charged, but knowing it was unlikely Tennant would ever appear in a U.S. court to be tried on them.

For his part, Taubman staunchly maintained his innocence throughout the investigation, but not so with Dede Brooks. White-collar crime investigations place tremendous pressure on those being targeted. The investigations can be prolonged and their existence a matter of public knowledge, yet exactly what the outcome will be and when is often uncertain. Many white-collar offenders find themselves in an embarrassing and uncomfortable position being viewed as a criminal and possibly facing the consequences of a conviction, for example, imprisonment. Thus, it is not uncommon for those in this situation to seek leniency in return for their cooperation. When Brooks outlined her involvement to her attorney, he advised her to take this path in order to avoid jail time. While not without remorse, she did so, and obligated herself to plead guilty and to testify against Taubman in the event of a trial. She entered a guilty plea on October 5, 2000, to one count of conspiracy to violate antitrust laws, and on the same day, Sotheby's entered a corporate guilty plea to antitrust violations and was fined $45 million.

On May 2, 2001, a federal grand jury in New York City returned an antitrust indictment charging both Taubman and Tennant. Taubman continued to maintain his innocence and elected to go to trial, while Tennant chose not to participate by remaining in England. The trial began in New York on November 8, 2001, and both Davidge and Brooks testified against Taubman. On December 4, 2001, the jury returned a guilty verdict against him. In April 2002, Taubman was sentenced to one year in prison and fined $7.5 million. About one week later, Brooks was sentenced to three years probation, with the first six months in home confinement; 1,000 hours of community service; and a fine of $350,000.

Should we be surprised to find the type of wrongdoing more frequently associated with the business world in the art world? Some research on antitrust offending suggests not. For instance, highly regarded criminologist Gilbert Geis produced one of the classic pieces of antitrust research in 1970 when he studied the prosecution of Westinghouse and General Electric for their collusive activity in attempts to share government contracts for electrical equipment. In this case, 45 executives from both firms were prosecuted. His analysis of this case resulted in an observation that can be applied to the Sotheby's-Christie's antitrust conspiracy: criminal behavior in these types of cases can be attributed to corporate pressure and not avarice or the lack of law-abiding character on the part of the participants. The Sotheby's-Christie's antitrust conspiracy was a tale of both firms wanting to prosper; and their otherwise law-abiding executives conspired unlawfully in this cooperative direction. A more recent study of antitrust offending that appeared in the *Journal of Quantitative Criminology* in 1997 by Simpson and Koper identified common characteristics associated with this type offending that can be applied to the Sotheby's-Christie's case: (1) the financial success of the organizations involved was dependent on only one market (neither Sotheby's nor Christie's was diversified into other businesses or markets; they competed against each other only in the art-auction market) and (2) most antitrust offending arose in organizations where the leadership was oriented toward administration or finance (both Taubman and Tennant were corporate executives from outside the art world while Brooks was a banker by trade). Thus, when the art world engages in high-stakes business, it must expect at times to suffer the ills of corporate crime.

CHAPTER 8

Vandalism and Malicious Destruction

Our tour of the crimes of the art world has covered a lot of ground thus far, both literally and figuratively. As represented at the outset of this volume, art crime is worldwide in scope and as you look back, our discussions and examples have been drawn from nearly every quarter of the globe. We have also covered a lot of ground in terms of the varieties of crimes that impact the art world. Most recently, we examined white-collar offending among the art world's elite, art professionals/executives, and wealthy collectors. Other varieties of crime in the art world are perhaps more well-known, for example, art theft and art forgery; and the most common motivation behind these acts, that is, financial gain, while not condoned, is at least widely understood. Moreover, the theft and trafficking of cultural-heritage objects has taken on a greater profile in recent years, and monetary motivations are clearly evident at some levels of this type of activity as well. As we have seen, however, as these objects reach the end-user, that is, private collectors and museums, crass monetary motivations are often muted by arguments that question whether any one nation has sole rights to early human history, as well as those that cite the need for proper preservation, academic research, and public education. Ironically, some collectors and institutions that have championed such arguments have done so to the reckless extreme of committing white-collar crimes along the way. In doing so, they have sometimes brought into question whether they are really putting forth philosophical values to thinly veil attempts at self-aggrandizement, whether financial or professional in nature. We have also examined how the art world has been impacted by war and civil/religious unrest. While personal financial motivations have been apparent in some notable instances, political/military leaders have historically stolen the art of the vanquished to augment their popularity among their own constituents. Not only has bringing home works of art from conquered lands provided visible evidence of victory, but also these works are viewed as the "spoils of war" and become valuable national assets.

As we have seen, war and civil/religious unrest have also resulted in the destruction of artwork because of either collateral damage or deliberate attempts to obliterate vestiges of a national or social group culture. In addition, art has been damaged and destroyed by looters of archeological sites. Unfortunately, however, art has also been desecrated outside of war and civil/religious unrest environments. Although often bewildering to comprehend, art has been victimized by the malicious hands of vandals, a term derived from one of the Germanic barbarian tribes that wreaked havoc throughout the Roman Empire and elsewhere in Europe in the fourth and fifth centuries, and which *Merriam-Webster's Collegiate Dictionary* (11th ed.) very aptly defines as "those who willfully or ignorantly destroy, damage or deface property belonging to another, or to the public." It is to this type of disturbing conduct that we now turn our attention, as it has affected the art world. Specifically, we will consider deliberate acts that result in physical harm to works of art where the motivations are less profound (if understood at all) than those associated with cultural-heritage looting, war, and civil/religious unrest, and more clearly associated with conventional criminal conduct, that is, destructive/malicious behavior (sometimes in the name of personal protest or social statement) and ad hoc financial gain.

However, just as we have been unable to quantify conventional crimes against art such as larceny, theft, and robbery in terms of frequencies and monetary losses, here too we lack any specific database that captures the number of such incidents, the number of objects affected, and the value of the art that is lost through such acts. For instance, the *Uniform Crime Report* does track vandalism of all varieties but as a Part II (or more minor) offense, only arrest data is captured, thus limiting opportunities to identify art-related incidents. While the still-evolving *National Incident Based Reporting System* (NIBRS) upgrades vandalism into its most serious crime category and will collect more information about vandalism incidents (that might permit an art connection), it is not an art-specific database; and of course, it tracks U.S. incidents only.

A limited attempt to quantify the frequency of art vandalism was undertaken by researchers in Great Britain in the early 1990s through a questionnaire sent to 92 museums and art galleries in England, Scotland, and Wales. Sixty responses were received. Thirty-seven respondents reported some vandalism incidents over a 10-year period while 18 reported none. The remaining five declined to provide any information. Thus, of those who responded just over one-half experienced vandalism incidents over the preceding 10-year period. Only nine of those respondents who reported incidents of vandalism described the events as major in nature, that is, slashing, stabbing, shooting of canvases, arson, or smashing sculptures or vases. Four of these respondents suffered 16 major vandalism incidents. However, the majority of vandalism incidents reported were characterized as minor in nature, that is, acts of scratching and scribbling with pencils, pens, and so forth. The respondents reported that major acts of vandalism tended to be public events aimed at generating publicity and the vandals did little to avoid apprehension. The minor incidents tended to be surreptitious and anonymous and consequently most of these offenders were not apprehended. Of the 15 minor offenders that were caught, few faced formal charges and prosecution, either because the institution wished to avoid publicity or out of compassion for the vandal. Respondents that suffered major acts of vandalism tended to characterize these acts as a consequence of mental disturbance and expressions of a grudge or envy (e.g., hatred of perceived excellence by nonachievers) and they noted that in at least half of these cases, the apprehended vandals received court-ordered mental-health treatment. While not diminishing the costs associated with the minor incidents, the respondents found these incidents most often connected to the daring behaviors of children and adolescents, and drunkenness was seldom a factor.[1]

While the British study provides us a much-needed empirical view of art vandalism, we still don't even have the estimates of frequency and losses that are proffered for art thefts. As we have already seen, assessing the damage and destruction to art objects through cultural-heritage looting, wars, and civil/religious unrest also defies precise evaluation. Thus, seeking an empirical comparison of the amount of damage and destruction to art through acts of vandalism versus the amount caused by cultural-heritage looting, war, and civil unrest is problematic. Anecdotally, however, the widespread and relentless destruction of art through wars, civil/religious unrest, and looting at archeological sites would seem clearly to surpass the losses attributable to the more conventional crimes of vandalism, at least in terms of number of objects damaged and monetary value. Nevertheless, garden-variety vandalism and malicious destruction to art is disturbing in its own right due to its often senseless nature and/or callous disregard for aesthetic value. One need only peruse the vandalism incidents to paintings by well-known artists as reported in table 8.1 to appreciate the serious impact this form of crime has had on the art world.

Our further review of art vandalism and malicious destruction will focus on the categories of this form of art crime that were outlined earlier in an attempt to differentiate it from damage that was caused by wars and civil/political/religious unrest: destructive/malicious behavior, personal protests or social statements, and ad hoc financial gain.

Table 8.1
Vandalism to Paintings by Well-Known Artists: Selected Incidents in Recent History*

Artist	Painting/Year	Place of Vandalism	Year of Vandalism
Cranach, Lucas the Elder	*Martin Luther*, 1529	Hanover, Germany	1977
da Vinci, Leonardo	*The Virgin and Child with St. Anne*, 1510	National Gallery, London, England	1962
da Vinci, Leonardo	*St John*, 1513–1516	National Gallery, London, England	1987
da Vinci, Leonardo	*Mona Lisa*, 1503–1505	Louvre, Paris, France	1956
Dürer, Albrecht	*Paumgartner Alta Triptych*, 1503	Alte Pinakothek, Munich, Germany	1988
Dürer, Albrecht	*Lamentation of Christ*, 1500–1503	Alte Pinakothek, Munich, Germany	1988
Dürer, Albrecht	*The Seven Sorrows of the Virgin: Mother of Sorrows*, 1496	Alte Pinakothek, Munich, Germany	1988
Klee, Paul	*Golden Fish*, 1925	Hamburg, Germany	1977
Michelangelo	*Pieta*, 1499	St. Peter's, Rome, Italy	1972
Michelangelo	*David*, 1501–1504	Piazza della Signoria, Florence, Italy	1991
Picasso, Pablo	*Guernica*, 1937	Museum of Modern Art, New York, United States	1974
Poussin, Nicolas	*Adoration of the Golden Calf*, 1633–1634	National Gallery, London, England	1978
Raphael	*The Marriage of the Virgin*, 1504	Brera, Milan, Italy	1958
Rembrandt	*The Nightwatch*, 1642	Rijksmuseum, Amsterdam, Netherlands	1911, 1975
Rembrandt	*Jacob Blessing Ephraim and Menasseh*, 1656	Gemaldegalerie, Kassel, Germany	1977
Rembrandt	*Self–Portrait*, 1634	Gemaldegelarie, Kassel, Germany	1977
Rembrandt	*Danae*, 1636	The Hermitage, St. Petersburg, Russia	1985
Rubens, Peter Paul	*Fall of the Damned*, 1620–1621	Alte Pinakothek, Munich, Germany	1959

(continued)

Table 8.1
(continued)

Artist	Painting/Year	Place of Vandalism	Year of Vandalism
Rubens, Peter Paul	*Virgin with the Innocents*, 17th century	Louvre, Paris, France	1968
Rubens, Peter Paul	*Adoration of the Magi*, 1624–1626	King's College, Cambridge, England	1974
Rubens, Peter Paul	*Archduke Albert*, 1615	Kunstakademie, Dusseldorf, Germany	1977
van Gogh, Vincent	*Berceuse*, 1889	Stedelijk Museum, Amsterdam, Netherlands	1977
van Gogh, Vincent	*Self–Portrait in Grey Hat*, 1887	Van Gogh Museum, Amsterdam, Netherlands	1977
Velázquez, Diego	*The Toilet of Venus*, 1647–1651	National Gallery, London, England	1914

* Incidents identified in Cordess, C. and Turcan, M. "Art Vandalism," *British Journal of Criminology* 33, no. 1 (1993): 95–102; by permission of Oxford University Press.

DESTRUCTIVE/MALICIOUS BEHAVIOR

For our purposes here, we will define destructive/malicious behavior as a category of vandalism in which art is maliciously and intentionally damaged for reasons not connected with any type of financial gain or making a philosophical/political statement. The motivations for such acts are not always apparent or explainable although one theory that will be introduced suggests that destroying art can be a pleasurable experience to some. Mental illness has also been blamed for this type of vandalism. Let's consider some examples and note these incidents have occurred in a variety of settings including museums, art exhibition halls, and archeological sites.

British Man Goes on Rampage at Art Exhibition

A 51-year-old man, so drunk he told police he could not remember what he did, damaged 300 paintings at an art exhibition in England in October 2006. He damaged the paintings while the exhibition hall was closed for the weekend, but a surveillance camera did record the incident that led to his apprehension. The man pled guilty to causing the damage and was placed on 12 months supervised probation and ordered to attend an alcohol rehabilitation course. His attorney also attributed the man's conduct to psychiatric problems.[2]

Vandalism at the Rijksmuseum, Amsterdam

The flagship museum in the Netherlands has suffered a series of attacks to paintings on display. In June 2006, a 69-year-old man threw an acid substance on a painting entitled *Celebration of the Peace of Munster,* a work dated 1648 by the Dutch artist Bartholomeus van der Helst. The man was immediately detained by museum security officials and only the varnish on the painting was damaged. Investigation determined that the vandal apparently had been planning the attack days in advance since he was previously observed in the area where it was on display; moreover, this individual was known to be responsible for similar attacks on Old Master paintings throughout Europe that have caused over $150 million in damage.

Previous incidents at the Rijksmuseum included an attack on another Van der Helst painting, a 1652 portrait of Princess Maria Henriette Stuart. A 43-year-old male caused a tear in the painting because he wanted to draw attention to his "personal difficulties." A man suffering from psychiatric problems but who was a self-proclaimed art lover was responsible for spraying sulfuric acid on a Rembrandt painting entitled *Nightwatch.* Fortunately, only the varnish was damaged due to quick response from museum security.[3]

Another "Art Lover"—This Time in France

In July 2007, a 30-year-old French woman was arrested for planting a kiss on an all-white painting by American artist Cy Twombly that was on display in Avignon, France. The kiss left an indelible lipstick smudge on the painting, a work that was valued at over $2.8 million. Restoration efforts to remove the smudge were unsuccessful. The woman, who described herself as an artist, told a judge her kiss was an act of love, an act that the artist Twombly would understand, and not a crime. The judge nevertheless found her guilty of voluntarily damaging a work of art, but her punishment consisted only of 100 hours of community service and payments for damages totaling about $2,100.[4]

Ancient Column in Pompeii Toppled

A huge fluted column in the garden of the ancient Roman villa in Pompeii, Italy, was found toppled over on Monday, March 19, 2007. Police believe that vandals or perhaps a disgruntled worker at the site entered a closed excavation area over the weekend and climbed scaffolding to push over the column. The column broke into five pieces, but fortunately, the damage was repairable, according to experts.[5]

Monet Painting "Punched" in Paris

In the early morning hours of October 7, 2007, five people broke into the Musée d'Orsay in Paris and damaged *Le Pont d'Argenteuil,* an Impressionist painting by Monet from 1874. A surveillance camera recorded the entry of these individuals, who appeared to be drunk and probably were participants in an annual all-night street festival and/or a rowdy celebration of a French victory in a world rugby tournament. The camera caught one of the individuals striking the painting with his fist, which resulted in a four-inch tear. An alarm did sound, but the intruders eluded guards who responded. Fortunately, the damage was repairable according to museum officials, who also termed the painting as "priceless." A few days later French police did apprehend five 18–19 year old men for their role in this incident.[6]

Museum Guard Damages Painting He Doesn't Like

Art is not even safe from vandalism by those employed to protect it. A guard at the Carnegie Museum in Pittsburgh was observed in May 2008 through video surveillance gouging a painting by Latvian artist Vija Celmins, a work that was on loan from the Art Institute of Chicago. The painting, entitled *Night Sky,* was valued at $1.2 million and suffered serious damage that required $5,000 in repairs. The guard used a key or other such implement to inflict the damage. A police investigation determined the guard caused the damage because he didn't like the painting. He was charged with institutional vandalism and subsequently pled guilty. The guard was fired from the museum and reportedly was undergoing mental-health counseling.[7]

Stonehenge Damaged by Souvenir Hunters

Monuments at the 5,000-year-old site in England were damaged in May 2008 by individuals who were suspected of souvenir hunting. They used a hammer and screwdriver to acquire chips from the ancient stones. The vandalism was interrupted by security officials on the scene and further damage was prevented. However, no apprehensions were made. Surveillance cameras had recorded two suspicious individuals days earlier at the site, but it is not known whether they were the same as those who actually inflicted the damage.[8]

Stained Glass Window by Marc Chagall in French Church Broken

Souvenir hunting was also blamed in connection with damage to a stained glass window that depicted Adam and Eve at Saint-Étienne Cathedral in

Metz. The window was a 1963 work by Marc Chagall. In August 2008, vandals smashed a hole in the window measuring 24 inches by 26 inches that allowed them to gain entry into the church. They then stole a few inconsequential items and littered the interior with graffiti. The damage to the window was repairable.[9]

UN Peacekeepers Vandalize Archeological Site

In a variation of "guards as vandals," members of a United Nations peacekeeping force in the Sahara desert sprayed graffiti on depictions of animals and humans that were painted on rocks up to 6,000 years ago. The UN peacekeeping force was multinational in its composition and some of those responsible for the graffiti were identified as holding officer ranks. Their role in the Sahara was to enforce a cease-fire agreement between Moroccan government forces and a separatist movement known as the Polisario Front.[10]

An Aesthetic Theory of Vandalism

Although drunkenness and psychiatric problems were blamed for the some of the incidents above, they were not factors in all cases. In fact, a Swedish study demonstrated that only when alcohol use was combined with a state of frustration did art vandalism occur.[11] In any event, inebriation seldom exonerates those charged with crimes; and while mental illness *can* form the basis for a successful insanity defense, not all such illnesses (at least in the United States) meet the legal threshold for an insanity judgment. Thus, attempts to understand why individuals inflict senseless damage on works of art force us to look beyond behaviors attributed to drunkenness and many psychiatric disorders. While acknowledging that no general theory of vandalism exists and that such acts are probably attributable to multiple factors, researchers at the University of Wisconsin have advanced the concept of an aesthetic theory of vandalism. This theory is formulated on the basic premise (for which they claim there is abundant anecdotal evidence) that those involved in vandalism derive sheer enjoyment from the destruction of an object. They go on to posit that the same variables that account for the pleasure that accompanies socially acceptable aesthetic experiences are responsible for enjoyment of socially unacceptable acts of destruction. These variables include an object's complexity; its incongruity or unexpected nature; its organization, patterning, or grouping; and its intensity, size and color. This theory argues that enjoyment of a destructive act derives primarily from the visual, auditory, and tactual-kinesthetic stimuli that occur during the rapid transformation of material (e.g., the destruction of an art object). Greater enjoyment will be derived when the process of breakage is complex, when this process results in an unexpected outcome, and/or is novel in some other way.[12]

Thus, to look upon some of the cases of art vandalism described above simply as pursuits of enjoyment probably offers our best chance at making some sense out of these senseless acts.

ART VANDALISM/DESTRUCTION AS A FORM OF PROTEST OR SOCIAL STATEMENT

While not excusable, some vandalism and/or destruction of art have occurred as a form of social protest or a (misguided) way of publicizing a social statement. It should be recognized that protests or social statements we are considering in this category are much more limited in scope than those we encountered when art is destroyed or damaged during war or civil/religious unrest. In fact, the motivations we are considering here are often personal in nature or reflect the sentiments of a limited group of people. While we might be able to attribute acts of vandalism or destruction to these motivations, as illustrated by the following incidents, the resulting damage is no less senseless and disturbing than those acts which lack any rational explanation.

Performance Artist Damages Marcel Duchamp's *Fountain*

Seventy-seven year old Frenchman Pierre Pinoncelli described himself as a performance artist; that is, he organizes and participates in bizarre acts or as he would describe them, "street happenings." In early January 2006, he engaged in a performance at the Pompidou Center in Paris in which he damaged and despoiled Marcel Duchamp's *Fountain*. Duchamp was a follower of the early 20th-century Dada movement that sought to destroy the conventional notion of art; and his work, *Fountain,* was simply a factory-made porcelain urinal. While on display at the Pompidou Center, Pinoncelli chipped *Fountain* with a hammer. He was arrested immediately whereupon he called his act a work of art and a tribute to Duchamp and Dadaist movement. His actions resulted in the imposition of a three-month suspended sentence and a fine of $18,600 to cover the cost of repairing the damage he inflicted on *Fountain,* which is valued at $3.6 million. For Pinoncelli, this was his second performance involving *Fountain.* In 1993 while on display at a museum in Nimes, France, he also struck it with a hammer and urinated into it as well.[13]

Personal Religious Protest by Egyptian Woman in Cairo Results in Damage to Antiquities

While in an earlier chapter we explored damage to art that can arise through widespread civil/religious unrest, similar events can occur on a more isolated and limited basis as well. Following the issuance of a fatwa by the Grand Mufti in Cairo against decorative statues of living beings,

a black-clad and veiled woman shouting "Infidels, Infidels!" damaged
three ancient Egyptian statues that were on display in a Cairo museum in
June 2006.[14]

Photography Exhibition in Sweden Elicits a Violent Rampage

Four masked individuals damaged an exhibition of photographs by
American artist Andres Serrano that were on display at a Swedish university museum in October 2007. The exhibition was entitled "The History
of Sex" and contained sexually explicit images. The vandals attacked the
photographs with crowbars and axes in front of other museum visitors
and while doing so verbally expressed their displeasure with the content
of the exhibition. They destroyed half the photographs on display resulting in a monetary loss of over $200,000; and upon their departure, they
left leaflets with the statement, "Against decadence and for a healthier culture." No organization took responsibility for the incident although police
believed those involved were part of a neo-Nazi movment.[15]

Ara Pacis Museum in Rome Vandalized

In 1998 American architect Richard Meier was commissioned by municipal leaders in Rome to design the Ara Pacis Museum that holds a ninth-
century B.C.E sacrificial altar to celebrate the peace brought by Rome's
first emperor, Augustus. The museum opened in 2006 and was the first
new public building to open in the city's historic center in more than
50 years. Meier's project was a source of controversy from the outset because of its modern design amidst an otherwise classical architectural environment. In June 2009, vandals pelted the exterior walls of the museum
with red and green paint (colors of the Italian flag) and left a toilet with
rolls of toilet paper outside the museum as well in an apparent continua-
tion of the social protest that this museum's design does not fit into to its
surroundings.[16]

DESTROYING ART FOR PROFIT

The final category of vandalism and malicious destruction we shall
cover is acts that damage and destroy works of art because of financial
gain. Up to this point, we have covered vandalism and malicious destruction of art that have been attributed to behaviors related to mental
problems, drunkenness, and perhaps misguided enjoyment. We have also
learned about destructive acts as a form of protest or social statement. But
a profit motive in destroying art? Unfortunately, the answer is "yes," a
tragic phenomenon driven by the value of the raw materials often used
by sculptors, that is, metals such as bronze and copper. Bronze objects

are particularly attractive because the copper alloy present in this metal is used in the manufacture of high-tech equipment, a strong demand that has caused prices for this material to soar. Once in the hands of a corrupt scrap metal dealer who destroys the art object by melting it down, a major piece of the evidence of the theft is forever gone while both the thieves and the complicit scrap-metal dealer profit handsomely.[17]

Large sculptures made from such materials are often placed in public, outdoor settings and often afforded little security protection. But then again, consider the logistics of covertly removing large, weighty objects and transporting them to scrap dealers. As we shall see in the examples that follow, such obstacles have not been a deterrent to some individuals. Arguably, such individuals could be considered thieves rather than vandals, but for our purposes, we will view them as the latter. Thievery as examined in earlier chapters at least had the goal of profiting from the sale (or ransom) of stolen art objects. Stealing art objects so that they might be destroyed for their raw material value seems to be an even more deplorable activity, thus earning those involved the title vandal, rather than thief.

New Orleans: Thieves Target Sculpture Studio

In late December 2006, thieves broke into a sculpture studio and dismantled and stole thousands of dollars worth of bronze sculptures by artist John T. Scott, whose works were well known throughout New Orleans. It was speculated that the thieves sought the sculptures only for their bronze content that would net them several hundreds of dollars. The thefts were discovered by another artist who shared the studio with him, and this loss represented another tragic episode in Scott's life. His studio had previously been ravaged by Hurricane Katrina, and the reason he was not there to discover the thefts himself was because he was in Houston recovering from lung transplants. [18]

Vermont: One Million Dollars of Bronze Sculptures Taken

Thirty bronze sculptures were stolen from the home and studio of American sculptor Joel Fisher in November 2007, while he was out of the country. His work has been displayed internationally in the Museum of Modern Art in New York, the Tate Museum in London, the Gallery Shimada in Japan, and the Stedelijk Museum in Amsterdam. The missing objects represented the majority of Fisher's work product that spanned a 25-year period. Some of the sculptures were as tall as eight feet and weighed as much as 1,000 pounds. In December, a scrap-yard operator called the Vermont state police with a tip about bronze statues that resulted in four arrests for possession and sale of stolen property. The motivation for the thefts was to obtain money for illegal drug purchases. One of those arrested, a 32-year-old male, subsequently was convicted and sentenced to prison for a period ranging from 5 to 20 years. Twenty-three of the 30 statues were recovered at another scrap yard in Vermont, fortunately before they were smelted into raw material. That scrap yard had paid the culprits $4,000 for them. Other sculptures taken from the Fisher property were located in Massachusetts.[19]

California Gold Miner Stolen from a Los Angeles Park

In January 2008, a statue of a California gold miner that had adorned a Los Angeles public park for 80 years was stolen. The sculpture was seven feet tall and weighed over 500 pounds. It was later found cut in two pieces at the knees at a local scrap-metal yard. The owner of the scrap yard paid $900 to thieves for the statue, which as an art object was valued at $125,000. In February 2008, police arrested two individuals in connection with the theft and these individuals are suspected of being responsible for a series of bronze-sculpture thefts throughout the Los Angeles area. Two business locations suffered losses of bronze sculptures valued at $30,000 and $35,000 respectively, and bronze sculptures and a mailbox were stolen from homes in the area.

In that same time period, another six-foot-tall bronze sculpture was stolen in Brea, California, and authorities noted it was the third bronze statue stolen in this jurisdiction within nine months. A scrap-metal dealer in Anaheim, California, who provided information to the police leading to the arrest of 18 individuals for metal theft, reported that most stolen metal is shipped overseas to China and India where it is refabricated.[20]

The practice of destroying art for its scrap metal is not limited to the United States. Similar incidents have been reported elsewhere, as evidenced below.

In England, Missing Metal Sculptures Become a Recurring Problem

Recall in chapter 2 that we considered the size of an art object as a function of theft and pointed to evidence that suggested that smaller objects were more likely to be theft targets. However, during this discussion, in order to acknowledge that art of all sizes has been stolen, the theft in December 2005 of a two-and-a-half ton bronze sculpture entitled *Reclining Figure* (1970) by Henry Moore in Hertfordshire, England, was provided as an example. This sculpture, which had a value of $18 million, has never been recovered and its theft is feared to have been motivated by the resale value of its bronze content as scrap metal. In fact, while no arrests have been made, police attribute the theft to a British travelers group (i.e., an organized band of itinerant thieves) that sold the sculpture for than less $3,000 to scrap dealers in Great Britain, who then shipped it abroad.

Unfortunately, metal sculptures have been popular targets for metal thieves in England as police there have encountered a series of such thefts beginning in 2005. Following the theft of the Henry Moore work at the end of 2005, one of three bronze figures that comprised *The Watchers* (1960) by sculptor Lynn Chadwick was stolen from the grounds of Roehampton University in southwest London in February 2006. This figure was over six feet tall and its removal would have required eight individuals according to one report. Its value as an art object was estimated to be over $1 million. A few months later, in May 2006, two more bronze statues were found removed, this time in Wiltshire and Gloucestershire. Both statues served as war memorials that depicted heroes from World War I and had a combined value of about $100,000 as art objects. One of these statues was by the noted British sculptor Henry Pegram and was considered a work of international importance. Metal sculptures displayed in public places continued to be targeted into 2007 and 2008. A bronze statue of Steve Ovett, the gold-medal winner in the 800-meter run at the 1980 Olympics, was found missing in September 2007 from a public park in his native Brighton, England. Police again feared it was melted down for its metal content, and they reported having no witnesses to its removal; nor were there any type of security devices such as surveillance cameras or security patrols at the park. By the summer of 2008, British police launched a nationwide crackdown on the theft of metal fueled by what they described as the insatiable demand from booming Asian economies. While the spate of missing artworks made from bronze were recognized as part of this problem, it was the brewing industry that was suffering losses of its aluminum kegs, along with the rail, telecom, and power industries that successfully lobbied the police for a more intensified effort to curb these thefts.[21]

A Monumental Sculpture Goes Missing in Spain

Not to be outdone by the sizable loss of the Moore sculpture in England, a 76,000-pound Richard Serra work entitled *Equal-Parallel/Guernica-Bengasi* (1986) was found missing at a private warehouse company where it had been stored by Madrid's Reina Sofia Museum after it had been put on display. The sculpture consisted of four steel slabs and was acquired by the museum in 1987. The warehouse company, however, went out of business in 1998, and it was not until 2005 that the museum inquired about the sculpture's status. As hope of locating the missing statue waned, Serra agreed to make an identical copy for the museum. It is feared that the original has been melted down for its scrap-metal value. [22]

Auguste Rodin's *The Thinker* Stolen in the Netherlands

A museum in Laren, Netherlands, suffered the loss of seven bronze sculptures in January 2007, including a casting of Rodin's *The Thinker*.

Police speculated that the thefts were motivated by the value of the sculptures' bronze contents, as iron objects were untouched. Museum officials placed the monetary loss of the statues in the range of hundreds of thousands of euros, and they noted that *The Thinker* was one of 74 castings (i.e., similar to limited edition prints) of this perhaps most well-known work by Rodin.[23]

In Australia, a Copper Statue That Adorned an Art Gallery for 50 years is Snatched

In July 2008, the Penrith Regional Gallery suffered the loss of one of its iconic pieces, a copper statue by the famed Australian sculptor, Gerald Lewers. In fact, the statue was taken from the grounds of the Lewers House, which is now part of the Penrith Regional Gallery. The theft occurred during the nighttime while the gallery was closed. The statue stood over three feet tall and weighed over 66 pounds. Police speculated the motive for taking the copper statue was to sell it for its scrap-metal value. As a work of art, it was valued over $20,000, but to a scrap dealer it would be worth only about 1 percent of that amount, $200.[24]

Of the cases briefed above, recoveries were made in only two instances, in Vermont and in Los Angeles (although the latter with the artwork in damaged condition). Thus, it *might* be premature to conclude that these and other missing metal sculptures have met the dire fate of being melted down for their valuable metal content. An optimistic view in this regard was voiced by Julian Radcliffe, chair of the *Art Loss Register,* who speculated that some of these missing pieces might have been stolen for resale abroad, much like the illicit trafficking in stolen paintings or antiquities. Unfortunately, when well-known pieces are involved, this line of thinking would work best if there were some basis to believe in the existence of individuals who secretly hoard well-known, stolen works of art for their private enjoyment, a theory that unfortunately does not receive widespread support. Thus, the fears expressed by many police authorities as well as many in the art world that a thriving scrap-metal market can result in the theft and destruction of metal sculptures is probably a sad reality.[25]

VANDALISM/MALICIOUS DESTRUCTION OF ART: DISHEARTENING, DISTURBING, AND SENSELESS

We have toured the crimes of the art world and now conclude on the very sour subject of art being purposely vandalized and damaged for reasons that are often incomprehensible; and even when motivations are apparent, they hardly justify the end result. Although far from condoning any of the art crimes covered heretofore, many of the theft scenarios as well as forgery/fakery have occurred in recognition of the aesthetic and/or monetary values associated with works of art. As we have seen, art objects have been damaged incident to their theft, but this outcome is often to the detriment of those who are looking to profit from such thievery. The damage to artworks inflicted by vandals does not fall into this category. Here the damage can be attributed to crazed behavior, brought on by mental disorders or substance abuse, or at least according to one theory, the sheer enjoyment that being involved in the destruction of an object. Some art vandals have also contended that their destructive actions are a form of social protest or statement. Not only does this type of rationale generally fail to justify such acts, but also the banner under which they perform their vandalism is often personal in nature, or at least does not receive widespread recognition. Finally, if there are any feelings of compassion for individuals who damage art because of behaviors they cannot control or for reasons most of us cannot fully comprehend, whether such gestures of humanity can be extended to those who have works of art destroyed for the value of their raw material should be held in doubt. The purposeful and calculated conduct of these individuals forever deprives the world of works of art that they unlawfully confiscate in order to receive remuneration for raw material that represents only a fraction of the value of the art objects. While it is acknowledged that such individuals must first steal the pieces, as suggested earlier, to accord them the status of thieves seems inappropriate. They are simply vandals.

CHAPTER 9

Responding to Art Crime

The preceding chapters have provided an account of art crime in its various manifestations. Along the way, mention has been made of efforts by public and private organizations to stem these activities although our focus so far has been more on the crimes themselves and less so on these organizations. Our attention in this chapter, however, shifts to law-enforcement agencies as well as private organizations that play a role in investigating art crimes. As has been demonstrated repeatedly here, art crime is global in its reach and accordingly we will be examining those organizations that play prominent enforcement roles on the world stage of art crime. Keeping in mind that art crimes often ignore international boundaries and, in turn, mandate international investigative/enforcement cooperation, it is in this direction that we first turn our attention, that is, the roles of worldwide organizations including the United Nations (U.N.) and Interpol. From there we will examine U.S. agencies and the laws that they enforce relative to art crime and then consider the role and activities of agencies located in Europe and elsewhere. Finally, we will review the efforts of private organizations that have provided investigative support on art crimes to the law-enforcement community.

INTERNATIONAL LAW ENFORCEMENT COORDINATION: THE ROLES OF THE UNITED NATIONS, INTERPOL, AND OTHER WORLDWIDE ORGANIZATIONS

To be clear, the United Nations is not a law-enforcement organization but rather a world diplomatic body that addresses a wide array of international issues that sometimes involve crime and law-enforcement issues.

Among these, art crime (and the illicit trafficking in cultural-heritage objects, in particular) has been of prominent concern. Interpol, however, can be characterized as a law-enforcement organization, although its role in this regard is largely one of coordination and liaison that help foster cooperative worldwide law-enforcement activities.

Early efforts by the United Nations to protect art can be traced to World War II when its membership consisted of the United States, the countries occupied by Nazi Germany, the British Commonwealth nations, China, and the Soviet Union. In January 1943, it issued a declaration that invalidated all forced transfers of property in enemy-controlled territory.[1] The U.N.'s landmark effort to curb the theft and illicit trafficking in art occurred years later and was brought under the banner of one its subsidiary organizations, the United Nations Educational, Scientific and Cultural Organization (UNESCO): the 1970 UNESCO Convention on the Means of Prohibiting and Preventing the Illicit Import, Export and Transfer of Ownership of Cultural Property. Parties to this convention agree to seek the return of cultural property to the country of origin even when current owners acquired it legally, although bona fide purchasers are entitled to just compensation (except in those countries such as the United States where good title cannot extend to stolen goods). Some criticize this convention for being more symbolic than effective because it operates at national government levels, thus requiring diplomatic negotiations to implement its provisions on a case-by-case basis. Perhaps the greatest weakness, however, has been that not all the major art-market nations have been signatories to the convention, although their participation has increased in recent years.[2] One notable major art-market nation that is a signatory is the United States, where legislation was enacted that has led to successes in implementing the spirit and terms of the convention. This legislation will be discussed in more detail later in this chapter.

In between World War II and the 1970 convention, the United Nations also enacted the UNESCO Convention for the Protection of Cultural Property in Armed Conflict in 1954. The purpose of this international agreement is to protect art and antiquities during times of war and military occupation. Ironically, however, it has not been particularly effective in the American-led military campaigns in Iraq and Afghanistan because it took 54 years (in 2008) for the United States to join 121 other nations in ratifying it.[3]

Although independent of the United Nations (but nevertheless tracing its origins to its predecessor, the League of Nations), the International Institute for the Unification of Private Law (UNIDROIT) in 1995 put forth an international agreement that attempted to address some of the deficiencies in the 1970 UNESCO convention: UNIDROIT Convention on Stolen or Illegally Exported Cultural Objects. Under this convention, signatories agree to permit owners of stolen or illegally exported art to seek redress in the courts of their own countries, as well as where the object(s) is (are) currently located.

Sixty-one nations participate in UNIDROIT, an organization that describes its purpose as to study needs and methods for modernizing, harmonizing, and coordinating private and, in particular, commercial law between states and groups of states. The effectiveness of its 1995 Convention on Stolen or Illegally Exported Cultural Objects has once again been limited by the failure of many major art-market countries to ratify it.[4]

On a regional level, the European Union has issued regulations for controlling illicit trafficking in stolen art. In 1993, it issued a directive that established a uniform system of export permits for art objects among European Union members as well as a system for restituting stolen objects between these nations. Then in 2003, incident to an increase in the smuggling of looted Iraqi antiquities that followed the fall of the Saddam regime, the European Union issued its own regulations to control this activity that eliminated any need to proceed under the terms of the 1970 UNESCO convention or the 1995 UNIDROIT convention.[5]

While the attempts by world organizations to control the trafficking in stolen and looted art and cultural-heritage objects have been imperfect, at the very least their efforts represent a global consensus that this type of criminal activity needs to be halted and, to that end, international coordination and cooperation are essential. The task of implementing this consensus, however, falls to the world's police agencies; and it is at this level that international coordination and cooperation are the sine qua non in achieving any success in halting illicit trafficking in stolen art and cultural-heritage objects. Playing a leading role in this manner is the International Criminal Police Organization, commonly known as Interpol.

Interpol

First, let's gain an understanding of what Interpol is and is not. While Interpol is the world's largest international police organization, it describes its roles as facilitating cross-border police cooperation and supporting and assisting all organizations, authorities, and services whose mission it is to prevent or combat international crime. Absent from this description is any role relating to the exercise of worldwide police or investigative authority. The notion of an Interpol field agent jetting from country to country to solve international crimes is largely mythical. Interpol began in 1923 and is headquartered in Lyons, France, where it maintains a workforce of employees involved in liaison activities among its 186 member nations and international crime-data collection, analysis, and reporting. In turn, each of the 186 member nations maintains a National Central Bureau, that is, the contact point for Interpol in a member country. National Central Bureaus are staffed by law-enforcement officials from the member nations.[6]

Although the theft of art and trafficking in looted cultural-heritage objects is not specifically listed as one of Interpol's crime priorities, Interpol has had a long history of involvement in this area and has been at the forefront in circulating information about these crimes worldwide. Interpol's first involvement with art theft can be traced to 1925, two years after its inception, when it circulated photographs of stolen miniatures and manuscripts. In 1947, Interpol began to publish and circulate International Notices on Stolen Art Works, an undertaking that since 1990 has evolved into a modern computer database containing about 34,000 stolen objects that is accessible online to member nations; as well as to other organizations/individuals who can gain access approval through an application process to Interpol.[7]

Contributions to this database are normally made through the National Central Bureaus. Interpol involvement is usually limited to losses of fine art and cultural-heritage items when there are international implications and substantial values involved. Submitting color photographs of the stolen/lost objects are usually requested along with accurate, detailed physical descriptions; any unique markings (including trademarks and serial numbers); circumstances of the loss or theft; value of the item; and any other pertinent information, including relevant history.[8]

ART-CRIME ENFORCEMENT IN THE UNITED STATES

While the efforts of international organizations vis-à-vis art crimes are largely diplomatic or liaison in nature, the investigation and prosecution of these crimes takes place within the justice systems of the world's nation-states. As a federal democracy, the justice system in the United States is bifurcated; that is, there is a national or federal justice system and then each state has its own system as well. Each system has its own set of laws, courts, and law-enforcement/investigative agencies. State-level enforcement/investigative agencies typically include state and municipal police departments that are responsible for a vast range of policing, investigation, and public safety responsibilities. At the same time, the legal authority of state-level agencies tends to be limited to the state in which they are located (if not in some instances to the municipal or county geographical areas in which they are employed). Federal agencies, on the other hand, have nationwide investigative authority, and these agencies have more specialized enforcement responsibilities. Art crimes that have interstate and international implications and/or connections and those that fall into the white-collar crime arena are usually investigated by federal agencies because of their broader investigative jurisdiction and their expertise in these highly specialized cases. Within the ranks of the federal agencies, the Federal Bureau of Investigation (FBI) arguably plays the leading role in art crime enforcement.

FBI

The leading role the FBI plays in art-crime enforcement in the United States can be attributed first to its investigative charter, which, in turn, has led to the development of specialized expertise and resources within its ranks to address cases of this nature. While most federal law-enforcement agencies have very defined and limited jurisdictions, the FBI is responsible for enforcing all federal criminal laws, except for a relatively small number of violations that are specifically assigned to other agencies. Several of the federal laws it has responsibility for have specific application to art-theft investigations: Title 18 of the United States, Section 668, makes it a federal offense to obtain by theft or fraud any object of cultural heritage from a museum and prohibits as well the fencing or possession of such objects, knowing them to be stolen; Section 1170 of Title 18 prohibits the illegal trafficking in Native American remains and cultural items. Section 668 is a felony violation as it provides for imprisonment up to 10 years while Section 1170 is a misdemeanor as it exposes an offender to an imprisonment of not more than one year (although a repeated offense by the same individual increases the penalty to 5 years imprisonment).[9]

The FBI also enforces federal laws that deal in theft, generally, and these have been applied to art-theft cases where the above-described circumstances are not present. Title 18, United States Code, Section 659, Theft from an Interstate Shipment, makes it a crime to steal or obtain by fraud anything from a conveyance, depot, or terminal and any shipment being transported in interstate or foreign commerce. The statute also prohibits fencing property that is knowingly stolen from an interstate shipment. Thus, in cases where an art object is stolen while in transit (although there must be an interstate or foreign commerce nexus), this violation could be applied and the penalty is 10 years imprisonment, providing the value of the stolen art exceeds $1,000 (absent this value, the imprisonment penalty is limited to a maximum of one year). Stolen property valued in excess of $5,000 that is transported across state lines or into the United States from abroad, or knowing possession of stolen property after such transportation has occurred is also a violation of federal law (18 USC, Section 2314 and 2315) with imprisonment penalties of up to 10 years.[10] In addition, the FBI enforces the federal wire-fraud statute, 18 USC 1343, a widely used law in white-collar crime cases. When the telephone system or the internet is used on an interstate or foreign basis to further a scheme to defraud within the art world, this felony statute would likely be charged.

As a result of these statutory responsibilities, the FBI has a long history in investigating a wide array of art crimes; and in the course of doing so, it has developed a recognized level of expertise in handling these investigations. On one level, this expertise could be described as institutional in nature, that is, the creation and maintenance of the *National Stolen Art File*, one of the primary computerized art-theft databases, as discussed in chapter 1. To review, this database contains reports of stolen art and cultural property submitted by U.S. and foreign law-enforcement agencies. It contains photographs of the stolen objects, detailed descriptions, and investigative information. Criteria for submission into this database include (1) historical or artistic significance, (2) a value of at least $2,000 (or less if associated with a major crime), and (3) a physical description (and photograph, if available) as well as a police investigative report accompanying the entry request. The primary purpose of this database is to provide investigative assistance to law enforcement. It is also represented to be of analytical value to law-enforcement officials with regard to art-theft investigations and intelligence.[11]

On another level, the FBI's art-crime expertise lies in its personnel. Throughout its history in investigating art crimes, a few of its agents have been able to specialize in these cases, and in some instances they were able to successfully assume undercover roles as rogue (and knowledgeable) art experts that led to the recovery of stolen artworks from thieves or their accomplices. Such feats, not surprisingly, are legend within the agency and among many in the art world (and deservedly so). However, the FBI perhaps more fully demonstrated its commitment to art-crime enforcement with the establishment of a national art-crime team in 2004. In doing so, it has replicated similar commitments to art crime that have been made by major police agencies in England, France, and Italy as will be discussed below. The FBI team members are spread across the country, but can be mobilized to respond to major art crimes. They receive special training not just in investigating these types of crimes, but they also are educated about art and art history generally, so that they have the necessary background to work in this environment.[12]

Other Federal Agencies

In addition to the FBI, other federal agencies also play a role in art-crime enforcement in the United States. Among these other agencies, Immigration and Customs Enforcement (ICE) is perhaps the most regular participant in these investigations because of its antismuggling responsibilities. As a major art-consuming nation, the United States is often a market of choice for stolen or looted works of art and cultural-heritage objects. When the United States ratified the 1970 UNESCO convention, Congress passed legislation to implement its provisions into law in the United States. The resulting statute in the United States Code, Section 2607 of Title 19, provides for import restrictions into the United States of archeological and ethnographic materials through bilateral and multilateral agreements where the requesting state can show that its cultural patrimony is in jeopardy and that it has taken measures to protect it. ICE is responsible for enforcing these import restrictions. Among the tools it can use incident to enforcing this statute is its broad authority to seize and forfeit objects at the border. This authority can also be applied when Customs Declarations falsely report the nature or identity of goods coming into the United States. Moreover, ICE can also apply the provisions of Title 18 of the United States Code, Sections 2314 and 2315, to individuals who bring stolen property into the United States from abroad or those who possess such property, knowing that it has been stolen.[13]

Other federal agencies that have roles in art-crime enforcement in the United States include the Internal Revenue Service and the Postal Inspection Service. The Postal Inspection Service is the investigative arm of the U.S. Postal Service and among other responsibilities, it investigates frauds and schemes that are carried on through the U.S. mails. As outlined in a press release in chapter 4 (see box 4.1), the investigation that led to the indictment of seven individuals in a counterfeit fine art prints scheme was jointly conducted by the Postal Inspection Service and the FBI. While the Internet continues to challenge the viability of the type of hard copy communication that is the bread and butter of the U.S. Postal Service, in other respects it has greatly expanded opportunities to service those who enjoy the conveniences of shopping from their homes (if not their workplaces as well!). The vast array of goods and services offered over the Internet has arguably penetrated this market beyond what even the glossiest catalogs and flyers were able to accomplish, and for lesser cost. However, there is still the matter of submitting payment and then shipping the goods. While customers can submit their payments online using credit cards, others still mail checks and money orders; and many shippers use the U.S. Postal Service for order fulfillment (although other interstate conveyances fall under the purview of the federal mail-fraud statute as well). Modern-day Internet marketing notwithstanding, the age-old problem of materially misrepresenting what is being offered for sale or, in some cases, never providing what is ordered at all, continues on unabated. As discussed in chapter 4, marketing phony works of art is tailor-made for the Internet/mail-order sales because it provides the distance and anonymity between seller and buyer that makes these schemes so viable. The case outlined in box 4.1 is only one of many that postal inspectors have tackled.

Intervention in the art world by the Internal Revenue Service (IRS) can occur in any number of scenarios where there are concerns about improper payment of federal income taxes. One scenario that was introduced in chapter 6 involves tax incentives for donating art works to nonprofit institutions such as museums. Collectors can purchase art objects and, at some point, donate them to a museum or educational institution. To be clear, this can be a win-win situation for all concerned. Art aficionados can pursue their collecting interests and then share their collection with the public (and add to a museum's collection in so doing) while reducing their tax liability. However, as the value of some art objects can be substantial (e.g., in the millions of dollars), tax deductions claimed can likewise be quite large. Although even sizable deductions can be legitimate, many art objects defy precise valuation, thus creating a murky area that can be exploited by tax dodgers who overvalue their donations in order to receive a greater tax deduction. This scenario can become aggravated when it takes on the characteristics of an organized scheme: dealers and/or nonprofit organizations (e.g., museums, educational institutions) recruit individuals to purchase art objects for donation and then provide them inflated appraisals for tax-deduction purposes. The following press release from the U.S. Attorney's Office in Los Angeles provides an example of this type of case (see box 9.1).

BOX 9.1 INFLATED APPRAISALS OF THAI ANTIQUITIES TIED TO TAX-FRAUD SCHEME

May 12, 2008

Asian Antiquities Expert Indicted For Wire Fraud

Charges Stem from Ongoing Federal Probe into Trafficking of Asian Antiquities

LOS ANGELES—An internationally recognized expert on Asian antiquities is expected to make her initial appearance this afternoon in federal court in Seattle where she was arrested late Friday on a federal wire fraud charge stemming from an ongoing multi-agency investigation into the importation of plundered antiquities from Southeast Asia.

Roxanna M. Brown, 62, director of the Southeast Asian Ceramics Museum at Bangkok University in Thailand, was indicted by a federal grand jury in Los Angeles on Friday. The indictment alleges that she allowed her electronic signature to be used on appraisal forms that, for tax purposes, inflated the value of antiquities donated to several Southern California museums.

The charges against Brown come four months after federal agents executed search warrants at four Southern California museums and the Silk Roads Gallery in Los Angeles. According to the affidavit filed in connection with the search of Silk Roads, the gallery's owners, Jonathan and Cari Markell, used Brown's electronic signature on several occasions to falsify appraisal forms so that collectors could claim increased tax deductions for objects donated to museums.

The search warrant affidavit details how an undercover agent posing as a collector approached the Markells in 2006 about donating several Asian antiquities to museums for charitable tax deductions. Jonathan Markell allegedly told the agent he normally charged $1,500 for an item or items that would be appraised at just under $5,000. Subsequently, the undercover agent met with the Markells at their home where he viewed a collection of Thai antiquities he had purchased from the gallery owners for $1,500 in cash. According to the affidavit, the Markells showed the agent an appraisal form purportedly prepared by Brown in which she claimed she had inspected the objects and valued them at $4,990. The items were ultimately donated to the Pacific Asia Museum in Pasadena.

An indictment contains allegations that a defendant has committed a crime. Every defendant is presumed innocent unless proven guilty in court.

The wire fraud charge carries a maximum penalty of 20 years in prison.

Brown was taken into custody by special agents with IRS-Criminal Investigation and the National Parks Service. U.S. Immigration and Customs Enforcement (ICE) is also involved in the ongoing investigation. Brown's prosecution is being handled by the United States Attorney's Office for the Central District of California.

Roxanna Brown died while in federal custody following her arrest on these charges. The search warrant affidavit discussed in the press release detailed conversations recorded by government investigators between museum officials and two antiquities dealers about smuggling of artifacts from China and Thailand, thus suggesting that this indictment was just an initial salvo in an ongoing investigation. In these conversations, an elaborate smuggling network was exposed from the grave robbers who transited looted artifacts through Myanmar to avoid customs detection to the tax fraud scheme in the Los Angeles area.[14] While responsibility for investigating the latter lies with the IRS, they often partner with other agencies when other illegalities precede the tax violations. Here, Immigration and Customs Enforcement became involved as a result of the smuggling feature (note: the undercover agent in this case was from the National Parks Service, an agency that might more frequently be involved in cases of looting of Native American remains and cultural objects).

State and Local Enforcement Efforts

As suggested at the outset of this section, federal agencies in the United States are most frequently in the forefront when it comes to art-crime enforcement efforts because of their nationwide jurisdiction and specialized investigative jurisdictions. However, there has been some notable work in this area at the state/local level in the nation's two largest cities, New York and Los Angeles. Surprisingly, it is not New York, the epicenter of the world's art market, which has a dedicated police unit to address art crime. That distinction goes to the Los Angeles Police Department, although the reality is that this unit has been typically staffed by only one or two detectives. However, the department does maintain a website of stolen art objects to assist in their recovery. The involvement of the New York City Police Department in art crime was most recently highlighted as a result of its involvement in a stolen antiquities task force established by the Manhattan District Attorney's Office. This task force operated under the direction of Matthew Bogdanos, the New York prosecutor/Marine officer who has gained wide acclaim for his investigation of thefts from the Iraqi National Museum while deployed in Baghdad during the U.S. invasion in 2003.[15] Bogdanos was preceded in New York City as an art-crime enforcer by the legendary (and late) Detective Robert Volpe. Volpe was formally trained as a painter and only became a police officer to earn a living. When art thefts were identified as increasing in New York City in the early 1970s, he was called upon to be the lone art-crimes specialist in the police department. With a combination of art knowledge and "street smarts," he proceeded to gain worldwide renown as an art-crime investigator and investigated art thefts that extended far beyond the borders of New York City at the request of foreign governments. In fact, his assistance was requested by the Hungarian government incident to the 1983, $35-million art theft from the Budapest Museum of Art, a case discussed earlier in chapter 3. By his own estimate, he recovered tens of millions of dollars worth of art objects during his career, including Byzantine ivories, Oriental rugs, Greek marble heads, Tiffany glass, and paintings by Matisse and Raphael. So unique and illustrious were his early days as an art-crime investigator that author Laurie Adams memorialized them in a book entitled *Art Cop* published in 1974.[16]

Ironically, while the federal government is usually at the forefront in the investigation and prosecution of white-collar crime, several of these cases reported in chapter 7 were handled by state/local authorities: the Salander gallery prosecution in New York City, the gallery frauds in Seattle and Milwaukee, and the auction fraud in Houston. Moreover, it was the California attorney general who investigated the misconduct at the Getty.

ART-CRIME ENFORCEMENT BEYOND THE UNITED STATES

The level of attention given to art crime by police agencies in other nations varies widely. Many countries recognize the problem of art theft and antiquities looting, either because they are a source of such objects or because they are a market/transit point for them. Many countries, unfortunately, find themselves in the position of being rich sources of art objects and/or antiquities but with little in the way of resources and expertise to address looting, theft, and illicit trafficking. There are notable exceptions, however, Italy being the prime example.

The Carabinieri

Within Italy's Carabinieri, its nationwide commando police organization, is a special unit identified as the Carabinieri for the Protection of Cultural Patrimony. From all accounts, this unit is the world's largest armed force whose sole mission is the investigation of art and antiquities theft and looting; and among the agencies worldwide that deal with these crimes, many would argue that it is the most effective as well. Its 300 officers are highly trained investigators as well as knowledgeable in art and antiquities. They have been called upon to assist other governments in the protection of their own national treasures, including Hungary, Greece, Kosovo, Iraq, Cuba, and Peru. They are able to draw upon the full array of law-enforcement tools and services that only the most modern and well-equipped police agencies enjoy, for example, aerial surveillance, dive teams, electronic surveillance, and a paid-informant program. Its specific investigative mandates include thefts of art and receipt of stolen art, damage to monuments and archeological sites, illegal exports of art and antiquities, counterfeiting, and organized trafficking in art and antiquities and any accompanying money laundering activities. Recall from chapter 1 that the Carabinieri also maintains a public-access database of stolen art objects and antiquities. This database is called Leonardo and is probably the world's largest and most advanced database of its kind.[17]

New Scotland Yard

In addition to New York, the other world art-market epicenter is London. Recognizing the need for specialized investigative expertise to handle the unique crimes that arise in this milieu, the London Metropolitan Police Department, commonly referred to as New Scotland Yard, transformed its Philatelic Squad (organized in 1968 to combat a rash of stamp robberies) into the Arts and Antiques Squad in 1976. Its activities include investigating art theft and forgery (and any accompanying money laundering) and intelligence gathering relative to art crimes, and it maintains the London Stolen Art Database (as discussed in chapter 1; see box 1.1). The latter was initially a manual system but was computerized in 1984 and now holds about 54,000 records. While well-regarded worldwide in the fight against art crime and with numerous high-profile cases to its credit, the Arts and Antiques Squad has nevertheless struggled to survive due to other priorities within New Scotland Yard. The year 1984 not only saw its database become computerized, but ironically, the squad was also abandoned that year as well, in order to divert resources to street crime. Five years later, it was reformulated in response to a growing need for art-crime expertise. Then in 2007, London police officials sought to cut the squad's funding by 50 percent and suggested that the art industry, which directly benefits from this service, make up the shortfall. Given the uncertainties surrounding the acquisition of private funding, the squad approached their budget problem from an alternative direction, that is, seeking the services of art professionals from universities, museums, and insurance companies as "special constables." This concept brought into the Art and Antiques Squad art experts who were then trained as police officers and given police powers, after which these "special constables" reported to work at the Art and Antiques Squad two days each week while on their employers' payrolls. Hopefully, this type of innovative thinking will keep the Arts and Antiques Squad in the art-crime wars for years to come.[18]

OCBC

The French national art police is the OCBC, Office central de lutte contre le trafic des biens culturels, which is headquartered in Paris. As discussed in chapter 2, France has a substantial problem of art- and cultural-objects theft from chateaux and churches and, as a result, OCBC has been a very active enforcement organization. In fact, the French government has designated the protection of its national heritage as a key task for the state. Some credit OCBC as being the most effective art-theft-fighting agency in the world based on arrests and recoveries, given its nationwide staff of 35.[19]

Art Policing Elsewhere in the World

Elsewhere in world, the commitment to art-crime enforcement does not rival the efforts being made by the United States, Italy, England, and France. Most nations do recognize the magnitude of the problem. The amounts of money associated with art theft and cultural-heritage looting/trafficking are large. For art-rich nations, such thefts have an adverse impact on their own cultural resources; and for art consuming nations, crimes such as smuggling and money laundering occur within their borders incident to the theft and trafficking of art and cultural-heritage objects. In fact, because of the international implications of art- and cultural-heritage-objects theft, in many countries the national customs authorities carry out whatever art-crime enforcement takes place, while the remainder of the law-enforcement resources tend to be diverted to other priorities.

Not surprisingly, many underdeveloped nations lack the personnel and training to wage an effective fight against those who steal and loot art and cultural-heritage objects, especially when their adversaries are well-organized and armed criminals; for instance, the illicit antiquities trade in Pakistan reportedly involves those who smuggle heroin out of Afghanistan. Moreover, many of these nations are also unable to pay their police adequately, a situation that contributes to corruption among those who are on hand to protect their nation's cultural treasures. In Cambodia, for example, while a 520-officer force has been established to protect the Angkor Historic Zone through the efforts of UNESCO and the French government, it is inadequate in size to be effective, and there have been allegations that some officers accept bribes to cooperate with antiquities dealers. Belize, a country with a treasure trove of Mayan artifacts, is another example where police efforts to protect the national heritage have been less than diligent, recording only 87 arrests for antiquities over a 29 year period. The national department of archeology does assist the police in attempting to control illicit smuggling, but the number of expert personnel it can provide is very limited. In Eastern Europe where countries in many respects have been enjoying their democratic renaissance, art thieves have been looting the churches and museums with abandon, due to police agencies being over-whelmed with an array of organized-crime problems.[20]

Some promising enforcement initiatives have been undertaken. For ex-ample, in antiquities-rich Greece, there is an increasingly aggressive spe-cial police squad that monitors illicit trafficking in its national-heritage objects, and legislative enhancements to strengthen these efforts have been sought. The Greeks have entered into a bilateral agreement with the Ital-ians over reclaiming antiquities, and there has been cooperation between their respective law-enforcement agencies on antiquities investigations. Combating illicit antiquities trafficking has also been given a higher prior-ity in Algeria where such activity is viewed as a form of organized crime. Four regional police units to address this illicit trafficking have been estab-lished along with increased border and port surveillance.[21]

In contrast, consider the Netherlands, which disbanded the government agency that inspected national museums and private collections and is-sued export permits in 2002, notwithstanding a series of art thefts that began a year earlier. Likewise, Canadian law enforcement has been crit-icized for a lack of art-crime expertise, although the establishment of a four-person art-crime task force in 2008 consisting of Quebec provincial police officers, an officer from the Royal Canadian Mounted Police, and an art historian provides some evidence of enforcement commitment in this area. Belgium does have a specialized art-theft unit as part of its national police force, but its efforts have largely been confined to thefts within its borders with little attention to international cooperation and smuggling of artifacts, especially from Africa. In Germany, efforts to combat art crime have varied, depending upon the priority given to it by its state-level police agencies.[22]

Art Crime Enforcement: A Worldwide Assessment

Although not comprehensive, this review suggests that the level of at-tention given to art crime (in it various manifestations) by police agen-cies on a worldwide basis is quite uneven. As policing in general in many underdeveloped countries has suffered from staffing, training, and re-source problems, the struggles in these nations to protect their cultural heritage from looting and curb smuggling in these objects should come as no surprise. Unfortunately, so many of these very nations are as rich in cultural resources as they are poor in government resources to protect their own cultural history. What is surprising, however, is that only a handful of nations in the developed world devote specialized resources to art-crime enforcement; and even in some of these countries, their resource com-mitment has been inconsistent over time. Given the volume of art theft and looting activity worldwide and the substantial amounts of money associated with these activities, the rather tepid global law-enforcement response arguably contributes to art theft and cultural-heritage looting/trafficking being ranked among the world's biggest crime problems.

Before we leave on this somber note, however, let's look at how the private sector is assisting governmental efforts.

ART-CRIME ENFORCEMENT: PRIVATE-SECTOR CONTRIBUTIONS

Nongovernmental organizations have made significant contributions in combating art crime. Although not possessing law-enforcement type investigative powers, these organizations have the advantage of a single focus, that is, art crime; and they employ individuals that have specialized expertise in this area. While these organizations typically provide support and assistance to law-enforcement agencies, they also tend to be more accessible to the general public, compared to law-enforcement agencies. Their primary activities are maintaining databases, usually of stolen art, and analyzing the data collected. As covered in chapter 1, although we do not have any type of comprehensive art-crime database(s) on a worldwide or even national basis (i.e., a mandated system of records), we do have databases that collect voluntary and/or selective submissions. The major indices in this regard are summarized in box 1.1. Through these databases, the details of a reported incident can be made rapidly available worldwide, often with accompanying photographs to facilitate identification. Not only can such information possibly assist in the investigation and recovery of lost, missing, or stolen art, but these types of indices can also provide a means for those in the private sector (gallery owners, museums, private collectors) to check on the bona fides of an object before acquiring it. It is believed that the availability and, in turn, increased use of these indices act as deterrents to at least some art crime.

Of the databases reviewed in box 1.1, two are maintained by private organizations, the *Art Loss Register* and *Trace Looted Art*. The *Art Loss Register* was created as a commercial enterprise by the International Foundation for Art Research (IFAR), a not-for-profit educational and research organization that was established in 1969. IFAR is an impartial, scholarly body that educates the public about problems and issues in the art world including art theft and looting, and it also conducts research on the attribution and authenticity of artworks. In the 1970s, in response to a rash of art thefts, IFAR established the first international archive of stolen art and then in 1991 it launched the *Art Loss Register* as a separate business entity. Searches of the database can be requested by members of the general public and are conducted by the *Art Loss Register* professional staff. A search fee is charged. The stolen artwork in the database is typically valued at over $2,000, and most items are those stolen from private residences.

IFAR also publishes the *IFAR Journal* on a quarterly basis that contains a section entitled, "Stolen Art Alert." This section highlights art thefts from around the world that have been reported to the *Art Loss Register* and Interpol.[23]

Trace Looted Art is a database limited to Holocaust-era looted art. Art objects that were stolen by the Nazis and their accomplices can be entered by those who suffered these losses, including individuals, government agencies, and museums. When artworks surface either in the marketplace or through police investigation, this database can be searched to determine whether the ownership of a work can be linked to those who suffered at the hands of Hitler and his henchmen. This is a free service offered by the organization Trace. Trace also maintains a general stolen-property database that was originally created by Swift-Find. Stolen art that is not related to the Holocaust-era looting can be entered into this database, and it can be queried by both the art-consuming public as well as law-enforcement officials when researching the provenance of an artwork that is on the market or recovered incident to an investigation.[24]

While the efforts made by public and private organizations to halt art crime through diplomatic, investigative, and prosecutorial powers are laudable, the impact of these approaches has been blunted by the limited resources that have been allocated to address what is an overwhelming problem. In this sense, art crime is not unlike other worldwide crime problems such as drug trafficking and terrorism; they have all been somewhat resistant to effective control through law-enforcement intervention. When faced with such situations, perhaps the more realistic response is not how do we investigate and prosecute these crimes, but rather how do we prevent them from occurring, in the first place? Our concluding chapter will pursue this theme as it examines how the art world can protect itself and the works of art it so treasures, from criminal activity through security and prevention measures.

CHAPTER 10

Security and Prevention:
The Best Response to Art Crime

In this final chapter, we examine ways that art crime can be prevented. Preventing art crime is a twofold undertaking. On the one hand, art objects themselves need to be protected from various forms of crime victimization such as theft, looting, and vandalism. On the other hand, those who own or seek to own art and those who are custodians of art represent the human side of art-crime victimization and, thus, benefit from protective measures that can reduce the chances for such victimization. Of course, many protective measures that can be implemented serve to protect both the objects themselves and the individuals who own them or have custody of them. Such steps range from maintaining collection inventories to the installation of electronic/technical surveillance equipment to security-guard staffing. In the following pages, we will examine these and other options that can safeguard art from theft, looting, and vandalism, as well as facilitate the recovery of objects that are stolen.

Owners, prospective owners, and custodians of artworks have also been victimized by forgery, fakery, and counterfeiting of artworks. In fact, it can be argued that all consumers of art are victimized when they view a work that is falsely represented as authentic. Steps can be taken to prevent such victimization by evaluating the authenticity of art objects. In this respect, the role of connoisseurship will be discussed, and applications of science and technology in identifying forgeries, fakes, and counterfeits will be reviewed.

PROTECTING ART FROM THEFT, LOOTING, AND VANDALISM

As a visual medium, the purpose of art is to be viewed. Thus, art is displayed in various settings to be observed, inspected, discussed, and enjoyed. Particularly in residential and even workplace settings, works of art are also displayed to add beauty to the environment and to enhance the décor. Other settings where art can be viewed include commercial galleries where works of art are displayed for sale. Of course, museums come readily to mind as institutions that house works of art. In these settings, art is not only displayed to provide enjoyment to those who visit the collections but also most museums engage in art-related educational and research activities. Works of art also adorn many churches. These works complement the religious rituals conducted in these houses of worship and add to the spirituality of that environment. Art is also displayed in public outdoor areas, where large sculptures are placed, and in locations where cultural-heritage objects are in situ. The point to this discussion is simply to state the obvious: art is meant to be viewed and not hidden away from the public eye in a vault or in some other place of safekeeping, notwithstanding that the latter scenarios provide better opportunities for protection. Thus, the dilemma for those who own art, who are art custodians, and those who wish to view art is the balance between providing maximum viewer access while protecting the works from theft, looting, and vandalism. The following pages explore some of the basic considerations that should be weighed in attempting to achieve the desired balance of access versus protection.

Records and Inventories

Although not a step that offers physical protection per se, maintaining a complete collection inventory that includes identifying information for each piece and photographs is a basic security measure for any art owner or custodian, whether a private collector, gallery owner, museum, church, or organization/government agency responsible for artworks and/or cultural-heritage sites. Identifying missing pieces in large collections, especially among those in storage or otherwise not on display, can be problematic without an inventory of objects that should be on hand. These latter scenarios are a point of vulnerability for theft since an object that is not on display might not be found missing for some time; and if not listed on an inventory, this type of theft might never be detected. Thus, not only is the compilation of an inventory a must, it should also be used as a basis periodically to inspect the holdings.

In addition to helping identify missing objects in a timely manner, inventories that contain physical descriptions including photographs facilitate the recovery of these objects. Art-theft databases work best when a detailed description of a stolen object is provided along with photographs. Such information aids investigators in their search for missing objects and helps to prevent stolen works from entering the legitimate art marketplace incident to due diligence searches.

Conventional wisdom might suggest that failure to develop and maintain inventories would be more characteristic of private collectors whose art is on display at their residences. Conversely, such wisdom might also suggest that for professional art custodians maintaining complete and current collection inventories would be routine. Unfortunately, however, examples abound where museums failed to have a current and/or complete inventory of their holdings and then accounting for losses became difficult, if not impossible. Such a problem confronted Matthew Bogdanos when he and his team attempted to assess losses due to looting from the Iraq National Museum in Baghdad following the 2003 U.S.-led invasion. Although Saddam Hussein took great pride in this great museum and looked upon it as his personal preserve, he also failed to staff it adequately. Thus, the inventory system on hand was antiquated and the staff had been unable to keep it current because new holdings poured in from archeological sites throughout Iraq. Media reports placed the losses from the museum at 170,000 objects, a figure that seemed exaggerated to Bogdanos given the 48-hour period in which widespread looting was thought to have taken place. However, the lack of viable inventory to work from was a great disadvantage in establishing a more realistic loss total. More importantly, however, efforts to recover missing objects from the museum were stymied by the failure to maintain a current inventory, notwithstanding the many successes that were achieved in this respect.[1]

In neighboring Turkey, another antiquities-rich nation, in 2006 the government for the first time launched a nationwide program to match museum holdings with inventory records, a process that was anticipated to take more than two years due to the large number of museums in this country. The government is now also leading an effort to automate inventory records incident to the verification process. In India, a 2005 government report criticized the Indian Museum in Kolkata for failing to establish a centralized inventory that reflects its entire holdings. Instead, each of the museum's six sections maintained its own inventory. The call for centralization arose incident to finding a wide discrepancy between objects on hand at the museum versus those reflected on the separate inventories. As in Iraq, the museum blamed staffing cutbacks for its inability to establish a centralized record-keeping system. The holdings of the Egyptian Museum in Cairo are believed to number at least 120,000, an assessment museum officials hope will become more accurate once a long overdue inventory process is completed.[2]

New Scotland Yard recommends a two-step approach in developing an inventory: a written description accompanied by photographs of each object. The written description should include the following:

- Type of object (e.g., painting, sculpture, etc.)
- Title
- Subject (i.e., what is represented)
- Artist/Sculptor (or creator; if known)

- Date or Period of the Work
- Materials and Techniques (e.g. oil on canvas, brass, etched)
- Size and Weight
- Signature, Inscriptions, Markings
- Distinguishing Features (e.g., damage, repairs, defects)

Multiple photographs of the object should be taken from different angles and for paintings, both the front and back. When feasible, placing a ruler next to an object helps to provide size context in a photograph. Photographs should show any distinguishing characteristics and damage or repair marks. Objects should be photographed against a white or gray background using natural light. The photographs should be attached to each written description and stored in a safe place.[3] These rudimentary steps can be taken even under relatively modest circumstances such as small private collections or church holdings with the expectation that this process would be more sophisticated/automated for works under the care of professional custodians.

Residential Collections

As may be recalled from chapter 2, most art thefts are reported incident to residential burglaries. Unlike hardened targets such as museums or banks, private residences are relatively soft targets for burglars, professional or otherwise. Many homeowners, regardless of the value of their personal property, opt for private security systems that detect unauthorized entries into the premises and are actively monitored to enable police response. Needless to say, the presence of an art collection in a home makes it a more attractive target for some burglars. Bear in mind that even a collection of nicely framed limited edition prints can have a substantial value. Thus, it only makes sense for private residential collections to be protected by a monitored security system. Once installed, such systems should be maintained in working order. They should always be armed when the residence is vacant, upon retiring in the evening, and perhaps at other times when prudent. Access to entry codes should be strictly limited.

Additionally, private collectors should be cautious as to the placement of their art. Their pieces should not be easily on view through exterior windows nor displayed near exterior windows or exterior doors, as such placements facilitate entry and escape. The identities of visitors and guests to the premises should be determined and unless trusted friends or relatives, they should not have unfettered access throughout the residence. The bona fides of regularly employed service people such as housekeepers and landscapers should be established. Finally, residential entry doors should be locked, always!

Commercial Art Galleries

Commercial art galleries are in business to sell art to the public. They are typically located in areas zoned for retail business and often housed in storefront settings. They are open to the public during business hours and sometimes staffed by employees. During nonbusiness hours, typically nights and portions of weekends and holidays, these premises are vacant. Effective sales practices require that the art be prominently displayed for examination by potential buyers to include window displays and/or interior placements that permit viewing from the street. During business hours, commercial galleries are vulnerable to larceny and robbery while burglary would be a concern during nonbusiness hours. It should be noted that some galleries only permit entry of known customers and/or by appointment to reduce larceny and robbery probabilities. Monitored security systems, which should include covertly placed keypads to summon police assistance in the event of larceny or robbery, should be installed in commercial galleries. Limited edition prints are particularly susceptible to theft because they might not be missed when there are multiple copies of the same image on hand. While safeguarding against customer larceny, the unfortunate reality is that gallery owners need to be cognizant of employee theft as well.

Ideally, potential commercial art-gallery locations should be evaluated from a security perspective before commencing business. Both geographic location and building characteristics should be considered. High-traffic business areas that are relatively free from crime would be preferable as would retail space that provides an on-site security guard presence. Absent the latter, building vulnerability to burglary should be assessed. For example, is there sufficient exterior lighting to discourage burglars from attempting a nighttime entry and are there any obstructions that would prevent observation of individuals attempting to gain access to the building? How accessible is the roof and how easily can entry be made from it? In multistory and/or multitenant buildings, do neighboring tenants (whether commercial or residential) affect the vulnerability risk and can access to the art gallery be gained through any of the adjoining (including above and below) office or residential space? Exterior doors should be reinforced, particularly those that provide access from nonpublic areas such as rear entrances.

Churches

The theft of art objects from churches has gained particular notoriety throughout Europe, including Eastern Europe. However, the scope of this problem probably extends to other corners of the world, with Central and South America coming readily to mind. Thus, thefts of religious art are probably grossly underreported, and bear in mind that we are limiting our consideration here to churches in the more modern-day tradition as

opposed to objects associated with religious practices found in archeological settings. The context of art in churches differs from other settings
in which art is displayed. Art adorns churches as an adjunct to the spirituality of the environment and to enhance the religious rituals that are
carried out there. This unique context poses a threefold problem in terms
of protecting the art. First, awareness that religious art objects have some
worldly value outside of their roles in the church and can be targets for
thieves has been slow to evolve. Second, in order to be part of the spiritual
environment and the religious rituals, worshippers and even guests must
feel a connectedness and proximity to artworks on display. They cannot
be segregated from the worship areas of a church in a museum or gallery-
like fashion, if they are to fulfill their roles in this context. Third, churches
have a tradition of openness in terms of their physical accessibility, often
with little oversight when services are not underway. Given this scenario,
it should not be surprising that art thieves have been frequent visitors to
churches and, unfortunately, not to engage in worship.

Protection of art in churches must begin with greater security awareness
on the part of clergy and lay leaders. Many churches have valuable art
collections and they need to be recognized as such. As described above,
the development of inventories and regular inspections is a commonsense first step in protecting art collections and obviously has no impact
on placement or accessibility concerns. However, the latter cannot be ignored. Whether it is to deter the theft of art or other valuables, vandalism
or other problems, churches should not remain open to the public without
oversight from clergy, parishioners, custodial/maintenance personnel, or
security guards. Church doors (and locks), both those for public entrance
and those for private or service entry, should be reinforced and resistant
to break-in. Ample exterior lighting (perhaps triggered by movement if
continuous lighting would be aesthetically inappropriate for these premises) to permit observation of individuals on church grounds when dark is
a burglary deterrent. Likewise, the removal of large objects such as trash
dumpsters from locations that would block observation of individuals attempting to break in is also another deterrent step. Moreover, the installation of a monitored security system to detect break-ins when the church is
closed and vacant should be considered, based on a burglary risk assessment of the church (e.g., the crime rate in the neighborhood and the value
of art and other objects that are on the premises). Finally, where possible,
art objects in churches should be displayed in locations that would make
their theft difficult. Avoiding placements near exit doors and windows
reduces theft vulnerability, especially when the objects are within reach,
are not affixed in any manner, and/or are small in size.

Public Art Displays

Art that falls into this category includes sculptures in parks and other
outdoor settings; sculptures, paintings, and other art objects in public

buildings such as lobbies in office buildings, shopping malls, and transportation terminals; and cultural-heritage sites. The common feature among these different settings is that art is displayed in areas open to the public and with the exception of cultural-heritage sites, these areas are not art forums per se. Parks provide areas for relaxation and recreation, but are also sometimes convenient thoroughfares for pedestrians, cyclists, and motorists. People frequent office buildings to conduct business, shopping malls to shop, and transportation terminals to begin or conclude travel. Art is displayed in these settings for both decorative and cultural reasons. While cultural-heritage sites differ from these settings in that they are art-specific in nature, they also tend to be located in more open and often remote areas while at the same time open to public visitation. Thus, in this sense they share similar security concerns that arise in public parks, office buildings, shopping malls, and transportation terminals.

At the risk of being repetitive, the need for inventorying art objects on display in public settings is a necessary step in providing protection. Like churches, an awareness to take this step and to periodically verify that the objects on the inventory list are in fact, on hand, might not be well developed among the types of government agencies or business organizations that are responsible for areas where this art is located. Custodians of cultural-heritage sites should be well aware of this basic step but are cautioned to ensure continual updating of their inventory along with regularly scheduled verification inspections.

While perhaps not universal, one advantage in many public office buildings, shopping malls, and transportation terminals is the presence of security personnel, often on a 24-hour basis, who will help to deter theft and vandalism of artwork on display. In addition, where these facilities do not afford 24-hour public access, monitored security systems are commonplace to deter break-ins. Sculptures located in outdoor areas tend to be under less scrutiny and, thus, easier targets for thieves and vandals. Ample lighting that permits observation of would-be thieves and vandals when dark, coupled with regular security/police patrols and/or monitored surveillance cameras, offers the best opportunities to protect outdoor, public-access sculptures from theft and vandalism.

Protecting cultural-heritage sites from looting and vandalism presents another unique set of problems that might be even more complex than other public art displays discussed so far. These locations can be located in remote areas and expansive in size. Thus, controlling access to these sites can require a substantial commitment of resources on a 24-hour-a-day basis in order to facilitate tourism on the one hand and to protect them from looting and vandalism on the other. Ideally, a trained and sufficiently staffed security-guard force should be on hand to provide round-the-clock coverage on the site premises. Physical security measures should augment the guard force to the extent possible including fencing and other access barriers, exterior and interior lighting as appropriate in order to provide ample illumination when dark, monitored closed-circuit television cameras to provide surveillance throughout the site, and alarm systems to detect intrusion into prohibited areas and the attempted removal of objects on display.

Museums

Among the various categories of art custodians, conventional wisdom would likely draw a parallel between museums and banks in terms of the level of protective measures employed to safeguard their valuables. To be sure, many museums, particularly those that are large and well funded, would not disappoint in this regard. However, while the events of theft and vandalism detailed throughout this volume are well known to museum officials worldwide, the level of security at museums is nevertheless inconsistent. As noted earlier in this chapter, even basic inventory procedures and verifications are not universally practiced. Even when these practices are in place, smaller, less well-funded museums can struggle to maintain the latest in security technology and/or an adequate guard force. In addition, museums in many parts of the underdeveloped world struggle with underfunding and inadequate training for security and yet house some of the most important collections of art and artifacts from ancient civilizations. Sharon Waxman, while researching her book, *Loot: The Battle Over the Stolen Treasures of the Ancient* (2008), observed few guards at the Egyptian Museum in Cairo, and those who were present allowed visitors to touch objects on display and even sit on the one of the sphinxes for photo opportunities. And, of course, whether large or small, well-funded or struggling, all museums strive to display their collections in a manner that is most accessible to visitors. Unfortunately, thieves have recognized and taken advantage of this vulnerability, especially at the smaller, less well-protected institutions. Moreover, as one Interpol official noted incident to the theft at the Bührle Collection in Switzerland in 2008, the advent of armed robberies at museums has introduced a further complication in protecting art, even at institutions with otherwise sound security measures against burglary, larceny, and vandalism.[4] The brazen use of firearms and physical force has compelled some museums to adopt security measures that are more similar to post-9/11 air travel than they would be to a museum visit. For instance, after *The Scream* robbery in 2004, the Munch Museum began requiring visitors to be scanned by a metal detector and their belongings examined through an X-ray machine. Once inside, to the dismay of many, they found themselves traversing a predetermined tour through the museum and viewing their favorite paintings from behind bulletproof screens. At the Uffizi Museum in Florence, Italy, increased security procedures in response to terrorist threats have resulted in longer waits to enter and higher admission costs to pay for screening equipment and additional personnel.[5]

Thus, the goal of providing accessibility to the art while affording it adequate protection continues to be an ongoing challenge, even at large, well-funded museums. Best practices in museum security combine the latest in high technology with a guard force that is adequate in number and well trained. These practices are discussed in more detail below.

Museum Security: Technology

Security technology for museums falls into two general categories: equipment that provides perimeter security and equipment that provides interior security. Perimeter security equipment detects intrusions through exterior entry points such as doors and windows. Electronic sensor devices can be installed at exterior entry points and when armed, send signals to monitoring stations and/or sound alarms when intrusions occur. This category of equipment can also include exterior lighting systems, exterior surveillance cameras, and reinforced doors and windows. Interior security equipment detects intrusions into protected areas through visual observation and motion, the removal of objects from their display positions, and even violation of the secure space between an object and museum visitors.[6]

Just as keeping pace with technology developments generally can prove frustrating, so too it is with the advent of new gadgetry for protecting art objects. Some of the new directions focus on protecting individual objects through smart tags and fingerprinting. Radio-frequency identification tags (RFID) can be affixed to objects, thus permitting wireless-tracking capability, at least while on the premises. In addition, the tags can emit signals that distinguish light touches versus a heavy touch and lift.[7] Methods to provide positive identification to art and cultural-heritage objects without tagging or other forms of alteration are also a possibility. While some works of art are one of kind and easily identifiable, cultural-heritage objects in particular can lack unique characteristics that could facilitate their theft and then impede recovery. One effort in this direction focuses on the use of scanning technology that would record unique texture and color characteristics in a small area of an object, thus resulting in the equivalent of a fingerprint. The scanned data would be then entered into a computer. Like automated fingerprint systems (AFIS) widely in use in crime labs, the texture and color characteristics of an object in question could be scanned and compared to data on file to determine if it has a known owner or origin. A unique fingerprint of a stone, ceramic, or wood object can also be obtained through sonic tomography. This process is based on the principle that objects emit distinct vibrations. Objects are fitted with sensors on an object and tapped with a small rubber hammer. A recording of the vibrations is made that can be used for comparison purposes in the future, if identification becomes an issue. While providing an effective form of identification, it is also expensive in terms of equipment and trained personnel. Since vibration patterns can change over time on the same object, the process would have to be repeated every few years.[8]

Security Officers

Notwithstanding the sophistication and advances in security technology at museums, the other part of the equation for providing protection to art is the human resource. Security-officer presence at museums, of course, is a well-established protective measure, and it continues to play an essential role in this regard. After all, who is it in this high-tech era that monitors all the sophisticated security equipment, including closed-circuit TV monitors providing real-time images? However, these are behind-the-scenes roles for security personnel. In many ways, security officers are still the public face of the museum to many visitors, and as such, they need to be more than just a physical presence. They need to be vigilant and observant in ways that permit them to be preemptive, that is, be able to identify suspicious behaviors, thus permitting early intervention to theft or vandalism, if necessary. The development of such skills should be part of formal training for museum security personnel along with first aid and CPR techniques, responding to fires, evacuation procedures, handling confrontational visitors, and so forth. Most museums do not arm their security officers with firearms, notwithstanding an increase in violent crimes at museums. The prevailing sentiment is that the risk that firearms present in the hands of museum security officers (even with proper training) outweighs any benefit of increased art security and protection of visitors. In terms of personal qualities, security officers should possess a congenial attitude toward visitors and museum staff (who should also be under their watchful eyes) that is pleasant and helpful. While security officers can be trained in the needed job skills, evaluating these requisite personal qualities at the time of hire requires special care. Although unfortunately not predictive of people skills per se, preemployment background checks should be performed that verify prior employment and education, check credit history, conduct drug testing (and on an ongoing basis while in service), and make criminal-history inquiries. Staffing a museum with a professionally trained guard force represents a substantial, but necessary, commitment of human resources in terms of the number of personnel required and the money needed for salaries, benefits, and training. Remember, security officers should be on duty 24 hours a day, seven days a week. While more officers might be required during visitor hours, a continuing need for both a physical presence and security-equipment monitoring exists on an around-the-clock basis. It is not uncommon, however, to augment a museum's permanent security staff with contract officers in the event of special exhibitions that draw larger-than-normal crowds and extended visitor hours. In any event, protecting art in museums requires a two-pronged approached: the application of security technology and a trained, adequately staffed security force. These two approaches complement each other; one cannot replace the other.[9]

Other Security Considerations: Storing and Transporting Art

Before leaving the subject of protecting art from theft, two other scenarios warrant special consideration: thefts of art while in storage and thefts of art while in transit. Notwithstanding the need for the two-pronged security approach described above that largely focuses on visitors and intruders, according to security experts, most museum art thefts are committed by individuals employed or contracted by the museum. Moreover, why steal from a public display where a missing object would be quickly noticed when museum employees and contractors can have access to art objects in storage areas and/or while being transported where thefts can go unnoticed (at least for awhile)? Again, however, applying the combination of security technology with security-officer presence can help to reduce the theft risks at these vulnerable points. Art that is not on display should be stored in defined storage rooms that have limited access and are under lock and key. Electronic access to these rooms would be preferable since such systems can record and identify those that enter and leave along with the date and time; although at a minimum, a manual entry-log system should be maintained when a standard lock-and-key system controls access. Alarms can also be installed to alert when an unauthorized intrusion occurs, and the entrance to these areas as well as the rooms themselves can be under actively monitored video surveillance. Nonpublic areas of museums need to be under the watchful eye of security officers, and constant vigil needs to be maintained when service and construction work is being performed within the museum. Many museums require employees and contractors to wear identification badges and to enter and exit the building through specially designated portals staffed by security officers. Security-officer duties at these stations can include subjecting employees and contractors to the same types of procedures as museum visitors undergo, for example, bag checks. Museum mail-room procedures must preclude the sealing of any outgoing mail prior to mail-room acceptance so that stolen art objects cannot leave the building in this manner. The safe transport of valuable art can be a complex undertaking, in terms of both preventing damage as well as theft. Experienced museum security officials should be involved in planning transportation arrangements, to include working through law-enforcement agencies on domestic and/or international levels to provide adequate protection. Interpol has facilitated such cooperation when valuable art is transported internationally.[10]

FORGERIES, FAKES, AND COUNTERFEITS: PREVENTING VICTIMIZATION AND DETERRING THESE PRACTICES

While perhaps complex in their application, the concepts of security and prevention as a way to protect art from theft and looting is a straightforward, commonsense approach to reduce the risks of these crimes. Thinking back to chapter 4, however, recall that art forgeries, fakes, and counterfeits are crimes of a different sort. Victimization in these instances occurs not because art is stolen; rather, victimization occurs through fraud and misrepresentation; that is, the art is falsely described to be authentic in order to induce a purchase. When a purchaser is duped under these circumstances, he/she acquires a phony piece of art and, in many instances, parts with a substantial amount of money in so doing. Of course, just as there are individuals who knowingly purchase fake Rolex watches to impress others, there are individuals of a similar mind-set who will knowingly purchase an art forgery or fake or do not care about the details of authenticity as long as it looks like the real thing. But for those prospective art purchasers who do want the real thing, the prevention measures discussed below focus on how they can protect themselves from being scammed.

Taking these measures, however, addresses another form of victimization as well. The expectation of visitors to museums is that they will be able to view and enjoy original and authentic art objects. Although perhaps in an intangible sense, museum visitors who view a painting that is not really the work of a famous master they so admire, or examine an object from an ancient civilization that was really not created in that era are also victims of forgery, fakery, and counterfeiting. Thus, art institutions should undertake due diligence steps to ensure that they are presenting authentic works to their patrons. Finally, just as a guarded and/ or alarmed premises might deter some thieves from stealing art located therein, the tools available to detect forgeries and fakes might have some deterrent value as well.

The Authentication Process

When questions or suspicions arise about whether an art object is a fake or forgery, the work's authenticity can be subjected to scrutiny through three lines of inquiry. Connoisseurship, that is, visual inspection of the object by an expert in the field, has been the traditional means for establishing or refuting authenticity; and this line of inquiry continues to be the gold standard. The other lines of inquiry include establishing the provenance (or history) of the work and examining the work through scientific testing. Through connoisseurship, an expert renders a judgment on authenticity based on an informed perception and interpretation of the forms and features specific to the artist in question. In this sense, such examinations are similar to forensic handwriting analysis where features such as slope, angle, and looping of letters are considered. While not to diminish the skill and training of forensic handwriting analysts, the knowledge a connoisseur has acquired on a particular artist or era is comprehensive in all respects and not just limited to stylistic and design features. Thus, connoisseurs will also consider the provenance of the piece in question.

This line of inquiry attempts to trace the history of the work back to its creator, which includes identifying transfers of ownership and possession and its locations. However, what is learned through such research likewise requires the interpretation of an expert, especially when the history surrounding a work is incomplete or unclear (circumstances that are not unusual). Provenance can be established through both oral and written evidence, with the latter consisting of such documentary items as bills of sale, recorded testimony, gallery/museum catalogs, and catalogues raisonnés (i.e., a scholar's definitive compilation of an artist's works). The final line of inquiry, scientific testing, is a still-evolving field in terms of art authentication because of the ever-increasing sophistication of the technology that is available for application in this context. It has proven to be more useful in refuting authenticity than in confirming it, which, of course, is significant for purposes being considered here. In any event, results from scientific testing are best understood when combined with information gained through visual inspection and provenance research.[11]

Scientific testing also can be very expensive although initial laboratory examination steps are typically low tech and, thus, lower in cost. These initial steps can consist of examinations using ultraviolet light and low-power microscopy as well as a visual inspection. The use of ultraviolet light is a familiar examination to many, as both real art experts and those who pretend to be (e.g., undercover law-enforcement agents posing as art experts) commonly use this tool to examine the surface of a painting. Ultraviolet light is able to differentiate paint on the surface of a work from underlying paint, thus highlighting any additions or alterations that have been made. Whether such a discovery is relevant, however, requires the interpretative knowledge of a true expert. It can also be used to evaluate sculptures made from stone and terra cotta and ceramic objects when authenticity is in question based on color variations in stone due to age and the identification of cracks and repairs. Microscopic examination permits detailed observation of texture and paint application, although making sense of these observations again requires an expert's knowledge and judgment. Finally, a visual inspection will look at such features as the carpentry methods and tools used to make the frame, the canvas on which the painting was created, and the tacks or nails that hold the frame together and affix the painting to it. The question to be answered is whether the observed methods and materials are consistent with the purported era of the painting, another assessment requiring specialized knowledge and judgment.[12]

Other Scientific Examinations

As suggested earlier, scientific examination of artworks to address authenticity questions is an ever-evolving area due to the proliferation of technologies that can be applied. In the paragraphs that follow, scientific examinations that can be employed beyond the basic inquiries discussed above are described. Many of these examinations fall into the cutting edge of technology category, notwithstanding the initial focus on handwriting analysis.

- Handwriting Analysis—Document examination is a well-established field within forensic science. Among the analyses within this discipline is handwriting examination, the results of which can be accepted by courts as positive identification. And, in fact, courts have given substantial weight to handwriting-examination results involving an artist's signature in litigation over the authenticity of a work, although art experts are less supportive of positive signature identification as being definitive of a work's authenticity.[13] Along these lines, two realities need to be pointed out about pursuing forensic examination of an artist's signature. First, not all artists place their signature on their works, thus making this examination a moot issue in some cases. Second, forensic handwriting examination is conducted comparing known specimens of a person's handwriting to handwriting that is in question. Thus, a handwriting examiner would need multiple known signatures of an artist to compare to a questioned signature. Finally, it must be recognized that handwriting-examination results are sometimes expressed in less than conclusive terms, for example, "the author of the known specimens *probably* wrote the questioned signature." In criminal proceedings, a less-than-positive handwriting identification would not provide a sole basis for a conviction due to the proof-beyond-a-reasonable-doubt standard; and moreover, such a conclusion would probably become fodder for defense arguments in these proceedings. In civil litigation, however, because of the lower burden of proof, a less-than-conclusive opinion *might* be material, especially when combined with other supporting evidence. The issue of a less-than-positive result could be particularly relevant when examining signatures made with an artist's brush. Many document examiners prefer to deal with writing that was authored using a standard writing instrument such as a ballpoint pen or pencil as these types of instruments tend to produce consistency in a writer's style. Most writers control these types of instruments better than nonstandard writing tools such as brushes, and even felt-tipped pens. Also, the manner in which ink, or in this case paint, is absorbed onto a surface can also be a troubling factor in handwriting identification. If the ink or paint tends to bleed into the surface to which it is applied, changes in character formation will likely occur, thus possibly adding inconsistencies that cannot be explained within a set of known specimens. All of which is to say that the reality of obtaining probative handwriting-analysis results in support of authenticity litigation can be a less than certain venture.
- Age Determinations—Establishing the age of an object or materials used in its creation can be an indicator of authenticity. For instance, thermoluminescence can measure accumulated radiation in a ceramic object, which is an indicator of the length of time that has elapsed since it was fired. Likewise, radio carbon dating can also be used to determine the age of materials used in creating an object. When results from these tests are inconsistent with the purported age of an object, the authenticity of the object would be in question.[14]
- Dendrochronology—This is the science of studying growth rings in trees to determine their age, which in turn provides a method for establishing the age of

wood used in art frames and panels. New developments in this field often allow for identification of the species of the wood in question and, occasionally, close approximations of the date the tree was felled. When available, this latter information has proved helpful in identifying forgeries and fakes that were created long ago, but still after the era they purport to represent.[15] Pigment Analysis—Raman spectroscopy, although costly, is a noninvasive procedure that conducts pigment analysis through laser-microscope examination. The process involves shining infrared beams on the painting's surface in order to identify the chemical composition of the various color pigments. Micro-chemical testing is another form of pigment analysis although one that is more invasive as it involves introducing a reagent to a paint layer to observe a reaction for a specific pigment. The presence of chemical compositions not known to be in use at the time the painting was created would raise authenticity concerns, at least when there is a firm understanding of the chemical evolution of color pigment(s) in question. Such findings might also indicate that the painting had undergone restoration in some later period.[16]

- Imaging Technology—Imaging procedures akin to those used in medicine produce views of art objects that can be useful in identifying forgeries and fakes. Radiographs assist in comparing known works to questioned works in terms of how the artist created the painting. They can also examine the interior of wooden or metal objects in order to establish authenticity. CAT scans provide three-dimensional views of objects made from materials ranging from wood and marble to terra cotta.[17]

- Infrared Examination—This procedure will reveal underdrawings or grids made by the artist when using carbon inks or paints on light backgrounds. These observations, however, require interpretation and expert knowledge of the artist who purportedly created the work.[18]

- Computer-Assisted Art Authentication—The application of computer technology to painting authenticity evaluations is among the newer directions for scientific examination in this area. It is based on the premise that an artist will adhere to certain patterns in creating his/her work in terms of color, contrast, brush strokes, structures, and so forth. Computer software can scan for the presence and/or frequency of these characteristics in known works by an artist, and then this data can be compared to the presence and/or frequency of similar characteristics in works of questioned origin through a subsequent scanning process. The identification of similar patterns would suggest the work in question is authentic while wide variations would argue against this assessment. So far, computer-assisted art authentication has met with cautious optimism among art experts.[19]

Forward-Looking Approaches

A measure current-day artists might consider to safeguard their works from forgery and counterfeiting is to seek protection under trademark laws. In the United States, artists would be able to design and register through the U.S. Copyright Office a distinct logo or monogram that would appear on their works. This form of identification would be superior to an artist's signature on a work (if one appears at all) in terms of establishing authenticity in a litigation. Moreover, the unauthorized importation of goods bearing a federally registered trademark can result in a seizure at the border by government officials. Such actions could prevent counterfeit artworks from entering the U.S. market. And if adopting such an identification scheme seems "un-artist-like" consider this: in the 16th century, Albrecht Dürer identified his works using a distinctive monogram inside an Egyptian-style cartouche, while the American master James McNeill Whistler used a combination of his name and a butterfly as a way of personal branding.[20]

Another direction that is being pursued for providing positive identification to artworks is through DNA encryption. Technology has been developed whereby an artist's DNA is used to make a unique anticounterfeit inkpad; that is, the artist's DNA is encrypted in the ink. Each piece of art the artist produces is then accompanied by a DNA-artwork certificate that is printed using this inkpad; thus, the certificate contains the unique DNA of the artist. The certificate contains such information as the name of the artwork, time/date of production, serial number, photographs, information on the art collection, and so forth.[21]

Finally, let's revisit our need for that comprehensive art-crimes database again. In addition to detailed information on thefts and missing artwork and cultural-heritage objects, let's consider another data field that would attempt to track and monitor known forgeries, fakes, and counterfeits. Just as the marketing of stolen artworks can be curbed through registering them in our existing databases, so too could we limit the marketability of forgeries, fakes, and counterfeits if a similar type of database were available. Given the proliferation of limited edition prints in the art market and the ever-improving technology that facilitates art forgery, fakery, and counterfeiting, our database needs have clearly expanded into this direction as well.[22]

Appendix A

COMMON ART-OBJECT CATEGORIES: DEFINITIONS

American painting and sculpture: Portraits, landscapes, history paintings, still lifes, folk art, and sculpture from colonial times through the early 20th century.

Ancient Near Eastern art: Stone reliefs and sculpture, ivory, and objects of precious metal from a vast area and time span: Anatolia to the Indus Valley, Neolithic period (ca. 8,000 B.C.E.) to the Arab conquest (7th century C.E.).

antiquities: A general category that includes Ancient Near Eastern art; arts of Africa, Oceania, and the Americas; Egyptian art; and Greek and Roman art. Some typologies might include archeological objects in this category.

arms and armor: Armor for men, horses, and children; weapons; and martial accoutrements of sculptural and ornamental beauty from Europe, Asia, the Middle East, and America.

arts of Africa, Oceania, and the Americas: Ritual objects and monuments, articles of personal adornment, and utensils for daily life from three continents (including Native American objects) and dozens of Pacific islands, 2,000 B.C.E. to the present. Some typologies might include archeological objects in this category.

Asian art: Paintings, calligraphy, prints, sculpture, ceramics, bronzes, jades, lacquer, textiles, and screens from ancient to modern China, Japan, Korea, and South and Southeast Asia.

costumes: Fashionable dress, regional costumes, and accessories for men, women, and children, up to the present.

Based on definitions from the Metropolitan Museum of Art at http://www.metmuseum.org/Works_of_Art/curatorial_departments (accessed April 16, 2008).

decorative arts: Furniture, silver, pewter, glass, ceramics, and textiles, as well as domestic architecture in furnished period rooms.

drawings and prints: Graphic art of the Renaissance and after, encompassing prints in all techniques, sketches to highly finished drawings, illustrated books, and other works on paper.

Egyptian art: Statuary, reliefs, stelae, funerary objects, jewelry, daily implements, and architecture from prehistoric Egypt through the Old, Middle, and New Kingdoms to the Roman period (fourth century C.E.).

ethnographic objects: Ritual objects and monuments, articles of personal adornment, and utensils for daily life dating from the earliest human civilizations to the present. Some typologies might include archeological objects in this category.

European paintings: Major canvases, panels, triptychs, and frescoes by Italian, Flemish, Dutch, French, Spanish, and British masters, from the 12th through the 19th century.

European sculpture and decorative arts: Sculpture, furniture, ceramics and glass, metalwork, scientific instruments, textiles, and period rooms of the major Western European countries from the Renaissance through the early 20th century.

fine arts: A general category that typically encompasses paintings, photographs, prints, drawings, and sculpture.

Greek and Roman art: Arts of Greece, Rome, Etruria, Cyprus, and Greek and Roman settlements until the fourth century C.E., including marble, bronze, and terracotta sculpture, vases, wall paintings, jewelry, gems, glass, and utilitarian objects.

Islamic art: Manuscripts and miniatures, carpets, intricately decorated objects in many media, and architectural elements from the founding of Islam in the seventh century C.E. onward, from Morocco to India. Sometimes this category is also labeled as Oriental and Islamic art, thus expanding its content into Asia.

medieval art: Early European, Byzantine, Carolingian, Romanesque, and Gothic works from the 4th to 16th century, including sculpture, tapestries, reliquaries, liturgical vessels, illuminated manuscripts, stained glass, metalwork, enamels, ivories, paintings, and so forth.

modern art: American and European paintings, works on paper, sculpture, design, and architecture representing the major artistic movements since 1900.

musical instruments: Instruments of historical, technical, and social importance, as well as tonal and visual beauty.

photographs: Prints and daguerreotypes from the early history of the medium to present.

textiles: Tapestries, velvets, carpets, embroideries, laces, samplers, quilts, and woven and printed fabrics from all periods and civilizations.

Appendix B

SELECTED ART-LOSS DATABASES

National Government Agencies

Argentina
National Police: http://www.interpol.gov.ar/patrimonio/patrimonio_menu.asp

Austria
BM.I: http://www.bmi.gv.at/fahndung/

Belgium
Federal Police for the judicial district of Oudenaarde: http://users.pandora.be/
fedpol.far.oudenaarde/engels/page3.htm

Chile
PICH: http://www.investigaciones.cl/paginas/arterb/arterb_dspl.htm

France
Gendarmerie Nationale: http://www.gendarmerie.defense.gouv.fr/judiciaire/
Police Nationale: http://193.252.228.130/osvnaviguer.asp?N=18

From STOLEN ART (Listings on Line), "A Search for the World's Most Wanted Art," http://
www.saztv.com/page9.html (accessed September 30, 2007).

Romania
Polita Romana: http://www.politiaromana.ro/obiecte/obdetalii.aspx

Serbia
Policija: http: //www.mup.sr.gov.yu/domino/objave.nsf/uudela

Slovenia
Policija: http://www.policija.si/si/kriminal/ukradene_slike/slk_prikaz.php

Spain
Guardia Civil: http://www.guardiacivil.org/patrimonio/obrec_princip.jsp

Switzerland
Swiss Police: http://www.swisspolice.ch/e/4_sachfdg/aktuell_kg1.htm

Local Police Agencies

Canada
Quebec: http://www.suretequebec.gouv.qc.ca/lutte/objets_perdus.html

Germany
Baden-Württemburg: http://www.polizei-bw.de/fahndung/
Berlin: http://www.berlin.de/polizei/presse-fahndung/sachfahndung.html
Thüringen: http://www.thueringen.de/de/lka/fahndung/sachfahndung/

Switzerland
Lucerne: http://www.kapo.lu.ch/index/fahn_sachfahndung.htm
Zurich: http://www.kapo.zh.ch/internet/ds/kapo/de/fahndungen.html

United States
Los Angeles: http://www.lapdonline.org/art_theft_detail/
San Antonio: http://www.ci.sat.tx.us/sapd/StolenArt2003.htm; http://www.ci.sat.tx.us/sapd/statues.htm

Private Sector Databases

Australia
Jinta Fine Arts: http://www.jintaart.com.au/stolen_works/stolenpaint.htm

Belgium
Stolenart.be: http://www.stolenart.be/Classifieds/home.asp

Denmark
Antikbrevkassen: http://www.antikbrevkassen.dk/katindex.asp?kukat=83

Germany

www.Kidnapped-art.com: http://www.kunstraub.de/KRaub_Frame.htm

Lost Art Internet Database: http://www.lostart.de/recherche/index.php3?lang=
english

Iraq

Lost Treasures from Iraq: http://oi.uchicago.edu/OI/IRAQ/dbfiles/Iraqdatabase
home.htm

Italy

City of Palermo: http://www.comune.palermo.it/Chilehaviste/varie/oggetti_vari.
html

InvestigArte: http://www.investigarte.com/bancadati_eng.htm

Mexico

Arte Mexico: http://www.arte-mexico.com/robada.htm

Nepal

Stolen Art of Nepal: http://asianart.com/kvpt/stolen/

Netherlands

Gestolen Kunst: http://www.gestolenkunst.nl/index.htm

Poland

War Time Losses: http://www.polamcon.org/lostart/intro.htm

United Kingdom

Antique Tribal Art Dealers Association: http://www.atada.org/theft.html

The Bryan Roberts H. Gallery: http://robertsgallery.com/stolen_art_and_art_theft_
update.htm

Find Stolen Art: http://www.findstolenart.com/

MissingFortunes.com: http://www.missingfortunes.com/cgi-bin/Forums/YaBB.
pl?board=Unclaimed_Art

Theft-Alerts.com: http://www.theft-alerts.com/index-2.html

Selected Bibliography

Adler, F., Mueller, G.O.W, and Laufer, W. S. 2007. *Criminology.* 6th ed. New York: McGraw-Hill.

Alford, K. D. 1994. *The Spoils of World War II: The American Military's Role in the Stealing of Europe's Treasures.* New York: Carol Publishing.

Atwood, R. 2004. *Stealing History: Tomb Raiders, Smugglers, and the Looting of the Ancient World.* New York: St. Martin's Press.

Barelli, J. J. 1986. "On Understanding the Business of Art and Antique Theft: An Exploratory Study." PhD diss., Fordham University.

Becker, H. S. 1982. *Art Worlds.* Berkeley: University of California Press.

Berouigeut, B. 1986. "Interpol and the Fight Against Art Thefts." *International Police Review* 395: 30–37.

Bogdanos, M. (with W. Patrick). 2005. *Thieves of Baghdad: One Marine's Passion for Ancient Civilizations and the Journey to Recover the World's Greatest Stolen Treasures.* New York: Bloomsbury.

Bresler, F. 1992. *Interpol.* London: Sinclair-Stevenson.

Brodie, N. Doole, J. and Refrew, C. eds. 2001. *Trade in Illicit Antiquities: The Destruction of the World's Archaeological Heritage,* Oxford, UK: Oxbow Books.

Conklin, J. E. 1994. *Art Crime.* Westport, CT: Praeger.

Cuno, J. 2008. *Who Owns Antiquity?: Museums and the Battle Over Our Ancient Heritage.* Princeton, NJ: Princeton University Press.

Dolnick, E. 2005. *The Rescue Artist: A True Story of Art Thieves, and the Hunt for a Missing Masterpiece.* New York: Harper Collins.

Dolnick, E. 2008. *The Forger's Spell.* New York: Harper Collins.

Edsel, R. M. 2006. *Rescuing Da Vinci: Hitler and the Nazis Stole Europe's Great Art; America and Her Allies Recovered It.* Dallas, TX: Laurel Publishing.

Esterow, M. 1973. *The Art Stealers.* Rev. ed. New York: MacMillan.

Feliciano, H. 1995. *The Lost Museum: The Nazi Conspiracy to Steal the World's Greatest Works of Art.* New York: Harper Collins.

Grampp, W. D. 1989. *Pricing the Priceless: Art, Artists, and Economics.* New York: Basic Books.

Hart, M. 2004. *The Irish Game: A True Story of Crime and Art.* New York: Plume.

Hebborn, E. 1997. *The Art Forger's Handbook.* Woodstock, NY: The Overlook Press.

Ho, Truc-Nhu Thi. 1992. "Art Theft in New York City: An Exploratory Study in Crime Specificity." PhD diss. Rutgers, The State University of New Jersey, Newark.

Houpt, S. 2006. *Museum of the Missing: A History of Art Theft.* New York: Sterling Publishing.

Hoving, T. 1996. *False Impressions: The Hunt for Big-Time Art Fakes.* New York: Simon and Schuster.

LaFont, M. 2004. *Pillaging Cambodia: The Illicit Traffic in Khmer Art.* Jefferson, NC: McFarland and Co. Publishers.

Mason, C. 2004. *The Art of the Steal: Inside the Sotheby's-Christie's Auction House Scandal.* New York: Berkley.

Mason, D. L. 1979. *Fine Art of Art Security: Protecting Public and Private Collections Against Theft, Fire, and Vandalism.* New York: Van Nostrand Reinhold.

Mason, D. L. 1993. "Purloining the World's Art." In *Criminal and Civil Investigation Handbook,* ed. J. J. Grau, 54–59. New York: McGraw-Hill.

McLeave, H. 1981. *Rogues in the Gallery: The Modern Plague of Art Thefts.* Boston: David R. Godine.

Meyer, K. E. 1973. *The Plundered Past.* New York: Atheneum.

Nicholas, L. H. 1994. *The Rape of Europa: The Fate of Europe's Treasures in the Third Reich and the Second World War.* New York: Vintage Books.

Radnóti, S. 1999. *The Fake: Forgery and Its Place in Art.* Lanham, MD: Rowman and Littlefield.

Schmidt, P. R. and McIntosh, R. J., eds. 1996. *Plundering Africa's Past.* Bloomington: Indiana University Press.

Smith, C. W. 1989. *Auctions: The Social Construction of Value.* New York: The Free Press.

Spencer, R. D., ed. 2004. *The Expert vs. The Object: Judging Fakes and False Attributions in the Visual Arts.* New York: Oxford University Press.

Spiel, R. E., Jr. 2000. *Art Theft and Forgery Investigation: The Complete Field Manual.* Springfield, IL: Charles C. Thomas.

Sutherland, E. 1940. "White-Collar Criminality." *American Sociological Review* 5 (1):1–12.

Tijhuis, A.J.G. 2006. *Transnational Crime and the Interface between Legal and Illegal Actors: The Case of the Illicit Art and Antiquities Trade.* The Netherlands: Wolf Legal Publishers.

Tubb, K. W., ed. 1995. *Antiquities Trade or Betrayed: Legal, Ethical and Conservation Issues.* London, Archetype.

Watson, P. 1997. *Sotheby's: Inside Story.* London: Bloomsbury.

Watson, P. and Todeschini, C. 2006. *The Medici Conspiracy: The Illicit Journey of Looted Antiquities from Italy's Tomb Raiders to the World's Greatest Museums.* New York: Public Affairs.

Waxman, S. 2008. *Loot: The Battle Over the Stolen Treasures of the Ancient World.* New York: Times Books.

Notes

CHAPTER 1: ART AND CRIME?

1. Dolnick, E. 2005. *The Rescue Artist: A True Story of Art Thieves, and the Hunt for a Missing Masterpiece.* New York: Harper Collins, 11.

2. Adler, F., Mueller, G.O.W, and Laufer, W. S. 2007. *Criminology.* 6th ed. New York: McGraw-Hill, 397–98.

3. Barlow, H. D. 1996. *Introduction to Criminology.* 7th ed. New York: Harper Collins, 7.

4. *Merriam Webster's Online Dictionary.* n.d. http://www.m-w.com/cgi-bin/dictionary (accessed August 31, 2007).

5. Adler, F., Mueller, G.O.W, and Laufer, W. S. 2007. *Criminology.* 6th ed. New York: McGraw-Hill, 11.

6. *Merriam Webster's Online Dictionary.* n.d. http://www.m-w.com/cgi-bin/dictionary (accessed August 31, 2007).

7. Barelli, J. J. 1986. "On Understanding the Business of Art and Antique Theft: An Exploratory Study." PhD diss., Fordham University, 11–12.

8. Conklin, J. E. 1994. *Art Crime.* Westport, CT: Praeger, 2.

9. Federal Bureau of Investigation. n.d. "Art Theft Program." http://www.fbi.gov/hq/cid/arttheft/nationalstolen.htm (accessed August 27, 2007).

10. Grampp, W. D. 1989. *Pricing the Priceless: Art, Artists, and Economics.* New York: Basic Books, 38.

11. Conklin, J. E. 1994. *Art Crime.* Westport, CT: Praeger, 7.

12. Frey, B. S. and Pommerehne, W. W. 1989. "Art Investment: An Empirical Inquiry." *Southern Economic Journal* 56 (2): 396–409.

13. Grampp, W. D. 1989. *Pricing the Priceless: Art, Artists, and Economics.* New York: Basic Books, 166.

14. Conklin, J. E. 1994. *Art Crime.* Westport, CT: Praeger, 45–46.

15. Houpt. S. 2006. *Museum of the Missing: A History of Art Theft.* New York: Sterling Publishing, 15.

16. Ho, Truc-Nhu Thi. 1992. "Art Theft in New York City: An Exploratory Study in Crime Specificity." PhD diss., Rutgers, The State University of New Jersey, Newark, 7–8.

17. Dolnick, E. 2005. *The Rescue Artist: A True Story of Art Thieves, and the Hunt for a Missing Masterpiece.* New York: Harper Collins, 132.

18. Ho, Truc-Nhu Thi. 1992. "Art Theft in New York City: An Exploratory Study in Crime Specificity." PhD diss., Rutgers, The State University of New Jersey, Newark, 5, 9.

19. Ibid., 50.

20. Grampp, W. D. 1989. *Pricing the Priceless: Art, Artists, and Economics.* New York: Basic Books, 37.

21. Spiel, R. E., Jr. 2000. *Art Theft and Forgery Investigation: The Complete Field Manual.* Springfield, IL: Charles C. Thomas, 10–11.

22. Ibid., 16–18.

23. Smith, C. W. 1989. *Auctions: The Social Construction of Value.* New York: The Free Press, x.

24. Ibid., 205.

25. Sotheby's. n.d. http://www.sothebys.com/help/ref/ref_liveterms.html#d1 (accessed September 3, 2007).

26. Watson, P. and Todeschini, C. 2006. *The Medici Conspiracy: The Illicit Journey of Looted Antiquities from Italy's Tomb Raiders to the World's Greatest Museums.* New York: Public Affairs, 28, 39.

27. Houpt. S. 2006. *Museum of the Missing: A History of Art Theft.* New York: Sterling Publishing, 157.

28. Watson, P. and Todeschini, C. 2006. *The Medici Conspiracy: The Illicit Journey of Looted Antiquities from Italy's Tomb Raiders to the World's Greatest Museums.* New York: Public Affairs, 261–62.

29. Sutherland, E. 1940. "White-Collar Criminality." *American Sociological Review* 5 (1): 1–12.

30. Adler, F., Mueller, G.O.W, and Laufer, W. S. 2007. *Criminology.* 6th ed. New York: McGraw-Hill, 1.

31. Spiel, R. E., Jr. 2000. *Art Theft and Forgery Investigation: The Complete Field Manual.* Springfield, IL: Charles C. Thomas, 112.

32. Conklin, J. E. 1994. *Art Crime.* Westport, CT: Praeger, 3.

33. Ibid., 4; Spiel, R. E., Jr. 2000. *Art Theft and Forgery Investigation: The Complete Field Manual.* Springfield, IL: Charles C. Thomas, 31.

34. Conklin, J. E. 1994. *Art Crime.* Westport, CT: Praeger, 3; Houpt, S. 2006. *Museum of the Missing: A History of Art Theft.* New York: Sterling Publishing, 11.

35. Houpt, S. 2006. *Museum of the Missing: A History of Art Theft.* New York: Sterling Publishing, 11; Adler, F., Mueller, G.O.W, and Laufer, W. S. 2007. *Criminology.* 6th ed. New York: McGraw-Hill, 294.

36. Houpt, S. 2006. *Museum of the Missing: A History of Art Theft.* New York: Sterling Publishing, 11.

37. Watson, P. and Todeschini, C. 2006. *The Medici Conspiracy: The Illicit Journey of Looted Antiquities from Italy's Tomb Raiders to the World's Greatest Museums.* New York: Public Affairs, 47.

38. Interpol. n.d. "Stolen Works of Art: Frequently Asked Questions." www. interpol.int/Public/WorkOfArt/woafaq.asp (accessed September 12, 2007).

39. Interpol. n.d. "Stolen Works of Art: Frequently Asked Questions." www. interpol.int/Public/WorkOfArt/woafaq.asp (accessed September 12, 2007). *Data sources:* www.artloss.com/home/content retrieved September 18, 2007; and Houpt, S. 2006. *Museum of the Missing: A History of Art Theft.* New York: Sterling Publishing, 8.

40. Kinsella, J. 2009. "Judge Gives Robert R. Mardirosian 7 Years in Prison, $100,000 Fine." *Cape Cod Today,* January 2 (accessed through Museum Security Network, http://groups.google.com/group/museum-security-network/t/ 9724cc35cdbfc955?hl=en, January 2, 2009); Saltzman J. 2008. "Ex-Lawyer Found Guilty in Stolen Art Trial; Had Discovered Paintings in 1980." *Boston Globe,* August 19 (accessed through Museum Security Network, http://groups.google.com/group/ museum-security-network/browse_thread/thread/1bdaef763578c7c3?hl=en, August 19, 2008); Saltzman, J. 2008. "Former Lawyer, 74, Sentenced to 7 Years in Stolen Art Case." *Boston Globe,* December 16 (accessed through Museum Security Network, http://groups.google.com/group/museum-security-network/t/ 1effeea62943411a?hl=en, December 16, 2008).

CHAPTER 2: ART THEFT

1. Federal Bureau of Investigation. n.d. *Uniform Crime Report.* http://www.fbi. gov/ucr/cius2006/index.html (accessed October 3, 2007).

2. United Nations. n.d. "Eighth United Nations Survey on Crime Trends." www.undoc.org/undoc/en/crime_cicp_survey_eighth.html (accessed October 2, 2007).

3. Houpt, S. 2006. *Museum of the Missing: A History of Art Theft.* New York: Sterling Publishing, 77–83; Dolnick, E. 2005. *The Rescue Artist: A True Story of Art Thieves, and the Hunt for a Missing Masterpiece.* New York: Harper Collins, 144–45; *St. Petersburg Times* (FL). 2009. "Art Thief Sentenced." January 8: 2A.

4. Edward Dolnick (2005) chronicles in detail the events of this case and the exploits of Charley Hill in his book, *The Rescue Artist: A True Story of Art Thieves, and the Hunt for a Missing Masterpiece,* New York: Harper Collins. The material reflected in this case study is largely drawn from this volume along with contributions from the following sources: Hart, M. 2004. *The Irish Game: A True Story of Crime and Art.* New York: Plume, 169; and Janson, H. W. 1966. *History of Art: A Survey of the Major Visual Arts from the Dawn of History to the Present Day.* 10th ed. Englewood Cliffs, NJ: Prentice Hall, 509.

5. Houpt, S. 2006. *Museum of the Missing: A History of Art Theft.* New York: Sterling Publishing, 11, 100; Dolnick, E. 2005. *The Rescue Artist: A True Story of Art Thieves, and the Hunt for a Missing Masterpiece.* New York: Harper Collins 241–43; *St. Petersburg Times* (FL). 2004. "Daylight Robbers Grab 'Scream,' 'Madonna.'" August 23: 1, 5A; *Art News.* 2006. "Three Convicted in Munch Museum Theft." Summer: 80; Associated Press. 2007. "Oslo Court Sentences Three in Theft of Munch Paintings." April 24 (accessed April 24, 2007 through Museum Security Network http://www.museum-security.org); Associated Press. 2008. "Munch Art Thieves Get Longer Sentences." January 11 (accessed April 29, 2008 through Museum Security Network, http://www.museum-security.org).

6. Adler, F., Mueller, G.O.W, and Laufer, W. S. 2007. *Criminology*. 6th ed. New York: McGraw-Hill, 294; Houpt, S. 2006. *Museum of the Missing: A History of Art Theft*. New York: Sterling Publishing, 11; Maneker, M. 2009. "Art Loss Register Data Dump." *Art Monitor*, April 23 (accessed through http://www.artmarket monitor.com/2009/04/23/art-loss-register-data-dump/, July 1, 2009).

7. Conklin, J. E. 1994. *Art Crime*. Westport, CT: Praeger, 154.

8. Weiss, C. H. 1998. *Evaluation*. 2nd ed. Upper Saddle River, NJ: Prentice Hall, 330.

9. Ho, Truc-Nhu Thi. 1992. "Art Theft in New York City: An Exploratory Study in Crime Specificity." PhD diss., Rutgers, The State University of New Jersey, Newark, 54.

10. Barelli, J. J. 1986. "On Understanding the Business of Art and Antique Theft: An Exploratory Study." PhD diss., Fordham University, 116–18.

11. Conklin, J. E. 1994. *Art Crime*. Westport, CT: Praeger, 156–57; Doland, A. and Satter, R. 2006. "At Least 170, 000 Stolen Artworks Remain Missing." *Tampa* (FL) *Tribune*, September 8: 13; Associated Press. 2005. "FBI Art-Theft Team Meets in Philly." January 14 (accessed January 14, 2005 through Museum Security, http://msn-list.te.verweg.com).

12. Barelli, J. J. 1986. "On Understanding the Business of Art and Antique Theft: An Exploratory Study." PhD diss., Fordham University, 116–18.

13. Ho, Truc-Nhu Thi. 1992. "Art Theft in New York City: An Exploratory Study in Crime Specificity." PhD diss., Rutgers, The State University of New Jersey, Newark, 54, 58.

14. Ibid., 87–89, 160.

15. *Merriam-Webster's Online Dictionary*. n.d. http://www.m-w.com/dictionary/anecdotal (accessed January 19, 2008).

16. Conklin, J. E. 1994. *Art Crime*. Westport, CT: Praeger, 119.

17. Doland, A. and Satter, R. 2006. "At Least 170, 000 Stolen Artworks Remain Missing." *Tampa* (FL) *Tribune*, September 8: 13; Associated Press. 2005. "FBI Art-Theft Team Meets in Philly." January 14 (accessed through http://msn-list.te.verweg.com/(accessed January 14, 2005); Burke, J. 2005. "Art Looting Smugglers Target French Churches." *Observer*, August 21, http://msn-list.te.verweg.com/ (accessed September 29, 2007).

18. Maneker, M. 2009. "Art Loss Register Data Dump." *Art Monitor*, April 23 (accessed through http://www.artmarketmonitor.com/2009/04/23/art-loss-register-data-dump/, July 1, 2009).

19. Barelli, J. J. 1986. "On Understanding the Business of Art and Antique Theft: An Exploratory Study." PhD diss., Fordham University, 8–9, 41; Maneker, M. 2009. "Art Loss Register Data Dump." *Art Monitor*, April 23 (accessed through http://www.artmarketmonitor.com/2009/04/23/art-loss-register-data-dump/, July 1, 2009).

20. Ho, Truc-Nhu Thi. 1992. "Art Theft in New York City: An Exploratory Study in Crime Specificity." PhD diss., Rutgers, The State University of New Jersey, Newark, 54.

21. Aarons, L. 2001. "Art Theft: An Exploratory Study of the Illegitimate Art Market in Australia." *Australia and New Zealand Journal of Criminology* 34 (1): 17–37.

22. Ho, Truc-Nhu Thi. 1992. "Art Theft in New York City: An Exploratory Study in Crime Specificity." PhD diss., Rutgers, The State University of New Jersey, Newark, 54; Houpt. S. 2006. *Museum of the Missing: A History of Art Theft*. New York: Sterling Publishing, 115.

23. Spiel, R. E., Jr. 2000. *Art Theft and Forgery Investigation: The Complete Field Manual.* Springfield, IL: Charles C. Thomas, 222.

24. Myers, S. L. 2006. "2 Arrested, Admit to Art Thefts." *Tampa* (FL) *Tribune,* August 6: 14; FitzGerald, N. 2006. "A Knife in Our Back." *Art News,* October: 84, 86; FitzGerald, N. 2007. "Hermitage Thief Sentenced." *Art News,* May: 90.

25. Conklin, J. E. 1994. *Art Crime.* Westport, CT: Praeger, 175–76.

26. Ho, Truc-Nhu Thi. 1992. "Art Theft in New York City: An Exploratory Study in Crime Specificity." PhD diss., Rutgers, The State University of New Jersey, Newark, 141.

27. Dolnick, E. 2005. *The Rescue Artist: A True Story of Art Thieves, and the Hunt for a Missing Masterpiece.* New York: Harper Collins, 11–12.

28. Hart, M. 2005. *The Irish Game: A True Story of Crime and Art.* New York: Plume, 59.

29. Spiel, R. E., Jr. 2000. *Art Theft and Forgery Investigation: The Complete Field Manual.* Springfield, IL: Charles C. Thomas, 42.

30. Houpt, S. 2006. *Museum of the Missing: A History of Art Theft.* New York: Sterling Publishing, 150.

31. Janson, H. W. 1966. *History of Art: A Survey of the Major Visual Arts from the Dawn of History to the Present Day.* 10th ed. Englewood Cliffs, NJ: Prentice Hall, 509.

32. Dolnick, E. 2005. *The Rescue Artist: A True Story of Art Thieves, and the Hunt for a Missing Masterpiece.* New York: Harper Collins; see unnumbered color plates.

33. Ibid., 14 and unnumbered color plates; Houpt, S. 2006. *Museum of the Missing: A History of Art Theft.* New York: Sterling Publishing, 170–71; Hennessee, J. 1990. "Why Great Art Always Will Be Stolen (And Seldom Found)." *Connoisseur,* July: 42.

34. Dolnick, E. 2005. *The Rescue Artist: A True Story of Art Thieves, and the Hunt for a Missing Masterpiece.* New York: Harper Collins, 14.

35. Ho, Truc-Nhu Thi. 1992. "Art Theft in New York City: An Exploratory Study in Crime Specificity." PhD diss., Rutgers, The State University of New Jersey, Newark, 141.

36. Barelli, J. J. 1986. "On Understanding the Business of Art and Antique Theft: An Exploratory Study." PhD diss., Fordham University, 37, 189, 194–95.

37. Esterow, M. 1973. *The Art Stealers.* Rev. ed. New York: Macmillan, 6.

38. Itoi, K. 2006. "Japanese Sting Nabs Art Thief." *Art News,* October: 90.

39. Dolnick, E. 2005. *The Rescue Artist: A True Story of Art Thieves, and the Hunt for a Missing Masterpiece.* New York: Harper Collins, 57, 128, 139, 152.

40. Hart, M. 2005. *The Irish Game: A True Story of Crime and Art.* New York: Plume, 134–36.

41. *St. Petersburg* (FL) *Times.* 2004. "Man to Serve Two Years for Role in Theft of Art." September 25: 7B; *St. Petersburg* (FL) *Times.* 2005. "French Police Find Museum's Missing Painting by Picasso." April 9: 2A.

42. Tijhuis, A.J.G. 2006. *Transnational Crime and the Interface Between Legal and Illegal Actors: The Case of the Illicit Art and Antiquities Trade.* The Netherlands: Wolf Legal Publishers, 140, 205.

43. Adler, F., Mueller, G.O.W, and Laufer, W. S. 2007. *Criminology.* 6th ed. New York: McGraw-Hill, 291.

44. Barlow, H. D. 1996. *Introduction to Criminology.* 7th ed. New York: Harper Collins, 171.

45. Sutherland, E. 1937. *The Professional Thief.* Chicago: University of Chicago Press; as cited in Adler, F., Mueller, G.O.W, and Laufer, W. S. 2007. *Criminology.* 6th ed. New York: McGraw-Hill, 291.

46. Conklin, J. 1972. *Robbery and the Criminal Justice System.* Philadelphia, PA: Lippincott; as cited in Adler, F., Mueller, G.O.W, and Laufer, W. S. 2007. *Criminology.* 6th ed. New York: McGraw-Hill, 257–58.

47. Cameron, M. O. 1964. *The Booster and the Snitch.* New York: Free Press; as cited in Adler, F., Mueller, G.O.W, and Laufer, W. S. 2007. *Criminology.* 6th ed. New York: McGraw-Hill, 292.

48. Shover, N. 1972. "Structures and Careers in Burglary." *Journal of Criminal Law and Criminology* 63: 540–49; and Decker, S., Wright, R., Redfern, A., and Smith, D. 1993. "A Woman's Place is in the Home: Females and Residential Burglary." *Justice Quarterly* 10: 143–62; as cited in Adler, et al., Ibid, 310.

49. Conklin, J. E. 1994. *Art Crime.* Westport, CT: Praeger, 166–67.

50. Wright, R. T. and Decker, S. H. 1994. *Burglars on the Job: Streetlife and Residential Break-ins.* Boston: Northeastern University Press; Letkemann, P. 1973. *Crime as Work.* Englewood Cliffs, NJ: Prentice Hall; as cited in Barlow, H. D. 1996. *Introduction to Criminology.* 7th ed. New York: Harper Collins, 176–77.

51. Barlow, H. D. 1996. *Introduction to Criminology.* 7th ed. New York: Harper Collins.

52. Adler, F., Mueller, G.O.W, and Laufer, W. S. 2007. *Criminology.* 6th ed. New York: McGraw-Hill, 257.

53. Conklin, J. E. 1994. *Art Crime.* Westport, CT: Praeger, 154.

54. Ho, Truc-Nhu Thi. 1992. "Art Theft in New York City: An Exploratory Study in Crime Specificity." PhD diss., Rutgers, The State University of New Jersey, Newark, 76; Barelli, J. J. 1986. "On Understanding the Business of Art and Antique Theft: An Exploratory Study." PhD diss., Fordham University, 209–10.

55. Barelli, J. J. 1986. "On Understanding the Business of Art and Antique Theft: An Exploratory Study." PhD diss., Fordham University 211, 213.

56. Ho, Truc-Nhu Thi. 1992. "Art Theft in New York City: An Exploratory Study in Crime Specificity." PhD diss., Rutgers, The State University of New Jersey, Newark, 71, 73–74.

57. Ibid., 87–89, 141.

58. Conklin, J. E. 1994. *Art Crime.* Westport, CT: Praeger, 166–67.

59. Barelli, J. J. 1986. "On Understanding the Business of Art and Antique Theft: An Exploratory Study." PhD diss., Fordham University, 184–87, 189, 191–96.

60. Bresler, F. 1992. *Interpol.* London: Sinclair-Stevenson, 359; Conklin, J. E. 1994. *Art Crime.* Westport, CT: Praeger, 6; Dolnick, E. 2005. *The Rescue Artist: A True Story of Art Thieves, and the Hunt for a Missing Masterpiece.* New York: Harper Collins, 13–14, 57, 128, 139, 152; Hennessee, J. 1990. "Why Great Art Always Will Be Stolen (And Seldom found)." *Connoisseur,* July: 42; Associated Press. 2005."FBI Art-Theft Team Meets in Philly." January 15 (accessed January 14, 2005, through Museum Security Network, http://msn-list.te.verweg.com/).

61. Hart, M. 2005. *The Irish Game: A True Story of Crime and Art.* New York: Plume, 59.

62. Spiel, R. E., Jr. 2000. *Art Theft and Forgery Investigation: The Complete Field Manual.* Springfield, IL: Charles C. Thomas, 96.

63. Ho, Truc-Nhu Thi. 1992. "Art Theft in New York City: An Exploratory Study in Crime Specificity." PhD diss., Rutgers, The State University of New

Jersey, Newark, 80; Houpt, S. 2006. *Museum of the Missing: A History of Art Theft.* New York: Sterling Publishing, 124.

64. Ozernoy, I. 2005. "The Art of the Heist." *U.S. News and World Report,* October 10: 44.

65. Conklin, J. E. 1994. *Art Crime.* Westport, CT: Praeger, 145.

66. *Art Loss Register.* n.d. http://www.artloss.com/Asp/TheftAndRecovery/mn_stats.asp (accessed October 19, 2006).

67. Dolnick, E. 2005. *The Rescue Artist: A True Story of Art Thieves, and the Hunt for a Missing Masterpiece.* New York: Harper Collins, 13–14.

68. Conklin, J. E. 1994. *Art Crime.* Westport, CT: Praeger 142; Hart, M. 2005. *The Irish Game: A True Story of Crime and Art.* New York: Plume, 59; Ho, Truc-Nhu Thi. 1992. "Art Theft in New York City: An Exploratory Study in Crime Specificity." PhD diss., Rutgers, The State University of New Jersey, Newark, 80; Mason, D. L. 1993. "Purloining the World's Art." In *Criminal and Civil Investigation Handbook,* ed. J. J. Grau, 54–59. New York: McGraw-Hill.

69. Barlow, H. D. 1996. *Introduction to Criminology.* 7th ed. New York: Harper Collins, 182.

70. Adler, F., Mueller, G.O.W, and Laufer, W. S. 2007. *Criminology.* 6th ed. New York: McGraw-Hill 311; Barlow, H. D. 1996. *Introduction to Criminology.* 7th ed. New York: Harper Collins,184.

71. Barelli, J. J. 1986. "On Understanding the Business of Art and Antique Theft: An Exploratory Study." PhD diss., Fordham University, 195.

72. Barlow, H. D. 1996. *Introduction to Criminology.* 7th ed. New York: Harper Collins, 184–85.

73. Barelli, J. J. 1986. "On Understanding the Business of Art and Antique Theft: An Exploratory Study." PhD diss., Fordham University, 189, 195.

74. Aarons, L. 2001. "Art Theft: An Exploratory Study of the Illegitimate Art Market in Australia." *Australia and New Zealand Journal of Criminology* 34 (1):17–37.

75. Barelli, J. J. 1986. "On Understanding the Business of Art and Antique Theft: An Exploratory Study." PhD diss., Fordham University, 194; Hart, M. 2005. *The Irish Game: A True Story of Crime and Art.* New York: Plume, 59; Ho, Truc-Nhu Thi. 1992. "Art Theft in New York City: An Exploratory Study in Crime Specificity." PhD diss., Rutgers, The State University of New Jersey, Newark, 73–74.

76. Conklin, J. E. 1994. *Art Crime.* Westport, CT: Praeger, 143–44; Doland, A. and Satter, R. 2006. "At Least 170,000 Stolen Artworks Remain Missing." *Tampa* (FL) *Tribune,* September 8: 13; Lyall, S. 2002. "A Titian Is No Longer At Large; Its Thief Is." *New York Times,* September 19: B1–2; McLeave, H. 1981. *Rogues in the Gallery: The Modern Plague of Art Thefts.* Boston: David R. Godine, 118–19; Ozernoy, I. 2005. "The Art of the Heist." *U.S. News and World Report,* October 10: 44; Thomas, K. D. 2006. "To Catch Art Thieves." *Art News,* May: 54.

CHAPTER 3: ART THEFT CONTINUED: SELECTED CASES

1. Hennessee, J. 1990. "Why Great Art Always Will Be Stolen (And Seldom found)." *Connoisseur,* July: 43.

2. Ibid., 47.

3. Houpt, S. 2006. *Museum of the Missing: A History of Art Theft.* New York: Sterling Publishing, 176.

4. Ibid., 174–76.

5. Ibid., 172–73.

6. Dolnick, E. 2005. *The Rescue Artist: A True Story of Art Thieves, and the Hunt for a Missing Masterpiece.* New York: Harper Collins, 125–27; Hart, M. 2004. *The Irish Game: A True Story of Crime and Art.* New York: Plume, 49–51, 55–56, 60, 190–92; Houpt, S. 2006. *Museum of the Missing: A History of Art Theft.* New York: Sterling Publishing, 95–96.

7. Hennessee, J. 1990. "Why Great Art Always Will Be Stolen (And Seldom found)." *Connoisseur,* July: 104.

8. Ibid., 104.

9. Agence France Presse. 2009. "Dutch Police Recover Long-lost Masters' Works." March 7 (accessed through Museum Security Network at http://groups. google.com/group/museum-security-network/t/61ead67ca9065572?hl=en on March 7, 2009); Hamilton, C. and Van Hecke, L. 2009. "Dutch Art Sting with a Twist." *National,* March 8, http://www.thenational.ae/ (accessed through Museum Security Network at http://groups.google.com/group/museum-security-network/t/00fb468274bc30f4?hl=en on March 8, 2009); Meijer, B. 2009. "Dealer Presumably Responsible For Stealing and Destroying Paintings Worth Millions." *ArtDaily.org,* March 10, http://www.artdaily.org (accessed through Museum Security Network at http://groups.google.com/group/museum-security-network/t/b16a43dea0a2338c?hl=en on March 10, 2009).

10. Houpt, S. 2006. *Museum of the Missing: A History of Art Theft.* New York: Sterling Publishing, 171.

11. Associated Press. 2008. "List of Notable Art Robberies," February 11, (accessed through http://nl.newsbank.com/nl-search/we/Archives?p_product=APAB&p_theme=apab&p_action=search&p_maxdocs=200&s_dispstring=List%20 of%20notable%20art%20robberies&p_field_advanced-0=&p_text_advanced-0=(%22List%20of%20notable%20art%20robberies%22)&xcal_numdocs=20&p_perpage=10&p_sort=YMD_date:D&xcal_useweights=no).

12. Ibid.

13. Houpt, S. 2006. *Museum of the Missing: A History of Art Theft.* New York: Sterling Publishing, 164.

14. Associated Press. 2008. "List of Notable Art Robberies," February 11, (accessed through http://nl.newsbank.com/nl-search/we/Archives?p_product=APAB&p_theme=apab&p_action=search&p_maxdocs=200&s_dispstring=List%20 of%20notable%20art%20robberies&p_field_advanced-0=&p_text_advanced-0=(%22List%20of%20notable%20art%20robberies%22)&xcal_numdocs=20&p_perpage=10&p_sort=YMD_date:D&xcal_useweights=no).

15. Lyall, S. 2002. "A Titian Is No Longer at Large; Its Thief Is." *New York Times,* September 12: B1–B2.

16. Houpt, S. 2006. *Museum of the Missing: A History of Art Theft.* New York: Sterling Publishing, 142, 164.

17. Dolnick, E. 2005. *The Rescue Artist: A True Story of Art Thieves, and the Hunt for a Missing Masterpiece.* New York: Harper Collins, 13.

18. Ibid., 13; Houpt, S. 2006. *Museum of the Missing: A History of Art Theft.* New York: Sterling Publishing, 163.

19. Houpt, S. 2006. *Museum of the Missing: A History of Art Theft.* New York: Sterling Publishing 163.

20. Ibid., 107–12.

21. Atwood, R. 2004. *Stealing History: Tomb Raiders, Smugglers, and the Looting of the Ancient World*. New York: St. Martin's Press, 263–64; Fitchett, J. J. 2001. "Stealing Goyas: They Made it Look Easy." *International Herald Tribune*, September 1 (accessed through http://iht.com/articles/2001/09/01/clyff_ed2_php on August 1, 2008); Thomas, K. D. 2006. "To Catch Art Thieves." *Art News*, May: 154–55.

22. Houpt, S. 2006. *Museum of the Missing: A History of Art Theft*. New York: Sterling Publishing, 159.

23. Ibid., 157, 159–60; Bloom, J. 2008. "Dutch Paintings Recovered." *New York Times*, September 16 (accessed through http://www.nytimes.com/2008/09/17/arts/design/17arts-DUTCHPAINTIN_BRF.html?_r=1&ref=arts&oref=slogin, September 17, 2008); "Major Art Heist Solved." n.d. (accessed through Museum Security Network, http://groups.google.com/group/museum-security-network/browse_thread/thread/ab8cacc8acbcfc9f?hl=en, September 16, 2008).

24. Hochwarter, T. 2009. "Saliera Cat Burglar Back Selling House Security." *Austrian Times*, March 5 (accessed through Museum Security Network at http://groups.google.com/group/museum-security-network/t/d9b38a1abc08031b?hl=en, March 5, 2009); Houpt, S. 2006. *Museum of the Missing: A History of Art Theft*. New York: Sterling Publishing 82.

25. Houpt, S. 2006. *Museum of the Missing: A History of Art Theft*. New York: Sterling Publishing, 154; Brown, C. 2007. "Stolen Painting: Lawyer Among Four Charged With Conspiracy to Rob." *Scotsman*, October 6, http://news.scotsman.com/ (accessed through Museum Security Network, msn-list@te.verweg.com, October 7, 2007); Lawless, J. 2007. "Police Recover Stolen Da Vinci Painting." Associated Press, October 7 (accessed via www.aol.com on October 7, 2007).

26. David, A. 2009. "Italy Police Recover Stolen Masterpieces." Associated Press, January 13 (accessed through Museum Security Network, http://groups.google.com/group/museum-security-network/t/88a4c0c072be359c?hl=en, January 14, 2009); Houpt, S. 2006. *Museum of the Missing: A History of Art Theft*. New York: Sterling Publishing, 154.

27. Houpt, S. 2006. *Museum of the Missing: A History of Art Theft*. New York: Sterling Publishing, 150–52; "Thieves Steal 17th Century Dutch Paintings Worth $13 Million; The Robbers Took 15 to 20 Paintings from the Westfries Museum." January 10, 2005 (accessed through Museum Security Network, msn-list@te.verweg.com, January 10, 2005); "Gang 'Scouted' Museum Before Theft." January 15, 2005 (accessed through Museum Security Network, msn-list@te.verweg.com, accessed January 15, 2005).

28. Houpt, S. 2006. *Museum of the Missing: A History of Art Theft*. New York: Sterling Publishing, 147–48; Associated Press. 2008. "List of Notable Art Robberies," February 11 (accessed through http://nl.newsbank.com/nl-search/we/Archives?p_product=APAB&p_theme=apab&p_action=search&p_maxdocs=200&s_dispstring=List%20of%20notable%20art%20robberies&p_field_advanced-0=&p_text_advanced-0=(%22List%20of%20notable%20art%20robberies%22)&xcal_numdocs=20&p_perpage=10&p_sort=YMD_date:D&xcal_useweights=no); Doland, A. and Satter, R. 2006. "At Least 170, 000 Stolen Artworks Remain Missing." *Tampa* (FL) *Tribune*, September 8: 13.

29. Associated Press. 2008. "List of Notable Art Robberies," February 11 (accessed through http://nl.newsbank.com/nl-search/we/Archives?p_product=APAB&p_theme=apab&p_action=search&p_maxdocs=200&s_dispstring=List%20of%20notable%20art%20robberies&p_field_advanced-0=&p_text_advanced-0=(%22List

%20of%20notable%20art%20robberies%22)&xcal_numdocs=20&p_perpage=
10&p_sort=YMD_date:D&xcal_useweights=no).

30. Associated Press. 2008. "French Man Charged in '07 Theft of Art." June 27 (accessed through Museum Security Network, http://groups.google.com/group/museum-security-network/browse_thread/thread/cd2d7541fb21b7cc?hl=en, June 28, 2008); U.S. Department of Justice. "French National Sentenced in International Stolen Art Conspiracy Involving Paintings by Monet, Sisley, and Brueghel." Press Release, September 24 (accessed through www.usdoj.gov/usao/fls, September 24, 2008).

31. Associated Press. 2008. "List of Notable Art Robberies," February 11 (accessed through http://nl.newsbank.com/nl-search/we/Archives?p_product=APAB&p_theme=apab&p_action=search&p_maxdocs=200&s_dispstring=List%20of%20notable%20art%20robberies&p_field_advanced-0=&p_text_advanced-0=(%22List%20of%20notable%20art%20robberies%22)&xcal_numdocs=20&p_perpage=10&p_sort=YMD_date:D&xcal_useweights=no); Associated Press. 2008. "Stolen Paintings Recovered in Brazil." January 9 (accessed through Museum Security Network, msn-list@te.verweg.com, January 9, 2008); Associated Press. 2008. "Suspect: Saudi Collector Wanted Stolen Art, Picasso, Portinari Paintings Stolen From Brazilian Museum Recovered." January 25 (accessed through Museum Security Network, msn-list@te.verweg.com, May 2, 2008).

32. "Art Theft is Worth UK Pounds 3bn a Year, and the Latest Heist Is One of the Biggest Ever; Andrew Johnson Reports on the Volatile Trade in Pictures, Antiques and Sculpture." February 17, 2008 (accessed through Museum Security Network, msn-list@te.verweg.com February 17, 2008); Esterow, M. and Granek, A. L. 2008. "Stealing Was the Easy Part." *Art News,* April: 76, 78; Harnischfeger, U. and Kulish, N. 2008. "At Zurich Museum, a Theft of 4 Masterworks." *New York Times,* February 12, http://www.nytimes.com/2008/02/12/world/europe/12swiss.html?_r=1&th&emc=th&oref=slogin (accessed February 12, 2008); Associated Press. 2008. "List of Notable Art Robberies," February 11 (accessed through http://nl.newsbank.com/nl-search/we/Archives?p_product=APAB&p_theme=apab&p_action=search&p_maxdocs=200&s_dispstring=List%20of%20notable%20art%20robberies&p_field_advanced-0=&p_text_advanced-0=(%22List%20of%20notable%20art%20robberies%22)&xcal_numdocs=20&p_perpage=10&p_sort=YMD_date:D&xcal_useweights=no); Reid, K. 2008. "Thieves Take $91 Million Masterworks in Swiss Art Heist." Reuters, February 11; Associated Press. n.d. "Two of 4 Paintings Stolen in Zurich Heist Are Recovered" (accessed February 19, 2008 through http://www.iht.com); Wolfsenberger, M. and Sandler, L. 2008. "Zurich Gang Grabs $163 Million Art Haul from Museum." (Update 3) Bloomberg, February 11 (accessed through Museum Security Network, at msn-list@te.verweg.com, February 12, 2008).

33. Bloom, J. 2008. "Another Art Theft in Sao Paulo." *New York Times,* June 14 (accessed through http://nytimes.com. June 14, 2008); Lehman, S. 2008. "Armed Robbers Steal Picasso Prints in Brazil." Associated Press, June 13(accessed through Museum Security Network, http://groups.google.com/group/museum-security-network/browse thread/thread/4bd8f9e94a9cedac, July 13, 2008); Sissaro, B. 2008. "Stolen Picasso Print Recovered in Brazil." *New York Times,* July 21 (accessed through http://nytimes.com July 21, 2008); "Two More Stolen Works Recovered and Second Man Arrested by the Brazilian Police." ArtDaily.org, August 12, 2008 (accessed through Museum Security Network http://groups.google.com/group/

museum-security-network/browse_thread/thread/2382b966e6c9692a?hl=en August 12, 2008).

34. Elsworth, C. 2008. "Chagall and van Dongen Paintings Worth Millions Stolen from Elderly Couple." *Telegraph,* September 10, www. telegraph.co.uk (accessed through Museum Security Network http://groups.google.com/group/museum-security-network/browse_thread/thread/2382b966e6c9692a?hl=en September 10, 2008).

35. Agence France-Presse. 2008. "Colombian Police Showcase Recovered Goya Masterpiece." October 14 (accessed through Museum Security Network, http://groups.google.com/group/museum-security-network/browse_thread/thread/c48fbd927872133d?hl=en, October 14, 2008); Agence France-Presse. 2008. "Thieves Pinch 'Priceless' Goya Engraving from Colombia Museum." September 13 (accessed through Museum Security Network, http://groups.google.com/group/museum-security-network/browse_thread/thread/3437c192a165202f?hl=en, September 13, 2008).

36. Bomsdorf, C. 2009. "Cranach Theft to be Used to Lure Visitors to Norwegian Church." *Art Newspaper,* March 25, http://www.theartnewspaper.com/ (accessed through Museum Security Network, http://groups.google.com/group/museum-security-network/t/aed5d60d65cb3760?hl=en March 27, 2009, 2009); Associated Press. 2009. "Norwegian Police Detain Suspect in Theft of Renaissance Painting." March 11 (accessed through Museum Security Network, http://groups.google.com/group/museum-security-network/t/6d415a6b95deb61a?hl=en March 11, 2009); Associated Press. 2009. "Renaissance Painting Stolen from Norwegian Church." March 8 (accessed through Museum Security Network, http://groups.google.com/group/museum-security-network/t/24815f76f17db71f?hl=en, March 8, 2009).

37. La Baume, M. 2009. "Picasso Sketchbook Is Taken in Paris." *New York Times,* June 9 (accessed through http://www.nytimes.com/2009/06/10/arts/design/10arts-PICASSOSKETC_BRF.html?scp=1&sq=picasso%20drawings&st=cse, June 11, 2009); *Tampa* (FL) *Tribune.* 2009. "Picasso Notebook Stolen from Museum in France." June 10: 14.

CHAPTER 4: ART FORGERIES AND FAKES

1. Hoving, T. 1996. *False Impressions: The Hunt for Big-Time Art Fakes.* New York: Simon and Schuster, 23.

2. Ibid., 15; Meyer, K. E. 1973. *The Plundered Past.* New York: Atheneum, 108.

3. Hoving, T. 1996. *False Impressions: The Hunt for Big-Time Art Fakes.* New York: Simon and Schuster, 17.

4. Porter, L. 2007. "Art Imitating Art." *The Age,* December 2 (accessed through Museum Security Network, msn-list@te.verweg.com, December 2, 2007).

5. Conklin, J. E. 1994. *Art Crime.* Westport, CT: Praeger, 47; Spiel, R. E., Jr. 2000. *Art Theft and Forgery Investigation: The Complete Field Manual.* Springfield, IL: Charles C. Thomas, 31.

6. *Art News.* 2007. "Rogues Gallery." September: 43.

7. Federal Bureau of Investigation. n.d. *Uniform Crime Report.* http://www.fbi.gov/ucr/cius2006/about/offense_definitions.html (accessed April 23, 2008).

8. Ibid.

9. Conklin, J. E. 1994. *Art Crime.* Westport, CT: Praeger, 48, 69.

10. Radnóti, S. 1999. *The Fake: Forgery and Its Place in Art.* Lanham, MD: Rowman and Littlefield, 5–6, 44, 116.

11. Grampp, W. D. 1989. *Pricing the Priceless: Art, Artists, and Economics.* New York: Basic Books, 123, 130.

12. Conklin, J. E. 1994. *Art Crime.* Westport, CT: Praeger, 47; Spiel, R. E., Jr. 2000. *Art Theft and Forgery Investigation: The Complete Field Manual.* Springfield, IL: Charles C. Thomas, 41.

13. Conklin, J. E. 1994. *Art Crime.* Westport, CT: Praeger, 51.

14. Esterow, M. 2005. "Fake, Frauds, and Fake Fakers." *Art News,* June: 102.

15. Mullarkey, M. 2007. "At the Bruce, the Art of Deception." *The New York Sun,* May 10 (accessed through Museum Security, msn-list@te.verweg.com Network, May 10, 2007); Meyer, K. E. 1973. *The Plundered Past.* New York: Atheneum, 108.

16. Meyer, K. E. 1973. *The Plundered Past.* New York: Atheneum, 108.

17. Tijhuis, A.J.G. 2006. *Transnational Crime and the Interface between Legal and Illegal Actors: The Case of the Illicit Art and Antiquities Trade.* The Netherlands: Wolf Legal Publishers, 132.

18. Hoving, T. 1996. *False Impressions: The Hunt for Big-Time Art Fakes.* New York: Simon and Schuster, 84.

19. Tijhuis, A.J.G. 2006. *Transnational Crime and the Interface between Legal and Illegal Actors: The Case of the Illicit Art and Antiquities Trade.* The Netherlands: Wolf Legal Publishers, 176.

20. Conklin, J. E. 1994. *Art Crime.* Westport, CT: Praeger, 76; Esterow, M. 2005. "Fake, Frauds, and Fake Fakers." *Art News,* June: 105; Hoving, T. 1996. *False Impressions: The Hunt for Big-Time Art Fakes.* New York: Simon and Schuster, 23, 331, 333.

21. Izenberg, D. 2005. "Israel Arrests Antiquities Forgers." *Art News,* March: 72; Shraga, N. 2008. "The Art of Authentic Forgery." *Haaretz Daily Newspaper,* (Israel), April 14 (accessed April 14, 2008 through Museum Security Network, msn-list@te.verweg.com, April 14, 2008).

22. Hoving, T. 1996. *False Impressions: The Hunt for Big-Time Art Fakes.* New York: Simon and Schuster, 56, 58; Janson, H. W. 1966. *History of Art: A Survey of the Major Visual Arts from the Dawn of History to the Present Day.* 10th ed. Englewood Cliffs, NJ: Prentice Hall, 388, 390.

23. Esterow, M. 2005. "Fake, Frauds, and Fake Fakers." *Art News,* June: 98–99, 101–2.

24. Dolnick, E. 2008. *The Forger's Spell.* New York: Harper Collins, 1, 215, 264, 268, 288; Esterow, M. 2005. "Fake, Frauds, and Fake Fakers." *Art News,* June: 98; Mullarkey, M. 2007. "At the Bruce, the Art of Deception." *New York Sun,* May 10 (accessed through Museum Security, msn-list@te.verweg.com Network, May 10, 2007); Nicholas, L. H. 1994. *The Rape of Europa: The Fate of Europe's Treasures in the Third Reich and the Second World War.* New York: Vintage Books, 427; *Independent.* 2007. "The Counterfeiters: Inside the World of Art Forgery." December 10 (accessed through Museum Security, msn-list@te.verweg.com Network, December 10, 2007).

25. Esterow, M. 2005. "Fake, Frauds, and Fake Fakers." *Art News,* June:104–5; *Independent.* 2007. "The Counterfeiters: Inside the World of Art Forgery." December 10 (accessed through Museum Security, msn-list@te.verweg.com Network, December 10, 2007).

26. Esterow, M. 2005. "Fake, Frauds, and Fake Fakers." *Art News,* June: 98, 102, 104; Hoving, T. 1996. *False Impressions: The Hunt for Big-Time Art Fakes.* New York:

Simon and Schuster, 190–92; Tijhuis, A.J.G. 2006. *Transnational Crime and the Interface between Legal and Illegal Actors: The Case of the Illicit Art and Antiquities Trade.* The Netherlands: Wolf Legal Publishers, 132.

27. Tijhuis, A.J.G. 2006. *Transnational Crime and the Interface between Legal and Illegal Actors: The Case of the Illicit Art and Antiquities Trade.* The Netherlands: Wolf Legal Publishers,147.

28. Akbar, A. 2006. "Exhibition Honours the Forger Who Fooled the World's Foremost Art Experts." *Independent,* April 29 (accessed through Museum Security Network, msn-list@te.verweg.com, April 29, 2006); Hegstad, M. 2006. "Art Dealers Learn to Ferret Out Fake Works." *Tampa* (FL) *Tribune,* November 27: 6.

29. Houpt, S. 2006. *Museum of the Missing: A History of Art Theft.* New York: Sterling Publishing, 76; *Independent.* 2007. "The Counterfeiters: Inside the World of Art Forgery." December 10 (accessed through Museum Security, msn-list@te.verweg. com Network, December 10, 2007).

30. Hegstad, M. 2006. "Art Dealers Learn to Ferret Out Fake Works." *Tampa Tribune,* November 27: 6; *Independent.* 2007. "The Counterfeiters: Inside the World of Art Forgery." December 10 (accessed through Museum Security, msn-list@ te.verweg.com Network, December 10, 2007).

31. Becker, H. S. 1982. *Art Worlds.* Berkeley: University of California Press, 168; Spiel, R. E., Jr. 2000. *Art Theft and Forgery Investigation: The Complete Field Manual.* Springfield, IL: Charles C. Thomas, 83, 89.

32. Akinsha, K. 2006. "The Scandal Sweeping Russia's Art Market." *Art News,* January: 114–19; Finn, P. 2006. "Who is Faking the Great Paintings of Russia? Rush to Buy 19th Century Landscapes Brings Forgers Out of the Woodwork." *Washington Post,* January 28 (accessed through Museum Security, msn-list@te.verweg.com Network, January 30, 2006).

33. Spiel, R. E., Jr. 2000. *Art Theft and Forgery Investigation: The Complete Field Manual.* Springfield, IL: Charles C. Thomas, 83.

34. Akbar, A. 2006. "Exhibition Honours the Forger Who Fooled the World's Foremost Art Experts." *Independent,* April 29 (accessed through Museum Security Network, msn-list@te.verweg.com, April 29, 2006); Esterow, M. 2005. "Fake, Frauds, and Fake Fakers." *Art News,* June: 98, 101–2, 104.

35. Esterow, M. 2005. "Fake, Frauds, and Fake Fakers." *Art News,* June: 104; Hebborn, E. 1997. *The Art Forger's Handbook.* Woodstock, NY: The Overlook Press, 38–41, 54–56, 95, 156, 165, 190.

36. Conklin, J. E. 1994. *Art Crime.* Westport, CT: Praeger, 45–46, 86.

37. Landi, A. 2008. "How a Faun Got Their Goat." *Art News,* April: 69; Spiel, R. E., Jr. 2000. *Art Theft and Forgery Investigation: The Complete Field Manual.* Springfield, IL: Charles C. Thomas, 96, 198–99, 222.

38. Hoving, T. 1996. *False Impressions: The Hunt for Big-Time Art Fakes.* New York: Simon and Schuster, 310.

39. Hebborn, E. 1997. *The Art Forger's Handbook.* Woodstock, NY: The Overlook Press, 156, 170–72, 175, 187–88.

40. Kalfrin, V. and Echegaray, C. 2008. "Man Accused of Selling Art Forgeries." *Tampa Tribune,* January 17: Metro. 2.

41. BBC News. 2007. "British Forger Fools US Museum." December 13 (accessed through Museum Security Network, msn-list@te.verweg.com, December 13, 2007); Associated Press. 2008. "Family That Forged Antiquities Told to Repay 400,000 Pounds." April 17 (accessed through Museum Security Network, msn-list@te.

verweg.com, April 18, 2008); Fulford, R. 2008. "The Artful Codgers." *National Post,* January 28 (accessed through Museum Security Network, msn-list@te.verweg.com, January 29, 2008); Keaveny, P. 2008. "Fears of Bolton's Master Forger in TV Spotlight," *This Is Lancashire,* May 13, http://www.thisislancashire.co.uk/ (accessed through Museum Security Network, msn-list@te.verweg.com, May 13, 2008); Landi, A. 2008. "How a Faun Got Their Goat." *Art News,* April: 68–69; Michel, A. 2008. "Duping the Experts." *Art News,* February: 58, 60.

CHAPTER 5: ART THEFT AND DESTRUCTION: THE PERILS OF WARS AND CIVIL/ RELIGIOUS UNREST

1. Alford, K. D. 1994. *The Spoils of World War II: The American Military's Role in the Stealing of Europe's Treasures.* New York: Carol Publishing, xii; Bogdanos, M. (with W. Patrick). 2005. *Thieves of Baghdad: One Marine's Passion for Ancient Civilizations and the Journey to Recover the World's Greatest Stolen Treasures.* New York: Bloomsbury, 122; Jardine, L. 2006. "Spoils of War: A Point of View." BBC News, June 27 (accessed through Museum Security Network, msn-list@te.verweg.com, June 27, 2006); Tijhuis, A.J.G. 2006. *Transnational Crime and the Interface between Legal and Illegal Actors: The Case of the Illicit Art and Antiquities Trade.* The Netherlands: Wolf Legal Publishers, 136.

2. Jardine, L. 2006. "Spoils of War: A Point of View." BBC News, June 27 (accessed through Museum Security Network, msn-list@te.verweg.com, June 27, 2006); Feliciano, H. 1995. *The Lost Museum: The Nazi Conspiracy to Steal the World's Greatest Works of Art.* New York: Harper Collins, 25; Tijhuis, A.J.G. 2006. *Transnational Crime and the Interface between Legal and Illegal Actors: The Case of the Illicit Art and Antiquities Trade.* The Netherlands: Wolf Legal Publishers, 135; Waxman, S. 2008. *Loot: The Battle Over the Stolen Treasures of the Ancient World.* New York: Times Books, 67.

3. Actual Films. 2008. *Rape of Europa,* aired by PBS on November 24; Edsel, R. M. 2006. *Rescuing Da Vinci: Hitler and the Nazis Stole Europe's Great Art; America and Her Allies Recovered It.* Dallas, TX: Laurel Publishing, 105.

4. Actual Films. 2008. *Rape of Europa,* aired by PBS on November 24; Cohan, W. D. 2008. "Put These Great Paintings Out There." *Art News,* October: 86; Feliciano, H. 1995. *The Lost Museum: The Nazi Conspiracy to Steal the World's Greatest Works of Art.* New York: Harper Collins, 4, 15–16.

5. Actual Films. 2008. *Rape of Europa,* aired by PBS on November 24; Edsel, R. M. 2006. *Rescuing Da Vinci: Hitler and the Nazis Stole Europe's Great Art; America and Her Allies Recovered It.* Dallas, TX: Laurel Publishing, 10; Nicholas, L. H. 1994. *The Rape of Europa: The Fate of Europe's Treasures in the Third Reich and the Second World War.* New York: Vintage Books, 8–9, 11.

6. Edsel, R. M. 2006. *Rescuing Da Vinci: Hitler and the Nazis Stole Europe's Great Art; America and Her Allies Recovered It.* Dallas, TX: Laurel Publishing, 10, 87; Feliciano, H. 1995. *The Lost Museum: The Nazi Conspiracy to Steal the World's Greatest Works of Art.* New York: Harper Collins, 107; Nicholas, L. H. 1994. *The Rape of Europa: The Fate of Europe's Treasures in the Third Reich and the Second World War.* New York: Vintage Books, 5, 11, 18, 23, 25, 166.

7. Actual Films. 2008. *Rape of Europa,* aired by PBS on November 24; Edsel, R. M. 2006. *Rescuing Da Vinci: Hitler and the Nazis Stole Europe's Great Art; America*

and Her Allies Recovered It. Dallas, TX: Laurel Publishing, 11, 87, 106, 111; Nicholas, L. H. 1994. *The Rape of Europa: The Fate of Europe's Treasures in the Third Reich and the Second World War.* New York: Vintage Books, 61.

8. Edsel, R. M. 2006. *Rescuing Da Vinci: Hitler and the Nazis Stole Europe's Great Art; America and Her Allies Recovered It.* Dallas, TX: Laurel Publishing, Nicholas; L. H. 1994. *The Rape of Europa: The Fate of Europe's Treasures in the Third Reich and the Second World War.* New York: Vintage Books, 8, 49, 78, 88, 107, 185.

9. Nicholas, L. H. 1994. *The Rape of Europa: The Fate of Europe's Treasures in the Third Reich and the Second World War.* New York: Vintage Books, 105–8, 166.

10. Feliciano, H. 1995. *The Lost Museum: The Nazi Conspiracy to Steal the World's Greatest Works of Art.* New York: Harper Collins, 15–16; Nicholas, L. H. 1994. *The Rape of Europa: The Fate of Europe's Treasures in the Third Reich and the Second World War.* New York: Vintage Books, 96, 143.

11. Henry, M. 2006. "A Victory in the Goudstikker Case." *Art News,* April: 80, 82; Nicholas, L. H. 1994. *The Rape of Europa: The Fate of Europe's Treasures in the Third Reich and the Second World War.* New York: Vintage Books, 84, 104–6; Riding, A. 2006. "Sleuthing for Looted Art." *New York Times,* March 26 (accessed through Museum Security Network, msn-list@te.verweg.com, March 27, 2006); Rottenberg, H. 2007."Repairing Injustice." *Art News,* January: 120–21; Smallenberg, S. 2007. "Piecing Together a Legacy." *Art News,* May: 84.

12. Actual Films. 2008. *Rape of Europa,* aired by PBS on November 24; Feliciano, H. 1995. *The Lost Museum: The Nazi Conspiracy to Steal the World's Greatest Works of Art.* New York: Harper Collins, 4, 120; Edsel, R. M. 2006. *Rescuing Da Vinci: Hitler and the Nazis Stole Europe's Great Art; America and Her Allies Recovered It.* Dallas, TX: Laurel Publishing, 12, 107; Nicholas, L. H. 1994. *The Rape of Europa: The Fate of Europe's Treasures in the Third Reich and the Second World War.* New York: Vintage Books, 5, 90–91, 96, 138–39.

13. Actual Films. 2008. *Rape of Europa,* aired by PBS on November 24; Feliciano, H. 1995. *The Lost Museum: The Nazi Conspiracy to Steal the World's Greatest Works of Art.* New York: Harper Collins, 120; Nicholas, L. H. 1994. *The Rape of Europa: The Fate of Europe's Treasures in the Third Reich and the Second World War.* New York: Vintage Books, 131, 135, 166, 170.

14. Dolnick, E. 2008. *The Forger's Spell.* New York: Harper Collins, 63–64; Feliciano, H. 1995. *The Lost Museum: The Nazi Conspiracy to Steal the World's Greatest Works of Art.* New York: Harper Collins, 40, 43–44; Nicholas, L. H. 1994. *The Rape of Europa: The Fate of Europe's Treasures in the Third Reich and the Second World War.* New York: Vintage Books, 131.

15. Edsel, R. M. 2006. *Rescuing Da Vinci: Hitler and the Nazis Stole Europe's Great Art; America and Her Allies Recovered It.* Dallas, TX: Laurel Publishing, 107, 119; Feliciano, H. 1995. *The Lost Museum: The Nazi Conspiracy to Steal the World's Greatest Works of Art.* New York: Harper Collins, 166; Nicholas, L. H. 1994. *The Rape of Europa: The Fate of Europe's Treasures in the Third Reich and the Second World War.* New York: Vintage Books, 314, 316–17.

16. Dolnick, E. 2008. *The Forger's Spell.* New York: Harper Collins, 254–55.

17. Actual Films. 2008. *Rape of Europa,* aired by PBS on November 24; Fitzgerald, N. 2005. "Return from Oblivion." *Art News,* Summer: 92; Lowenthal, C. 1997. "Art Theft and Its Control: Art Theft Since World War II." *Journal of Financial Crime* 5 (1): 39–44; Kozlov, G. 2007. "The Merovingian Question." *Art News,* May: 88; Nicholas, L. H. 1994. *The Rape of Europa: The Fate of Europe's Treasures in the Third Reich and the Second World War.* New York: Vintage Books, 323, 362.

18. Actual Films. 2008. *Rape of Europa*, aired by PBS on November 24,; Axelrod, T. 2008. "Loss and Return." *Art News*, October: 90–91; Fitzgerald, N. 2005. "Return from Oblivion." *Art News*, Summer: 92; Fitzgerald, N. 2006. "Politics and Populism." *Art News*, December: 133–35; Tijhuis, A.J.G. 2006. *Transnational Crime and the Interface between Legal and Illegal Actors: The Case of the Illicit Art and Antiquities Trade*. The Netherlands: Wolf Legal Publishers, 135.

19. Dyer, J. 2008. "Equivalent to a Theft." *Art News*, May: 98; Nicholas, L. H. 1994. *The Rape of Europa: The Fate of Europe's Treasures in the Third Reich and the Second World War*. New York: Vintage Books, 414, 421.

20. Feliciano, H. 1995. *The Lost Museum: The Nazi Conspiracy to Steal the World's Greatest Works of Art*. New York: Harper Collins, 155–56, 161–62.

21. Marton, A. 2006. "Plundered Art Plagues Museums All Across America." *New York Times*, July 10 (accessed through Museum Security Network, msn-list@ te.verweg.com, July 12, 2006); Nicholas, L. H. 1994. *The Rape of Europa: The Fate of Europe's Treasures in the Third Reich and the Second World War*. New York: Vintage Books, 442.

22. Henry, M. 2007. "Not a Priority." *Art News*, January: 122–23; Feliciano, H. 1995. *The Lost Museum: The Nazi Conspiracy to Steal the World's Greatest Works of Art*. New York: Harper Collins, 215–16, 118, 235–36.

23. Akinsha, K. 2006. "Restitution: Unfulfilled Promises." *Art News*, December: 129; Dempsey, J. 2008. "Germany Tracing Artwork and Its Nazi Past." *International Herald Tribune*, December 22 (accessed through Museum Security Network, http://groups.google.com/group/museum-security-network/t/02e627473 b44fffb?hl=en); Henry, M. 2007. "The Limitations of Statutes." *Art News*, June: 50, 52.

24. Rottenberg, H. 2007. "Repairing Injustice." *Art News*, January: 120–21.

25. Dempsey, J. 2008. "Germany Tracing Artwork and Its Nazi Past." *International Herald Tribune*, December 22 (accessed through Museum Security Network, http://groups.google.com/group/museum-security-network/t/02e627473b44 fffb?hl=en); Hickley, C. 2007. "Thousands of Nazi-Looted Works Are Held by Museums, Survey Says." Bloomberg, April 27 (accessed through Museum Security Network, msn-list@te.verweg.com, April 27, 2007); *Spiegel*. 2008. "There's No Point in Trying to Duck." December 3 (accessed through Museum Security Network, msn-list@te.verweg.com, December 3, 2008).

26. Falkenstein, M. 2006. "Far From the Goal." *Art News*, December: 130–32; Kennedy, R. 2006. "Research on Looting Seen to Lag." *New York Times*, July 25 (accessed through www.nytimes.com on July 25); "The Nazi Era Portal Project" n.d. (accessed through www.nepip.org, January 20, 2009).

27. Flamini, R. 2006. "Dutch to Give Back Stolen Art." United Press International, February 8 (accessed through Museum Security Network, msn-list@ te.verweg.com, February 8, 2006).

28. Glazer, A. 2006. "N.Y. Museum Buys Controversial Klimt Art." Associated Press, June 19 (accessed through Museum Security Network, msn-list@te.verweg. com, June 19, 2006); Knight, C. 2006. "L.A. Has Loved and Lost 'Adele.'" *Los Angeles Times*, June 19 (accessed through Museum Security Network, msn-list@te.verweg. com, June 19, 2006); Reynolds, C. and O'Connor, A. 2006. "Klimt Painting Sells for Record Amount." *Los Angeles Times*, June 19, (accessed through Museum Security Network, msn-list@te.verweg.com, June 19, 2006);Vogel, C. 2006. "Lauder Pays $135 Million, a Record, for a Klimt." *New York Times*, June 19 (accessed through Museum Security Network, msn-list@te.verweg.com, June 19, 2006).

29. Indo Asian News Service. 2006. "Bin Laden Ordered Bamiyan Buddha Destruction." March 28 (accessed through Museum Security Network, msn-list@ te.verweg.com, March 29, 2006); Bohlen, C. 2002. "Cultural Salvage in the Wake of Afghan War." *New York Times*, April 15: B1, B3; Jardine, L. 2006. "Spoils of War: A Point of View." BBC News, June 27 (accessed through Museum Security Network, msn-list@te.verweg.com, June 27, 2006); Smith, H., 2006. "We Will Have Nothing Left." *Art News*, December: 86; Smith, R. 2008. "Silent Survivors of Afghanistan's 4,000 Tumultuous Years." *New York Times*, May 23 (accessed through http://www. nytimes.com May 23, 2008).

30. Atwood, R. 2004. "Restoring Iraq's Cultural Legacy." *Art News*, Summer: 70; Atwood, R. 2008. "The Loot Root." *Art News*, June: 86, 88; Bogdanos, M. (with W. Patrick). 2005. *Thieves of Baghdad: One Marine's Passion for Ancient Civilizations and the Journey to Recover the World's Greatest Stolen Treasures*. New York: Bloomsbury, 136, 139, 141, 232, 270, and generally; Jardine, L. 2007. "Spoils of War: A Point of View." BBC News, June 27 (accessed through Museum Security Network, msn-list@te.verweg.com, June 27, 2006); Mohammed, A. and Kami, A. 2008. "Iraq Seizes Scores of Looted Artifacts." Reuters, December 16 (accessed through Museum Security Network, http://groups.google.com/group/museum-security-network/t/52d06404eb011b63?hl=en December 16, 2008); "Stolen From The National Museum, Baghdad, Iraq, and From Some 12,000 Archaeological Sites Across Iraq in 2003." n.d. Smithsonian.com (accessed through Museum Security Network, msn-list@te.verweg.com, May 30, 2008).

CHAPTER 6: STEALING THE PAST: THE LOOTING OF CULTURAL-HERITAGE OBJECTS

1. Renfrew, C. 1995. Foreword to *Antiquities Trade or Betrayed: Legal, Ethical and Conservation Issues*. K. W. Tubb. London: Archetype.

2. Meyer, K. E. 1973. *The Plundered Past*. New York: Atheneum, 64–65, 132–33; Waxman, S. 2008. *Loot: The Battle Over the Stolen Treasures of the Ancient World*. New York: Times Books, 7.

3. Harris, J. 2008. "Pressure For Frieze Heats Up." *Art News*, September: 102; Waxman, S. 2008. *Loot: The Battle Over the Stolen Treasures of the Ancient World*. New York: Times Books, 247.

4. Associated Press. 2005. "Egypt Wants Its Artifacts Returned." *St. Petersburg (FL) Times*, July 14: 4A; Agence France Presse. 2009. "Famed Nefertiti Bust a Fake: Expert." May 6 (accessed through Museum Security Network, http://groups. google.com/group/museum-security-network/t/7d6fef5f2b7bb775?hl=en, May 6, 2009); Halpern, O. 2005. "Nefertiti, Come Home." *Art News*, September: 64; Waxman, S. 2008. *Loot: The Battle Over the Stolen Treasures of the Ancient World*. New York: Times Books, 33, 40–41, 53–54, 74–75.

5. Cromwell, R. 2006. "Peru Tells Yale It Wants Its Machu Picchu Treasures Back (after 100 Years)." *Independent*, February 3, http://news.independent.co.uk/ (accessed through msn-list@te.verweg.com, February 3, 2006); Heaney, C. 2007. "Stealing from the Incas." *New York Times*, October 7 (accessed through msn-list@ te.verweg.com, October 8, 2007); Kennedy, R., 2007. "Yale Officials Agree to Return Peruvian Artifacts." *New York Times*, September 17 (accessed through http:// nytimes.com, September 17, 2007); Lowe, J. 2006. "Peru Pushes Claim for Machu Picchu Objects." *Art News*, March: 86; Montgomery, D. 2006. "Who Owns Inca

Treasures?" *Washington Post*, March 11 (accessed through msn-list@te.verweg.com, March 11, 2006); Needham, P. 2009. "Peru Sues Yale." *Art News*, February: 53.

6. Deliso, C. 2005. "Smugglers and Legends Complicate Fight Against Antiquities Theft (Part I)," November 16 (accessed through msn-list@te.verweg.com, November 16, 2005). *Economist*. 2006. "Protecting Archaeological Sites in Southeastern Europe: A Balkan Battle Is On to Save the Past." November 25 (accessed through msn-list@te.verweg.com, November 29, 2006).

7. Kimanuka, O. n.d. "Salvaging Our Cultural Heritage." (accessed through Museum Security Network, msn-list@te.verweg.com, June 26, 2006); Schmidt, P. R. and McIntosh, R. J. eds. 1996. *Plundering Africa's Past.* Bloomington: Indiana University Press, xi.

8. Watson, P. and Todeschini, C. 2006. *The Medici Conspiracy: The Illicit Journey of Looted Antiquities from Italy's Tomb Raiders to the World's Greatest Museums.* New York: Public Affairs, 310.

9. Elia, R. J. 1995. "Conservators and Unprovenanced Objects: Preserving the Cultural Heritage or Servicing the Antiquities Trade?" In *Antiquities Trade or Betrayed: Legal, Ethical and Conservation Issues,* K. W. Tubb ed., 244–55. London: Archetype; Interpol. n.d. "Frequently Asked Questions." (accessed through http://www.interpol.int/Public/WorkOfArt/woafaq.asp, September 12, 2007).

10. Atwood, R. 2004. *Stealing History: Tomb Raiders, Smugglers, and the Looting of the Ancient World.* New York: St. Martin's Press, 221; Elia, R. J. 2001. "Analysis of the Looting, Selling and Collecting of Apulian Red-Figure Vases: A Quantitative Approach. In *Trade in Illicit Antiquities: The Destruction of the World's Archaeological Heritage,* N. Brodie, J. Doole, and C. Renfrew ed., 145–53. Oxford, UK: Oxbow Books; LaFont, M. 2004. *Pillaging Cambodia: The Illicit Traffic in Khmer Art.* Jefferson, NC: McFarland and Co. Publishers, 78; "Policing Antiquities in Italy: The Carabinieri Art Squad." n.d. (accessed through http://74.125.47.132/search?q=cache:ys_a04dZx1cJ:www.savingantiquities.org/C on September 13, 2007).

11. Kean, T. 2008. "Asia Fights to Stem Loss of Cultural Treasures." December 22 (accessed through Museum Security Network, http://groups.google.com/group/museum-security-network/t/2849325d6fa4e300?hl=en, December 22, 2008); LaFont, M. 2004. *Pillaging Cambodia: The Illicit Traffic in Khmer Art.* Jefferson, NC: McFarland and Co. Publishers, 3, 34, 58, 72.

12. *India eNews.* 2007. "Culture Ministry Consults CBI to Curb Antique Theft." March 20, http://www.indiaenews.com/ (accessed through Museum Security Network, msn-list@te.verweg.com, March 20, 2007); Mujtaba, Syed Ali. 2007. "Loot of India's Antiquities Goes Unchecked." TwoCircles.net, November 1 (accessed through Museum Security Network, msn-list@te.verweg.com, November 1, 2007).

13. Kimanuka, O. n.d. "Salvaging Our Cultural Heritage." (accessed through Museum Security Network, msn-list@te.verweg.com, June 26, 2006); Schmidt, P. R. and McIntosh, R. J. 1996. "The African Past Endangered." In *Plundering Africa's Past,* Schmidt, P. R. and McIntosh ed., R. J., 1–17. Bloomington: Indiana University Press.

14. *Xinhuanet.* 2007. "Removal of Cultural Relics Older than 1911 Banned." May 29, http://news.xinhuanet.com/ (accessed through Museum Security Network, msn-list@te.verweg.com, June 1, 2007); Agence France Press. 2007. "Smuggling Fuels Worldwide Trade in Chinese Antiquities." September 30 (accessed through Museum Security Network, msn-list@te.verweg.com, September 30, 2007).

15. *Economist*. 2007. "An Overdue Effort to Protect Antiquities." September 6, http://www.economist.com/ (accessed through Museum Security Network, msn-list@te.verweg.com, September 10, 2007); "Looters Plunder Peru's Antique Treasures." April 2, 2007 (accessed through Museum Security Network, msn-list@te.verweg.com, April 5, 2007); LawFuel.com. 2006. "US Attorney Reports Three Charged for Smuggling—Press Release—Smugglers. Brought Pre-Columbian Artifacts into US." July 23 (accessed through Museum Security Network, msn-list@te.verweg.com, July 24, 2006).

16. Tuckman, J. 2006. "Art Thieves Threaten to Erase Mexico's Past." *Guardian,* November 24 (accessed through Museum Security Network, msn-list@te.verweg.com, November 26, 2006).

17. Grose. T. K. 2006. "Stealing History." *U.S. News & World Report,* June 19: 40–47; "Italy Art Trafficker Duped U.S. Museums, Police Say." January 15, 2005 (accessed through Museum Security Network, msn-list@te.verweg.com, January 15, 2005); Povoledo, E. 2006. "U.S. Antiquities Dealer at Center of Inquiry." *New York Times,* June 20 (accessed through Museum Security Network, msn-list@te.verweg.com, June 21, 2006); Thomas, K. D. 2006. "The Man Who Moved Kraters." *Art News,* April: 134–35; Watson, P., and Todeschini, C. 2006. *The Medici Conspiracy: The Illicit Journey of Looted Antiquities from Italy's Tomb Raiders to the World's Greatest Museums.* New York: Public Affairs; Waxman, S. 2008. *Loot: The Battle Over the Stolen Treasures of the Ancient World.* New York: Times Books, 288–89, 291; Willan, P. 2009. "Art Hit Squad Takes on Tomb Raiders After Relics Looted; Public Opinion Turning Against 'Tombaroli.'" *Sunday Herald* (UK), February 22 (accessed through Museum Security Network, http://groups.google.com/group/museum-security-network/t/f66ea4ead9335938?hl=en, February 27, 2009).

18. Kean, T. 2008. "Asia Fights to Stem Loss of Cultural Treasures." December 22 (accessed through Museum Security Network, http://groups.google.com/group/museum-security-network/t/2849325d6fa4e300?hl=en, December 22, 2008).

19. Bogdanos, M. (with W. Patrick). 2005. *Thieves of Baghdad: One Marine's Passion for Ancient Civilizations and the Journey to Recover the World's Greatest Stolen Treasures.* New York: Bloomsbury, 244.

20. Povoledo, E. 2008. "Collector Returns Art Italy Says Was Looted." *New York Times,* January 18 (accessed through http://nytimes.com, January 23, 2008).

21. Povoledo, E. 2008. "Tempelsman Sculptures Return to Italy." *New York Times,* February 26 (accessed through http://nytimes.com, February 26, 2008)

22. Elia, R. J. 1995. "Conservators and Unprovenanced Objects: Preserving the Cultural Heritage or Servicing the Antiquities Trade?" In *Antiquities Trade or Betrayed: Legal, Ethical and Conservation Issues,* K. W. Tubb ed., 247–48, 251. London: Archetype; Spiel, R. E., Jr. 2000. *Art Theft and Forgery Investigation: The Complete Field Manual.* Springfield, IL: Charles C. Thomas, 222.

23. Lawless, J. 2009. "Chinese Bronzes, Gandhi's Glasses in Art Tussle." Associated Press, March 8 (accessed through Museum Security Network, http://groups.google.com/group/museum-security-network/t/6883fc733f19b4c2?hl=en, March 8, 2009); Vasi, N. n.d. "India, China Face Auction Catch 22." (accessed through Museum Security Network, http://groups.google.com/group/museum-security-network/t/605f53c57fa1bc7c?hl=en, March 5, 2009).

24. Atwood, R. 2004. *Stealing History: Tomb Raiders, Smugglers, and the Looting of the Ancient World.* New York: St. Martin's Press, 142.

25. Cuno, J. 2008. *Who Owns Antiquity?: Museums and the Battle Over Our Ancient Heritage.* Princeton, NJ: Princeton University Press, 27; *Los Angeles Times.* 2005. "Several Museums May Possess Looted Art." November 8 (accessed through Museum Security Network, msn-list@te.verweg.com, November 8, 2005).

26. *Los Angeles Times.* 2005. "Several Museums May Possess Looted Art." November 8 (accessed through Museum Security Network, msn-list@te.verweg.com, November 8, 2005); Silver, V. 2006. "Getty Ex-Curator Says Antiquities Trade 'Corrupt,' Art Smuggled." Bloomberg, November 10 (accessed through Museum Security Network, msn-list@te.verweg.com, November 11, 2006); Waxman, S. 2008. *Loot: The Battle Over the Stolen Treasures of the Ancient World.* New York: Times Books, 361.

27. Povoledo, E. 2006. "Top Collector Is Asked to Relinquish Artifacts." *New York Times,* November 28, http://www.nytimes.com/ (accessed through Museum Security Network, msn-list@te.verweg.com, November 29, 2006); Povoledo, E. 2007. "Returning Stolen Art; No Easy Answers." *New York Times,* October 27 http://www.nytimes.com/ (accessed through Museum Security Network, msn-list@te.verweg.com, October 28, 2007); *Los Angeles Times.* 2005. "Several Museums May Possess Looted Art." November 8 (accessed through Museum Security Network, msn-list@te.verweg.com, November 8, 2005).

28. Litt, S. 2009. "A Negotiation among Gentlemen." *Art News,* January: 50.

29. Povoledo, E. 2007. "Princeton to Return Disputed Art to Italy." *New York Times,* October 27 (accessed through http://www.nytimes.com, October 27, 2007); *Los Angeles Times.* 2005. "Several Museums May Possess Looted Art." November 8 (accessed through Museum Security Network, msn-list@te.verweg.com, November 8, 2005).

30. Eakin, H. and Povoledo, E. 2006. "Met's Fears on Looted Antiquities Are Not New." *New York Times,* February 20, http://www.nytimes.com; Kennedy, R. 2006. "Met Sending Vase to Italy, Ending 30-Year Dispute." *New York Times,* February 2, http://www.nytimes.com; Meyer, K. E. 1973. *The Plundered Past.* New York: Atheneum, 86; Van Gelder, L. 2006. "The Mysterious Trail of a Treasure, Retraced." *New York Times,* February 5, http://www.nytimes.com; Vogel, C. 2008. "Ciao to a Met Prize Returning to Italy." *New York Times,* January 11, http://www.nytimes.com; Waxman, S. 2008. *Loot: The Battle Over the Stolen Treasures of the Ancient World.* New York: Times Books, 188–92.

31. Atwood, R. 2004. *Stealing History: Tomb Raiders, Smugglers, and the Looting of the Ancient World.* New York: St. Martin's Press, 154, 209; Cuno, J. 2008. *Who Owns Antiquity?: Museums and the Battle Over Our Ancient Heritage.* Princeton, NJ: Princeton University Press, xviii, 124–25, 141, 146, 161; Lowenthal, C. 1997. "Art Theft and Its Control since World War II." *Journal of Financial Crime* 5 (1): 39–44; Meyer, K. E. 1973. *The Plundered Past.* New York: Atheneum, 28; Waxman, S. 2008. *Loot: The Battle Over the Stolen Treasures of the Ancient World.* New York: Times Books, 142, 158, 172–74, 188–89.

32. Atwood, R. 2004. *Stealing History: Tomb Raiders, Smugglers, and the Looting of the Ancient World.* New York: St. Martin's Press, 209; Cuno, J. 2008. *Who Owns Antiquity?: Museums and the Battle Over Our Ancient Heritage.* Princeton, NJ: Princeton University Press, 124–25, 141, 146, 161; Lowenthal, C. 1997. "Art Theft and Its Control since World War II." *Journal of Financial Crime* 5 (1): 39–44; Watson, P. and Todeschini, C. 2006. *The Medici Conspiracy: The Illicit Journey of Looted Antiquities from Italy's Tomb Raiders to the World's Greatest Museums.* New York: Public Affairs, 28; Waxman, S. 2008. *Loot: The Battle Over the Stolen Treasures of the Ancient World.* New York: Times Books, 29–30, 142, 144, 165–66.

33. Atwood, R. 2004. *Stealing History: Tomb Raiders, Smugglers, and the Looting of the Ancient World.* New York: St. Martin's Press, 209; Cuno, J. 2008. *Who Owns Antiquity?: Museums and the Battle Over Our Ancient Heritage.* Princeton, NJ: Princeton University Press, xviii; Waxman, S. 2008. *Loot: The Battle Over the Stolen Treasures of the Ancient World,* New York: Times Books, 97.

34. Watson, P. and Todeschini, C. 2006. *The Medici Conspiracy: The Illicit Journey of Looted Antiquities from Italy's Tomb Raiders to the World's Greatest Museums.* New York: Public Affairs, 325; Waxman, S. 2008. *Loot: The Battle Over the Stolen Treasures of the Ancient World.* New York: Times Books, 9, 188–89, 194–95.

35. Cuno, J. 2008. *Who Owns Antiquity?: Museums and the Battle Over Our Ancient Heritage.* Princeton, NJ: Princeton University Press, xviii, xxxiv, xxxv, 127, 141, 154–55; Cuno, J. 2009. "Treaty on Antiquities Hinders Access for Museums." *Science News,* March 28, http://www.sciencenews.org/view/generic/id/41671/title/Treaty_on_antiquities (accessed through Museum Security Network, http://groups.google.com/group/museum-security-network/t/44798375027d583d?hl=en, March 13, 2009).

36. American Association of Museums. "Standards Regarding Archeological Material and Ancient Art." (accessed through http://www.aam-us.org/museumresources/ethics/upload/Standards%20Regarding%20Archaeological%20Material%20and%20Ancient%20Art.pdf on April 21, 2009); Association of Art Museum Directors. "New Report on Acquisition of Archeological Materials and Ancient Art Issued by Association of Art Museum Directors." (accessed through http://www.aamd.org/newsroom/documents/2008ReportAndRelease.pdf on April 21, 2009); Lush, T. 2008. "Antiquities Smuggling: Growing Problem at US Ports." Associated Press, September 15 (accessed through Museum Security Network at http://groups.google.com/group/museum-security-network/browse_thread/thread/03d93e714fcdcf4e?hl=en on September 15, 2008).

37. LaFont, M. 2004. *Pillaging Cambodia: The Illicit Traffic in Khmer Art.* Jefferson, NC: McFarland and Co. Publishers, 79; McIntosh, R. J. 1996. "Just Say Shame: Excising the Rot of Cultural Genocide." In *Plundering Africa's Past,* eds. P. R. Schmidt and R. J. McIntosh, 45–62. Bloomington: Indiana University Press; Meyer, K. E. 1973. *The Plundered Past.* New York: Atheneum, 28; Renfrew, C. 2001. Foreword to *Trade in Illicit Antiquities: The Destruction of the World's Archaeological Heritage,* N. Brodie, J. Doole, and C. Renfrew, eds. Oxford, UK: Oxbow Books.

CHAPTER 7: WHITE-COLLAR CRIME IN THE ART WORLD

1. Federal Bureau of Investigation. n.d. "Facts and Figures." (accessed through http://www.fbi.gov/libref/factsfigure/wcc.htm, May 23, 2009).

2. See Shapiro, S. P. 1984. *Wayward Capitalists: Target of the Securities and Exchange Commission.* New Haven, CT: Yale University Press; Weisburd, D., Wheeler, S., Waring, E., and Bode, N. 1991. *Crimes of the Middle Classes: White Collar Offenders in the Federal Courts.* New Haven, CT: Yale University Press.

3. Croall, H. 1992. *White Collar Crime.* Buckingham, UK: Open University Press, 10.

4. Eakin, H. and Povoledo, E. 2006. "Antiquities Trial in Rome Focuses on a London Dealer." *New York Times,* March 29 (accessed through Museum Security Network, msn-list@te.verweg.com, March 30, 2006); Eakin, H. 2007. "Treasure

Hunt: The Downfall of the Getty Curator Marion True." *New Yorker,* December 17; Farber, J. 2007. "Bringing Trust Back to the Getty." *Daily News,* May 5, http://www.dailynews.com/ (accessed through Museum Security Network, msn-list@te.verweg.com, May 6, 2007); Felch, J. and Frammolino, R. 2005. "Ex-Getty Curator Received 2nd Loan." *Los Angeles Times,* November 17 (accessed through Museum Security Network, msn-list@te.verweg.com, November 17, 2005); Frammolino, R. and Felch, J. 2006. "Getty Paid Trustee's Legal Fees Despite Lawyer's Warning." *Los Angeles Times,* June 29 (accessed through Museum Security Network, msn-list@te.verweg.com, June 29, 2006); Grohman, K. 2006."Former Getty Curator Charged with Greek Art Theft." Reuters, November 21 (accessed through Museum Security Network, msn-list@te.verweg.com, November 22, 2006); Knight, C. 2005. "Critics' Notebook: At Getty Trust, the Trust Part is Lacking." *Los Angeles Times,* November 13 (accessed through Museum Security Network, msn-list@te.verweg.com, November 13, 2005); *The Age.* 2006. "Their Hands in the Tombs." March 23, http://www.theage.com.au/ (accessed through Museum Security Network, msn-list@te.verweg.com, March 23, 2006); Waxman, S. 2008. *Loot: The Battle Over the Stolen Treasures of the Ancient World.* New York: Times Books, 300–301, 310–12, 314–17, 319, 339, 341.

5. Rosoff, S. M., Pontell, H. N., and Tillman, R. H. 2004. *Profit Without Honor: White-Collar Crime and the Looting of America.* 3rd ed. Upper Saddle River, NJ: Pearson Prentice Hall, 27.

6. Friedrichs, D. 1996. *Trusted Criminals: White Collar Crime in Contemporary Society.* Belmont, CA: Wadsworth, 55.

7. Pastore, A. L. and Maguire, K., eds., 2009. *Sourcebook of Criminal Justice Statistics* (online) (accessed http://www.albany.edu/sourcebook/, June 4, 2009), Table 3.111.

8. Andrews, S. 2008. "Art of the Steal." *Portfolio,* April, http://www.portfolio.com/ (accessed through Museum Security Network, msn-list@te.verweg.com, March 18, 2008); Barron, J. 2007. "Art Dealer Files for Bankruptcy, Delaying Suits Against Him." *New York Times,* November 6 (accessed through http://www.nytimes.com/2007/11/07/arts/07arts.html?_r=1&ref=arts&oref=slogin, November 7, 2007); Barron, J. 2009. "Upper East Side Art Dealer Is Charged With Stealing $88 Million." *New York Times,* March 27 (accessed through Museum Security Network, http://groups.google.com/group/museum-security-network/t/5aedd36f1383716a?hl=en, March 26, 2009); Boroff, P. and Pollock, L. 2009. "Gallery Director Pleads Guilty to Falsifying Records." Bloomberg, April 9 (accessed through Museum Security Network, http://groups.google.com/group/museum-security-network/t/5aedd36f1383716a?hl=en, April 10, 2009).

9. Ho, V. 2007. "Theft Sends Art Dealer to Prison." *Seattle Post-Intelligencer,* October 15 (accessed through Museum Security Network, msn-list@te.verweg.com, October 15, 2007); Johnson, A. 2006. "Art Dealer Sentenced to 14 Months in Prison." *Milwaukee Journal-Sentinel,* May 25 (accessed through Museum Security Network, msn-list@te.verweg.com, May 27, 2007); Nance, K. 2007. "Gallery Failed to Pay Consignors, Judge Rules." *Chicago Sun Times,* January 17 (accessed through Museum Security Network, msn-list@te.verweg.com, January 17, 2007).

10. Kaufman, J. E. 2007. "Slap on Wrist for Fraudulent Antiquities Dealer." *Art Newspaper,* October 4, http://www.theartnewspaper.com/ (accessed through Museum Security Network, msn-list@te.verweg.com, October 5, 2007).

11. Fehling, D. 2009 "Hundreds Claim to be Victims of Houston High-Society Couple." Khou.com., April 25 (accessed through Museum Security Network, msn-list@te.verweg.com, April 24, 2009); Whitely, J. 2007. "High Profile Auctioneers Accused of Cheating Clients." Khou.com, October 20 (accessed through http://www.khou.com/news/local/crime/stories/khou071019_jj_hartfelony.1884f03d0 on June 10, 2009).

12. Geis G. 1970. "White Collar Crime: The Heavy Electrical Equipment Anti-Trust Cases of 1961." In *Crime and Delinquency*, C.A. Bersani ed., 170–84. London: MacMillan; Mason, C. 2004. *The Art of the Steal: Inside the Sotheby's-Christie's Auction House Scandal.* New York: Berkley, 7, 34–37, 43, 51, 62, 96–97, 110, 121, 133–34, 139–40, 149, 157, 170, 199, 248–51, 278, 288, 299–300, 311–12, 332–33, 341–44, 354, 360, 363–64; Simpson, S. S. and Koper, C. S. 1997. "The Changing of the Guard: Top Management Characteristics, Organizational Strain and Anti-Trust Offending." *Journal of Quantitative Criminology* 13 (4): 373–403.

CHAPTER 8: VANDALISM AND MALICIOUS DESTRUCTION

1. Cordess, C. and Turcan, M. 1993. "Art Vandalism." *British Journal of Criminology* 33 (1): 95–102.

2. *Burnley Citizen.* 2007. "Man Went on Rampage at Art Exhibition." September 12, http://www.burnleycitizen.co.uk/ (accessed through Museum Security Network, msn-list@te.verweg.com, September 13, 2007).

3. "Rijksmuseum, Amsterdam, Evacuated After Acid Attack on Painting." June 26, 2006, msn-list@te.verweg.com; "Man Confesses to Attack on Masterpiece," June 26, 2006. msn-list@te.verweg.com; "Particulars plus photographs of man who threw a chemical substance on a 16th century painting in the Rijksmuseum, Amsterdam, are available online at: http://www.museum-security.org/hans_joachim_Bohlmann.pdf," msn-list@te.verweg.com, June 28, 2006.

4. Associated Press. 2007. "Woman Tried For Kissing Twombly Painting." October 9 (accessed through Museum Security Network, msn-list@te.verweg.com, October 9, 2007); CBS News. 2007. "Artist Twombly Gets One Euro Award for Unwanted Kiss." November 16 (accessed through http://www.cbc.ca/arts/art design/story/2007/11/16/twomby-kiss.html, June 24, 2008).

5. Associated Press. 2007. "Massive Pompeii Column Toppled." *The Tampa Tribune*, March 22: 14.

6. Associated Press. 2007. "Famous Monet Painting Vandalized in Paris." October 7 (accessed through Museum Security Network, msn-list@te.verweg.com, October 7, 2007); Kanter, J. 2007. "Vandal Punches Hole in a Monet in Paris." *New York Times*, October 8 (accessed through www.nytimes.com October 8, 2007); Kanter, J. 2007. "5 Held in Monet Attack." *New York Times*, October 11 (accessed through www.nytimes.com October 11, 2007).

7. Associated Press. 2008. "Museum Guard Caught Defacing Painting." June 5 (accessed through http://www.msnbc.msn.com/id/24993578/, June 24, 2008); Sherman, J. L. 2009. "Carnegie Museum Guard Admits Defacing Painting." *Pittsburgh Post-Gazette*, January 22 (accessed through Museum Security Network, http://groups.google.com/group/museum-security-network/t/7ff4cf09cb641362?hl=en, January 22, 2009).

8. BBC News. 2008. "Vandals in Attack on Stonehenge." May 22 (accessed through http://news.bbc.co.uk/go/pr/fr/-/2/hi/uk_news/england/wiltshire/74144, August 11, 2008).

9. Bloom, J. 2008. "Chagall Window Shattered in France." *New York Times,* August 14 (accessed through http://www.nytimes.com/2008/08/15/arts/design/15arts-CHAGALLWINDO_BRF.html?_r=1&ref=arts&oref=slogin, August 15, 2008).

10. Alberge, D. 2008. "UN Vandals Spray Graffiti on Sahara's Prehistoric Art." *Times On Line* (UK), January 31 (accessed through Museum Security Network, msn-list@te.verweg.com, January 31, 2008).

11. Nordmarker, A., Norlander, T. and Archer, T. 2000. "The Effects of Alcohol Intake and Induced Frustration Upon Art Vandalism." *Social Behavior and Personality* 28 (1): 15–28.

12. Allen, V. L. and Greenberger, D. B. 1978. "An Aesthetic Theory of Vandalism." *Crime and Delinquency* 24 (3): 309–21.

13. Hurwitz, L. 2007. "Sentence Upheld for Urinal Vandal." *Art News,* April: 72; Rider, A. 2006. "Conceptual Artist as Vandal: Walk Tall and Carry a Little Hammer (or Ax)." *New York Times,* January 7 (accessed through accessed through Museum Security Network, msn-list@te.verweg.com, January 7, 2006).

14. *Islamic and Jewish News.* 2006. "Attack on Egyptian Antiquities Fuels Fears of an Islamist Egypt." June 18 (accessed through accessed through Museum Security Network, msn-list@te.verweg.com, June 19, 2007).

15. Vogel, C. 2007. "Gallery Vandals Destroy Photos." *New York Times,* October 9 (accessed through accessed through Museum Security Network, msn-list@te.verweg.com, October 11, 2007).

16. Itzkoff, D. 2009. "Vandals Attack Roman Museum." *New York Times,* June 1; Winfield, N. 2009. "Vandals Hurl Paint-Filled Balloons at Rome Museum." *Associated Press,* June 1 (accessed through http://www.wtopnews.com/index.php?nid=105&sid=1686763, June 11, 2009).

17. Esterow, M. 2006. "If You Can't Sell It, Melt It." *Art News,* March: 74, 76.

18. United Press International. 2006. "Thieves Steal Valuable Art for Scrap Metal." December 27 (accessed through accessed through Museum Security Network, msn-list@te.verweg.com, December 29, 2006).

19. Baird, J. B. 2007. "Scrap Yard Tip Saves Sculpture From Smelters." *Burlington* (VT) *Free Press,* December 12 (accessed through accessed through Museum Security Network, msn-list@te.verweg.com, December 13, 2007); Associated Press. 2008. "Fourth Person Sentenced in Sculpture Heist." October 31 (accessed through accessed through Museum Security Network, http://groups.google.com/group/museum-security-network/browse_thread/thread/67bef507b6ebb710?hl=en, November 2, 2008); Rathke, L. 2007. "3 Arrested in Theft of Sculptures Worth an Estimated $1 Million." Associated Press, December 27 (accessed through accessed through Museum Security Network, msn-list@te.verweg.com, December 27, 2007); Silverman, A. 2007. "Police Investigate $1 Million Sculpture Heist." *Burlington* (VT) *Free Press,* December 7 (accessed through accessed through Museum Security Network, msn-list@te.verweg.com, December 5, 2007); WCAX TV News. 2008. "2nd Suspect Sentenced for $1M Art Heist." July 22, http://www.wcax.com (accessed through accessed through Museum Security Network, http://groups.google.com/group/museum-security-network/browse thread/thread/5aaf1cc5e2c7291e?hl=en, July 22, 2008).

20. Blankenship, A. 2008. "Howdy, Pardner! Missing Miner Statue Recovered." *Los Angeles Times,* February 15 (accessed through accessed through Museum

Security Network, msn-list@te.verweg.com, February 15, 2008); *Red Orbit News.* 2008. "Metal Thieves Lift 7-Foot Statue." February 13 (accessed through accessed through Museum Security Network, msn-list@te.verweg.com, February 15, 2008).

21. Addison, S. 2008. "Police Launch Two-Day Blitz on Metals Theft." Reuters, July 8 (accessed through Museum Security Network, msn-list@te.verweg.com, July 9, 2008); Bennetto, J. 2006. "Theft of Bronze Statues Worth £45,000 Linked to 'Artworks for Scrap' Gang." *Independent* (UK), May 31 (accessed through accessed through Museum Security Network, msn-list@te.verweg.com, May 31, 2006); *Zee News.com.* 2006. "Bronze Statues Go Missing From In & Around London." February 1 (accessed through accessed through Museum Security Network, msn-list@ te.verweg.com, February 2, 2006); Esterow, M. 2006. "If You Can't Sell, Melt It." *Art News,* March: 74–75; Houpt, S. 2006. *Museum of the Missing: A History of Art Theft.* New York: Sterling Publishing, 150; Townsend, M. and Davies, C. 2009. "Mystery of Stolen Moore Bronze Solved." *Observer,* May 17 (accessed through accessed through Museum Security Network, http://groups.google.com/group/ museum-security-network/t/a5cb66f6e603b325?hl=en May 17, 2009); Wareing, R. 2007. "Athlete's Statue Stolen From Park." *Argus* (UK) September 4 (accessed through accessed through Museum Security Network, msn-list@te.verweg.com, September 7, 2007).

22. Esterow, M. 2006. "If You Can't Sell, Melt It." *Art News,* March: 74–75.

23. Van der Starre, M. 2007. "Dutch Police Detain Two Men in Rodin's 'Thinker' Theft Inquiry." Bloomberg, January 18 (accessed through accessed through Museum Security Network, msn-list@te.verweg.com, January 21, 2007).

24. Morgan, C. 2008. "Thieves Melt into Night with Sculpture." *Sydney Morning Herald,* July 10 (accessed through accessed through Museum Security Network, http://groups.google.com/group/museum-security-network/browse_thread/ thread/107ea4417273c2b4?hl=en, July 10, 2008); "Stolen Sculpture may be Melted Down." 2008. *National Nine News,* July 10 (accessed through Museum Security Network, http://groups.google.com/group/museum-security-network/browse thread/thread/880d32dba5c7d1ce?hl=en, July 10, 2008).

25. Mulroney, P. 2005. "The Artful Dodgers." *Stuff.co.nz,* December 31 (accessed through accessed through Museum Security Network, msn-list@te.verweg.com, December 31, 2005).

CHAPTER 9: RESPONDING TO ART CRIME

1. Nicholas, L. H. 1994. *The Rape of Europa: The Fate of Europe's Treasures in the Third Reich and the Second World War.* New York: Vintage Books, 214–15.

2. Clément, E. 1995. "The Aims of the 1970 UNESCO Convention on the Means of Prohibiting and Preventing the Illicit, Export and Transfer of Ownership of Cultural Property and Action Being Taken by UNESCO to assist in Its Implementation." In *Antiquities Trade or Betrayed: Legal, Ethical and Conservation Issues,* K. W. Tubb, ed., 38–56. London: Archetype; Tijhuis, A.J.G. 2006. *Transnational Crime and the Interface between Legal and Illegal Actors: The Case of the Illicit Art and Antiquities Trade.* The Netherlands: Wolf Legal Publishers, 123–25.

3. Archaeological Institute of America. n.d. "U.S. Senate Gives Its Advice and Consent to the 1954 Hague Convention on Cultural Property." (accessed through Museum Security Network, http://groups.google.com/group/museum-security-network/browse_thread/thread/5794121cc01f3ce5?hl=en, September 27, 2008);

Tijhuis, A.J.G. 2006. *Transnational Crime and the Interface between Legal and Illegal Actors: The Case of the Illicit Art and Antiquities Trade.* The Netherlands: Wolf Legal Publishers, 123–25.

4. Tijhuis, A.J.G. 2006. *Transnational Crime and the Interface between Legal and Illegal Actors: The Case of the Illicit Art and Antiquities Trade.* The Netherlands: Wolf Legal Publishers, 123–25; International Institute for the Unification of Private Law. 2008. "UNIDROIT: An Overview." n.d. (accessed through http://www.unidroit. org/dynasite.cfm?dsmid=84219, August 29, 2008).

5. Tijhuis, A.J.G. 2006. *Transnational Crime and the Interface between Legal and Illegal Actors: The Case of the Illicit Art and Antiquities Trade.* The Netherlands: Wolf Legal Publishers, 123–25.

6. Interpol. "About Interpol." (accessed through http://www.interpol.int/, August 19, 2008).

7. Berouigeut, B. 1986. "Interpol and the Fight Against Art Thefts." *International Police Review* 395: 30–37; Bresler, F. 1992. *Interpol.* London, UK: Sinclair-Stevenson, 361; Interpol Media Release, August 17, 2009 (accessed through http://www.inter pol.int/Public/ICPO/PressReleases/PR2009/PR200978.asp); Interpol. "Property Crime." (accessed through http://www.interpol.int/Public/WorkOfArt/Default. asp, August 19, 2008); U.S. National Central Bureau of Interpol. n.d. "About the Cultural Property Program." (accessed through www.usdoj.gov/usncb/cult-prop/cultureabout.htm, September 12, 2007); 5th Meeting of the Interpol Expert Group (IEG) on Stolen Cultural Property-Lyon. 2008. "Recommendations." March 4 and 5 (accessed through accessed through Museum Security Network, msn-list@ te.verweg.com, March 7, 2008).

8. Berouigeut, B. 1986. "Interpol and the Fight Against Art Thefts." *International Police Review* 395: 30–37; Bresler, F. 1992. *Interpol.* London, UK: Sinclair-Stevenson, 358; U.S. National Central Bureau of Interpol. n.d. "About the Cultural Property Program." (accessed through www.usdoj.gov/usncb/cultprop/culture about.htm, September 12, 2007).

9. Federal Bureau of Investigation. n.d. "Legislation." (accessed through http://www.fbi.gov/hq/cid/arttheft/arttheft.htm, September 4, 2008).

10. Ibid.

11. Federal Bureau of Investigation. n.d. "National Stole Art File (NSAF)." (accessed through http://www.fbi.gov/hq/cid/arttheft/nationalstolen.htm, September 4, 2008).

12. Federal Bureau of Investigation. n.d. "Art Crime Team." (accessed through http://www.fbi.gov/hq/cid/arttheft/artcrimeteam.htm, September 4, 2008); Horn, P. 2005. "FBI Team to Target Art Thieves." *Philadelphia Inquirer,* January 15 (accessed through accessed through Museum Security Network, msn-list@ te.verweg.com, January 15, 2005).

13. Spiegler, H. N. and Kaye, L. M. 2001. "American Litigation to Recover Cultural Property: Obstacles, Options, and a Proposal." In *Trade in Illicit Antiquities: The Destruction of the World's Archaeological Heritage,* N. Brodie, J. Doole, and C. Renfrew, eds., 121–32. Oxford, UK: Oxbow Books.

14. Waxman, S. 2008. "Caught on Tape." *Art News,* March: 66, 68.

15. Bogdanos, M. (with W. Patrick). 2005. *Thieves of Baghdad: One Marine's Passion for Ancient Civilizations and the Journey to Recover the World's Greatest Stolen Treasures.* New York: Bloomsbury, 269.

16. Bernstein, A. 2006. "Robert Volpe—Renowned 'Art Cop.'" *Washington Post,* December 1 (accessed through accessed through Museum Security Network,

msn-list@te.verweg.com, December 2, 2006); Birnbaum, M. 2007. "New York's First 'Art Cop.'" *Art News,* February: 58.

17. "Commando Officers for the Protection of the Cultural Patrimony." n.d. (accessed through http://www.carabinieri.it/Internet, September 20, 2007); Gruner, S. 2006. "Italy's Special Carabinieri Unit Fights Art Looting." April 10, http://www.opinionjournal.com/la/?id=110008219 (accessed through accessed through Museum Security Network, msn-list@te.verweg.com, April 16, 2006); Tijhuis, A.J.G. 2006. *Transnational Crime and the Interface between Legal and Illegal Actors: The Case of the Illicit Art and Antiquities Trade.* The Netherlands: Wolf Legal Publishers, 115.

18. Butler, J. 1995. "The Arts and Antiques Squad." In *Antiquities Trade or Betrayed: Legal, Ethical and Conservation Issues,* K. W. Tubb, ed., 226–28. London: Archetype; Copping, J. 2007. "Police Seek Sponsors to Tackle Rising Art Crime." *The Sunday Telegraph* (UK), January 14 (accessed through Museum Security Network, msn-list@te.verweg.com, January 14, 2007); "Laville, S. 2007. "Met's Art Theft Squad Has to Go Cap in Hand." *The Guardian,* April 21 (accessed through Museum Security Network, msn-list@te.verweg.com, April 22, 2007). Lethbridge, L. 2007. "Adding Curators to the Force." *Art News,* April: 70.

19. Burke, J. 2005. "Art Looting Smugglers Target French Churches." *The Observer,* August 21 (accessed through Museum Security Network, msn-list@te.verweg.com, August 21, 2005); Tijhuis, A.J.G. 2006. *Transnational Crime and the Interface between Legal and Illegal Actors: The Case of the Illicit Art and Antiquities Trade.* The Netherlands: Wolf Legal Publishers, 114, 128.

20. Ellis, R. 1995. "The Antiquities Trade: A Police Perspective." In *Antiquities Trade or Betrayed: Legal, Ethical and Conservation Issues,* K. W. Tubb, ed., 222–25. London, Archetype; Fogel, D. 1994. *Policing in Central and Eastern Europe.* Helsinki, Finland: European Institute for Crime Prevention and Control, 9, 39; Gilgan, E. 2001. "Looting and the Market for Maya Objects: A Belizean Perspective." In *Trade in Illicit Antiquities: The Destruction of the World's Archaeological Heritage,* N. Brodie, J. Doole, and C. Renfrew, eds., 73–87. Oxford, UK: Oxbow Books; Thosarat, R. 2001. "The Destruction of Cultural Heritage of Thailand and Cambodia." In *Trade in Illicit Antiquities: The Destruction of the World's Archaeological Heritage,* N. Brodie, J. Doole, and C. Renfrew, eds., 7–17. Oxford, UK: Oxbow Books.

21. Aflou, L. 2007. "Algeria Is Stepping Up Efforts to Curb the Theft of Its Archaeological Treasures." *Magharebia,* January 28 (accessed through Museum Security Network, msn-list@te.verweg.com, January 29, 2007); *Kathimerini.* 2006. "Antiquities Squad Progress in UK." May 12, http://www.ekathimerini.com/ (accessed through Museum Security Network, msn-list@te.verweg.com, May 12, 2006); CBC. 2007. "Greece Closes Net on Antiquities Smuggling." July 9, http://www.cbc.ca (accessed through Museum Security Network, msn-list@te.verweg.com, July 10, 2007); Waxman, S. 2008. *Loot: The Battle Over the Stolen Treasures of the Ancient World.* New York: Times Books, 348.

22. CBC. 2009. "Canadian Police Unveil New Art-Fraud Task Force. Investigators Find Fake Riopelle Works in Quebec City Home." January 29, http://www.cbc.ca (accessed through Museum Security Network, http://groups.google.com/group/museum-security-network/t/212ec8388a7b6e12?hl=en, January 29, 2009); Knelman, J. 2007. "Art Thieves, Look Out." *Globe and Mail* (Canada), January 28 (accessed through Museum Security Network, msn-list@te.verweg.com, January 28, 2007); Tijhuis, A.J.G. 2006. *Transnational Crime and the Interface Between Legal and Illegal Actors: The Case of the Illicit Art and Antiquities Trade.* The Netherlands: Wolf Legal Publishers, 113, 127–28.

23. International Foundation for Art Research. n.d. "What is IFAR?" (accessed through http://www.ifar.org/what_main.htm, September 12, 2007); *Art Loss Register*. n.d. "Frequently Asked Questions." (accessed through http://www.artloss.com/content/frequently-asked-questions, September 18, 2007).

24. Leyden, J. 2005. "Stolen Property On-Line Registry Database Created By Swift-Find." Israeli News Agency, August 7 (accessed through http://www.israelnewsagency.com/stolenpropertydatabaseswiftfind440807.html, October 1, 2008); "Frequently Asked Questions." n.d. (accessed through http://www.mythings.com/transition/faq.aspx, October 1, 2008); Trace. n.d. "Looted Art." (accessed through http://www.tracelootedart.com/, September 12, 2007); Trace. n.d. "About Us." (accessed through http://www.trace.com/about.aspx, September 12, 2007).

CHAPTER 10: SECURITY AND PREVENTION: THE BEST RESPONSE TO ART CRIME

1. Bogdanos, M. (with W. Patrick). 2005. *Thieves of Baghdad: One Marine's Passion for Ancient Civilizations and the Journey to Recover the World's Greatest Stolen Treasures.* New York: Bloomsbury, 136.

2. *Express India.* n.d. "Neglected Indian Museum in Urgent Need of Reform." http://cities.expressindia.com/ (accessed through Museum Security Network, msn-list@te.verweg.com, October 28, 2007); *Today Szaman.* n.d. "Security to be Tightened Against Art Theft in Museums." http://www.todayszaman.com/ (accessed through Museum Security Network, msn-list@te.verweg.com, December 17, 2005); Waxman, S. 2008. *Loot: The Battle Over the Stolen Treasures of the Ancient World.* New York: Times Books, 109–12.

3. Metropolitan Police Service. n.d. "Protect Your Art and Antiques." (accessed through http://www.met.police.uk./crimeprevention/art.htm, June 9, 2007).

4. Associated Press. 2008. "Big Art Theft in Zurich Raises Fears for Smaller Museums." February 12 (accessed through Museum Security Network, msn-list@te.verweg.com, February 13, 2008); Waxman, S. 2008. *Loot: The Battle Over the Stolen Treasures of the Ancient World.* New York: Times Books, 109–10.

5. Campbell-Johnston, R. 2005. "Don't Scream at the Plate Glass—It's the Price Paid for Artful Robberies." *Arts Notebook,* August 18 (accessed through Museum Security Network, msn-list@te.verweg.com, August 19, 2005); Reuters. 2005. "Security Comes at a Price for Italian Art." August 25, http://today.reuters.co.uk (accessed through Museum Security Network, msn-list@te.verweg.com, August 25, 2005); "The Munch Museum Reopens with Strict Security Measures." August, 18, 2005 (accessed through Museum Security Network, msn-list@te.verweg.com, August 19, 2005).

6. Mason. D. L. 1979. *Fine Art of Art Security: Protecting Public and Private Collections Against Theft, Fire, and Vandalism.* New York: Van Nostrand Reinhold.

7. Baker, N. n.d. "New Museum and Gallery Security Products." (accessed through Museum Security Network, msn-list@te.verweg.com, February 25, 2005); O'Connor, M. C. 2008. "Art Dealer Finds Beauty in RFID Tracking System." *RFID Journal,* July 2 (accessed through http://www.rfidjournal.com/article/articleview/4174/, October 25, 2008).

8. "In Situ 3 Dimensional Non-Contact Microscale Documentation and Identification of Paintings and Polychrome Objects." n.d. (accessed through Museum Security Network, msn-list@te.verweg.com, March 28, 2006); *Tracing Your*

Treasures: FINGaRtPRINT. n.d. (accessed through http://www.fingartprint.org/ index.php?option=com_frontpage&Itemid=1, October 25, 2008); Martinelli, N. 2007. "Sonic Fingerprints Safeguard Art." *Wired,* January 9, http://www.wired. com/ (accessed through Museum Security Network, msn-list@te.verweg.com, January 9, 2007).

   9. Bennett, L. 2004. "Armed Guards Watch Dali Art." *St. Petersburg* (FL) *Times,* August 24: 1A, 6A; Falkenstein, M. 2005. "The Training of the Guards." *Art News,* May: 134–37.

   10. Berouigeut, B. 1986. "Interpol and the Fight Against Art Thefts." *International Police Review* 395: 30–37; Falkenstein, M. 2005. "The Training of the Guards." *Art News,* May: 134–37.

   11. Flesher, S. 2004. "The International Foundation for Art Research (IFAR)." In *The Expert vs. The Object: Judging Fakes and False Attributions in the Visual Arts,* R. D. Spencer, ed., 95–102. New York: Oxford University Press; Levenson, R. S. 2004. "Examining Techniques and Materials of Paintings." In *The Expert vs. The Object: Judging Fakes and False Attributions in the Visual Arts,* R. D. Spencer, ed., 111–22. New York: Oxford University Press; O'Connor, F. V. 2004. "Authenticating the Attribution of Art: Connoisseurship and the Law in Judging Forgeries, Copies and False Attributions." In *The Expert vs. The Object: Judging Fakes and False Attributions in the Visual Arts,* R. D. Spencer, ed., 3–27. New York: Oxford University Press; Spencer, R. D. 2004. "Authentication in Court: Factors Considered and Standards Proposed." In *The Expert vs. The Object: Judging Fakes and False Attributions in the Visual Arts,* R. D. Spencer, ed., 189–215. New York: Oxford University Press; Thaw, E. V. 2004. Foreword to *The Expert vs. The Object: Judging Fakes and False Attributions in the Visual Arts,* e.d. R. D. Spencer. New York: Oxford University Press; Thaw, E. V. 2004. (interviewed by R. D. Spencer). "The Authentic Will Win Out." In *The Expert vs. The Object: Judging Fakes and False Attributions in the Visual Arts,* R. D. Spencer, ed., 73–77. New York: Oxford University Press.

   12. Flesher, S. 2004. "The International Foundation for Art Research (IFAR)." In *The Expert vs. The Object: Judging Fakes and False Attributions in the Visual Arts,* R. D. Spencer, ed., 95–102. New York: Oxford University Press; Landi, A. 2005."Seeing Infrared." *Art News,* June: 108–9; Hoving, T. 1996. *False Impressions: The Hunt for Big-Time Art Fakes.* New York: Simon and Schuster, 116–17; Levenson, R. S. 2004. "Examining Techniques and Materials of Paintings." In *The Expert vs. The Object: Judging Fakes and False Attributions in the Visual Arts,* R. D. Spencer, ed., 111–22. New York: Oxford University Press.

   13. Siegel, P. 2004. "Signature Identification from Pen Stroke to Brush Stroke." In *The Expert vs. The Object: Judging Fakes and False Attributions in the Visual Arts,* R. D. Spencer, ed., 89–93. New York: Oxford University Press; Spencer, R. D. 2004. "Authentication in Court: Factors Considered and Standards Proposed." In *The Expert vs. The Object: Judging Fakes and False Attributions in the Visual Arts,* R. D. Spencer, ed., 189–215. New York: Oxford University Press.

   14. Landi, A. 2005. "Seeing Infrared." *Art News,* June: 108–9; Levenson, R. S. 2004. "Examining Techniques and Materials of Paintings." In *The Expert vs. The Object: Judging Fakes and False Attributions in the Visual Arts,* R. D. Spencer, ed., 111–22. New York: Oxford University Press.

   15. Landi, A. 2005. "Seeing Infrared." *Art News,* June: 108–9; Hoving, T. 1996. *False Impressions: The Hunt for Big-Time Art Fakes.* New York: Simon and Schuster, 116–17; Levenson, R. S. 2004. "Examining Techniques and Materials of Paintings."

In *The Expert vs. The Object: Judging Fakes and False Attributions in the Visual Arts,* R. D. Spencer, ed., 111–22. New York: Oxford University Press.

16. Landi, A. 2005. "Seeing Infrared." *Art News,* June: 108–9; Porter, L. 2007. "Art Imitating Art." *The Age,* December 2, http://www.theage.com.au/articles/ 2007/12/01/1196394679586.html (accessed through Museum Security Network, msn-list@te.verweg.com, December 2, 2007); Levenson, R. S. 2004. "Examining Techniques and Materials of Paintings." In *The Expert vs. The Object: Judging Fakes and False Attributions in the Visual Arts,* R. D. Spencer, ed., 111–22. New York: Oxford University Press.

17. "Art Authentication the Forensic Way." n.d. (accessed through Museum Security Network, msn-list@te.verweg.com, October 20, 2006); Landi, A. 2005. "Seeing Infrared." *Art News,* June: 108–9; Levenson, R. S. 2004. "Examining Techniques and Materials of Paintings." In *The Expert vs. The Object: Judging Fakes and False Attributions in the Visual Arts,* R. D. Spencer, ed., 111–22. New York: Oxford University Press.

18. Levenson, R. S. 2004. "Examining Techniques and Materials of Paintings." In *The Expert vs. The Object: Judging Fakes and False Attributions in the Visual Arts,* R. D. Spencer, ed., 111–22. New York: Oxford University Press; Porter, L. 2007. "Art Imitating Art." *The Age,* December 2, http://www.theage.com.au/articles/ 2007/12/01/1196394679586.html (accessed through Museum Security Network, msn-list@te.verweg.com, December 2, 2007).

19. Hanan, J. F. 2008. "Digital Imaging Helps Stop Art Forgies; Computer Program Can Scrutinize Brush Stroke." Newhouse News Service, July 11 (accessed through Museum Security Network, msn-list@te.verweg.com, July 11, 2008); Heingarter, D. 2004. "A Computer That Has an Eye for Van Gogh." *New York Times,* June 13 (accessed through http://www.nytimes.com/2004/06/13/arts/ design/13HEIN.html?ex=1088161930&ei=1&en, June 14, 2004); Landi, A. 2005. "Seeing Infrared." *Art News,* June: 108–9; O'Connor, F. V. 2004. "Authenticating the Attribution of Art: Connoisseurship and the Law in Judging Forgeries, Copies and False Attributions." In *The Expert vs. The Object: Judging Fakes and False Attributions in the Visual Arts,* R. D. Spencer, ed., 3–27. New York: Oxford University Press; *Newsweek.* 2008. "Teaching a Computer to Appreciate Art." February 29, http:// www.newsweek.com (accessed through Museum Security Network, msn-list@ te.verweg.com, March 2, 2008).

20. Gioconda, J.C. 2008. "Creative Approaches to Fighting Art Forgery." Law.com, October 14, http://www.law.com/jsp/nylj/PubArticleNY.jsp?id=1202425171321 (accessed through Museum Security Network, http://groups.google.com/group/ museum-security-network/browse_thread/thread/6ff7979c05218cdf?hl=en, October 13, 2008); Smith, G. 2006. "Copycat Paintings Concern Artists: Technology, Overseas Factories Add to Rising Tide of Cheap Knockoffs." *Post and Courier* (Charleston, SC), November 12 (accessed through Museum Security Network, msn-list@te.verweg.com, November 12, 2006).

21. *PRNewswire-FirstCall.* 2006. "Applied DNA Sciences, Inc., Announces DNA Encryption Technology to Protect Famous Chinese Artworks from Forgery and Counterfeiting." March 29 (accessed through Museum Security Network, msn-list@te.verweg.com, March 29, 2006).

22. Ashraf, G. 2008. "Set Up an Art Loss Register to Curb Forgery." *News* (Pakistan), April 20, http://www.thenews.com.pk/ (accessed through Museum Security Network, msn-list@te.verweg.com, April 20, 2008).

Index

About the Author

THOMAS D. BAZLEY received his MA and PhD in criminology from the University of South Florida, Tampa. He also holds a master's degree from Monmouth University, West Long Branch, New Jersey, and he received his BA from Rutgers University, New Brunswick, New Jersey. He maintains teaching affiliations with several universities in criminology/criminal justice and he pursues an active agenda of research and writing in these areas. His publications have appeared in *Justice Quarterly, The Journal of Criminal Justice,* and *Criminal Justice Review,* among others. He is also the author of an earlier book, *Investigating White Collar Crime* (Pearson Prentice Hall, 2008).

Prior to his academic career, Dr. Bazley served as a U.S. Postal Inspector for 27 years where he was primarily involved with white-collar crime cases. In this capacity, he held a variety of field and management/supervisory positions including assignments to the U.S. Department of Justice Organized Crime Strike Force in Newark, New Jersey and as an investigator on the staff of a Congressional subcommittee headed by the late Senator Claude Pepper.